ENTREPRENEURSHIP DEVELOPMENT

NIPA GENX ELECTRONIC RESOURCES & SOLUTIONS P. LTD.
New Delhi-110 034

nipa
Browse Subject
Agriculture Sciences (679)
Animal Husbandry and Veterinary Sciences (261)
Climate Change and Environmental Sciences (63)
Community Science (Home Science) (39)
Competitive Examinations and MCQ's (57)
Dairy Technology (91)
Fisheries Sciences (26)
Food Science and Technology (155)
Geological Sciences (50)
Horticultural Sciences (342)
Plant Sciences (151)
Skill and Entrepreneurship Development (47)
eBooks / eChapters / Articles
eBooks
scan for catalogue
Browse, Search, Read & Buy...
Subject Catalogues
eChapters
Publishers
Print Books
Forthcoming
eBooks
New Titles
NIPA
GENX
ONLINE RESOURCES
Publishing Books and Journals
Ebooks and e articles, Current Affairs
Reasoning, Logic and Aptitude
Competitive Examination Preparation
Language Learning and Development Programme
Document Quality Checker and Improvement Tool
Effective Public Speaking, Presentation and Interpersonal Skills
Online Programmes for Professional Development
Personality Development and Human Values
UPI
PayPal
PAY USING

Skill and Entrepreneurship Development Series Volume 02

ENTREPRENEURSHIP DEVELOPMENT

Sapna Jarial
Assistant Professor
Department of Agricultural Economics and Extension
School of Agriculture
Lovely Professional University
Phagwara, Punjab

NIPA GENX ELECTRONIC RESOURCES & SOLUTIONS P. LTD.
New Delhi-110 034

NIPA GENX ELECTRONIC RESOURCES & SOLUTIONS P. LTD.

101,103, Vikas Surya Plaza, CU Block
L.S.C.Market, Pitam Pura, New Delhi-110 034
Ph : +91 11 27341616, 27341717, 27341718
E-mail:newindiapublishingagency@gmail.com
www: www.nipabooks.com

For customer assistance, please contact
Phone: + 91-11-27 34 17 17 Fax: + 91-11- 27 34 16 16
E-Mail: feedbacks@nipabooks.com

ISBN: 978-93-95319-24-9

Composed and Designed by NIPA.

Preface

Entrepreneurship growth is essential for a country's economic prosperity. Farmers and farmers-turned-businesspeople are called agripreneurs. Agricultural extension advisory services gained a new perspective after research revealed that rural development cannot occur until agriculture is viewed as a business and the farmer as an entrepreneur. Entrepreneurs disrupt the market and the economy. In this sense, agripreneurs are the change agents. And universities create the change agents. The Deans Committee recommended that the course "Entrepreneurial Development and Communication Skills" be added to the curricula of Indian agricultural universities. The book explores entrepreneurship to help students become entrepreneurs. This book is intended for undergraduate agriculture students studying horticulture, home science, animal sciences, etc. Postgraduate students in agricultural and non-agricultural universities could use this as a reference book. Entrepreneurship education and training help young people improve their traits and attitudes. It helps them prepare business ideas, seek financial aid, and manage profitable company.

As with all textbooks, the present work is based on the research findings, books, and other resources of many academicians, researchers, and authors who have been fully acknowledged. Our experience in teaching, training, and extension has enabled us to gather sufficient material and concepts on the subject, as well as provide appropriate examples from field scenarios. The goal of adding another book to the ever-expanding list of publications on entrepreneurship is to put useful, relevant, updated and straightforward books in the hands of teachers and students in agricultural institutions and universities. Most of the essential concepts and principles have been clarified by the authors. The book is divided into 13 chapters, keywords, case studies are provided to explain entrepreneurship development with sufficient supporting details for novice learners.

Again, we thank the different sources and writers whose ideas and perspectives were included in the book, as well as those who directly and indirectly helped us to prepare the content.We are grateful to—NIPA publishers for publishing the present book. We hope that readers will warmly welcome the current work.

Editor

Contents

Preface v

List of Crontributors ix

1. **Introduction to Entrepreneurship** 1
   Sapna Jarial
2. **Characteristics of an Entrepreneur** 19
   Guneshori Maisnam and Nikita Khoisnam
3. **SWOT Analysis.** 39
   Roop Kumar and Sharad Sachan
4. **Achievement Motivation** 53
   Nidhi Thakur
5. **Role of Government in Entrepreneurship Development** 61
   Arnab Roy and Priyanka Lal
6. **Institutions for Entrepreneurship Development** 69
   Sapna Jarial, Haobijam James Watt, and Devina Seram
7. **Entrepreneurial Development** 103
   Abhilash Singh Maurya, Ayush Mishra and Sonia
8. **Impact of Economic Reforms on Agri-enterprises** 117
   Priyanka Lal and Arnab Roy
9. **Essential Skills for Entrepreneurship Development** 125
   Haobijam James Watt
10. **Entrepreneurial Characteristics** 143
    Nikita Khoisnam

11. Roadmap for Business Start-up: Project Planning Formulation and Report Preparation. 149

Sapna Jarial, Sharad Sachan, Haobijam James Watt and Devina Seram

12. Financing of An Enterprise 173

Sapna Jarial, Sharad Sachan, Haobijam James Watt and Devina Seram

13. Opportunities for Agri-entrepreneurship and Rural Enterprise 193

Sapna Jarial, Sharad Sachan, Haobijam James Watt Devina Seram and Roop Kumar

Bibliography 229

List of Contributors

Abhilash Singh Maurya, *Assistant Professor, Department of Agricultural Economics and Extension, School of Agriculture, Lovely Professional University, Phagwara Punjab*

Arnab Roy, *Department of Agricultural Economics and Extension, School of Agriculture, Lovely Professional University, Phagwara, Punjab*

Ayush Mishra, *Department of Extension Education at Chaudhary Charan Singh Haryana Agricultural University, Hisar, Harayana*

Devina Seram, *Assistant Professor, Department of Entomology, School of Agriculture Lovely Professional University, Phagwara, Punjab*

Guneshori Maisnam, *Assistant Professor, Department of Agricultural Economics and Extension, Lovely Professional University, Phagwara, Punjab*

Haobijam James Watt, *Assistant Professor in the Department of Agricultural Economics and Extension, School of Agriculture, Lovely Professional University, Phagwara Punjab*

Nidhi Thakur, *Assistant Professor, Department of Agricultural Economics and Extension, School of Agriculture, Lovely Professional University, Phagwara, Punjab*

Nikita Khoisnam, *Assistant Professor the Department of Agricultural Economics and Extension, School of Agriculture, Lovely Professional University, Phagwara Punjab*

Priyanka Lal, *Department of Agricultural Economics and Extension, School ofAgriculture, Lovely Professional University, Phagwara, Punjab.*

Roop Kumar, *Assistant Professor in the Department of Agricultural Economics and Extension, School of Agriculture, Lovely Professional University, Phagwara, Punjab*

Sapna Jarial, *Assistant Professor in Agricultural Extension, Department of Agricultural Economics and Extension, School of Agriculture, Lovely Professional University, Phagwara, Punjab*

Sharad Sachan, *Assistant Professor, Agricultural Economics, Lovely Professional University, Phagwara, Punjab*

Sonia, *Department of Agricultural Economics at CCS HAU, Hisar, Harayana*

1

Introduction to Entrepreneurship

Sapna Jarial

Department of Agricultural Economics and Extension, Lovely Professional University, Phagwara, Punjab

Concept of Entrepreneur

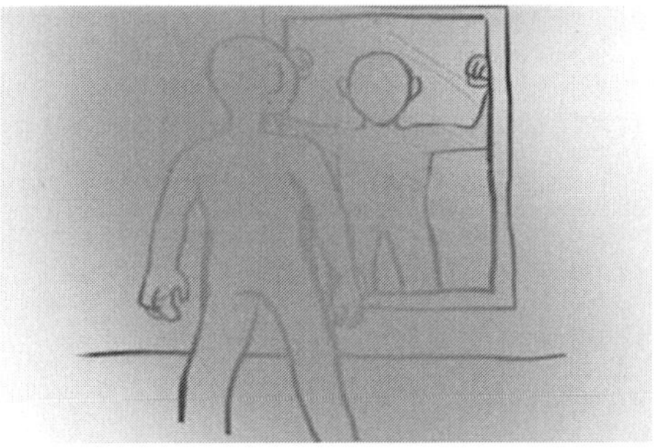

An entrepreneur is an economic man who seeks to maximize revenues by identifying and adopting innovations. However, entrepreneurs are willing to take risks and create change by organising human efforts. Entrepreneurs are vital to the country's economic growth. Entrepreneurial development as a component of economic growth has long been acknowledged.

Starting from the basics, etymologically, the word entrepreneur comes from the French word "entreprendre", which means "to do something", and, in the Middle Era, it was originally used in the sense of a person who is active, who gets things done. The study of entrepreneurship reaches back to work in the late 17th and early 18th centuries of Irish-French economist Richard Cantillon. "Entrepreneur" is a French word that first appeared in the French dictionary entitled *Dictionnaire Universel de Commerce,* compiled by **Jacques des Bruslons** and published in **1723.** Richard Cantillon's 1755 work "Essai sur la nature du commerce en general" changed the entrepreneurial concept. Risk has been used to identify entrepreneurs since ancient times. In India, entrepreneurship means Udyog.

Keywords

Entrepreneur: An entrepreneur starts and runs a business in uncertain conditions.

Entrepreneurship: Entrepreneurship is the process of planning, launching and running a new business with the motive of earning a profit and creating wealth.

Innovative entrepreneur: is one who assembles and synthesis information and introduces new combinations of factors of production.

Imitative/ Adoptive - entrepreneur: Imitative entrepreneur is also known as an adoptive entrepreneur. He simply adopts successful innovations introduced by other innovators.

Fabian: The Fabian entrepreneur is timid and cautious. He imitates other innovations only if he is certain that failure to do so may damage his business.

Drone: These entrepreneurs are conservative or orthodox in outlook. They never like to get rid of their traditional business and traditional machinery or systems of the business.

Inventors: These entrepreneurs primarily involve themselves in Research and Development (R and D) activities

Table 1. Entrepreneurs in different languages

Word	Language	Meaning
Entreprendre	French	To undertake
Unternehmen	German	To undertake or to do something
Adventurer	English	To undertake or to do something

The original entrepreneurs were merchants and traders who identified an economic opportunity and capitalised on it. Ancient and mediaeval examples indicate that the entrepreneur's "who" and "what" haven't altered much. The French verb *entreprendre* means 'to undertake', but it can also indicate 'to start a new endeavour' This is key to the English word 'entrepreneur.'

In French, entrepreneur implies builder or contractor. Thus, we can define an entrepreneur as someone who produces and innovates to construct something valuable around anticipated opportunities. The word 'someone' emphasises that a personality, rather than a system, is involved. 'Anticipated opportunities' are a must to provide direction and focus. The opportunity may or may not be novel to the entrepreneur, but identifying it is a trait. Entrepreneurs recognise good ideas others miss or only see in retrospect.

Due to the market's power, the number of entrepreneurs has expanded dramatically.

According to Cantillon-An entrepreneur buys factor services at certain rates to manufacture a product and sell it at uncertain prices, committing himself to his cost. It's not known if the person will recover their investment.

Schumpeter pioneered the concept of innovation in entrepreneurship in 1934 because he believed it was the key to success.

Brockhaus provided an outstanding historical summary of entrepreneur definitions in 1982. From a societal standpoint, innovation is the most significant trait. Innovation and entrepreneurship go hand-in-hand. Thus the writers were right.

Joseph Schumpeter suggested that an entrepreneur must combine his work with other pursuits. Knight, Marshal, and Clark assumed an entrepreneur is a person with directional skills; they believe an entrepreneur must have a company vision and be able to assume the role of Chief Executive Officer (CEO).

Entrepreneurs are balancing forces in the market process, according to Meir Kirzner, since they identify opportunities, may take advantage of them, make decisions to develop them, and compete with other entrepreneurs interested in entering the market and gaining benefits in a market economy.

Max Weber, on the other hand, said that a businessman needs to be in a capitalist world and that entrepreneurs are the leaders of social change and the pillars of growth. Zorrilla thinks it's very important not to mix up an entrepreneur with a businessman or an investor. An entrepreneur creates the idea and concept for a product or service; an investor is someone who gives the business the money it needs to get off the ground, and a businessman is a person in charge of running the business and keeping the books.

In the end, it's true that an entrepreneur can be both an investor and a businessperson, but to keep being called an entrepreneur, he or she needs to keep coming up with new ideas. After all the other ideas have been looked at, we can say that an entrepreneur is someone who can see what people need and make changes before anyone else. It's important to remember that being an entrepreneur doesn't always mean being successful, and there are always risks.

Definitions of Entrepreneur

An entrepreneur is a person who purchases the means of production to combine them into marketable products with a profit motive in future, or an entrepreneur is one who buys factor services at a "certain" price with a view to selling their product at "uncertain" prices in future (**Richard Cantillon (1775).**

Entrepreneurs as a group of experts who bears the risk of operating a business in the face of uncertainty about the future conditions for taking business advantages. **(Frenk Knight 1921)**

An entrepreneur is one who organises, operates and assumes the risk in a business venture with an expectation of making a profit (**Oxford dictionary 1933).**

Entrepreneurship: The process of setting up a business is known as entrepreneurship.

According to the oxford **dictionary definition, the entrepreneur is one who organises, manages and assumes the risk of a business enterprise.**

The **Center for American Entrepreneurship** defined entrepreneurship as "the process by which individuals or a group of individuals (entrepreneurs) exploit a commercial opportunity either by bringing a new product or process to the market or by substantially improving an existing good, service, or method of production. This process is generally organised through a new organisation (a startup company) but may also occur in an established small business that undergoes a significant change in product or strategy (see below on growth)." (Liang, 2021).

To summarise, an entrepreneur is a person who takes risks, integrates numerous production aspects, and exploits possibilities to elicit demand, produce money, and create jobs.

Furthermore, entrepreneurship can be interpreted as "entrepreneur's spirit." Entrepreneurs' spirit is built on invention and adventure, with innovation serving as the soul and adventure as nature. Entrepreneurs have a clear goal in mind and a well-planned approach for accomplishing it. They have a society-centred vision which is based on the societal challenge. Pain. They design and implement solutions that have a positive impact on society. Others see threats and gloom, but they see opportunities. Entrepreneurs might identify opportunities in adversity and avoid failure. People overcome difficulties and danger to attain their aim. They're comfortable with uncertainty and ambiguity, can spot possibilities others overlook and can endure without tiring. They're courageous and open to new ideas.

Concept of Enterprise

Entrepreneurship and business are linked. An entrepreneur's offshoot is an enterprise. Its success is determined by the entrepreneur. Enterprise is where Entrepreneurial activity is going on, for example, Company, Industry, Firm, organisation, office, agency, franchise, Shops etc.

Factors influencing entrepreneurship

Entrepreneurs emerge as a result of a complex interplay of social, religious, cultural, psychological, and economic factors.

1. Entrepreneurs internalise their family's and society's traditions, values and norms.
2. **Religious, social and cultural factors -** In some countries, religious and cultural beliefs that higher profit is unethical to inhibit entrepreneurship.
3. **Psychological factors -** Psychological factors like security orientation, conformity and compliance, and high need for affiliation inhibit entrepreneurship.
4. **Political system -** Free market, individual freedom, and private enterprise promote entrepreneurship.
5. **Economic policies-** Government and financial institution policies, and the opportunities they create, directly affect entrepreneurship.

Functions of Entrepreneur

- **Initiation** - Entrepreneurs start businesses. He/She must make production and marketing decisions.
- **Choice of Location** - The entrepreneur must locate where production and marketing facilities exist or can be created.
- **Innovation** - The entrepreneur introduces new scientific findings and technologies, new product uses, and/or new markets.
- **Coordination** - The entrepreneur must coordinate, direct, and supervise production.
- **Risk and uncertainties** - The entrepreneur must face risk and uncertainty and search for new alternatives. He or she organises and operates the business and is responsible for losses or gains.

In business terms, an entrepreneur isn't an employee, manager, or leader. An entrepreneur usually starts with an idea or plan, some money, and the ambition to develop a firm. Thousands of managers and executives start new enterprises in their organisations, industries, and economies. The question comes to mind, what distinguishes an entrepreneur from managers and leaders? An analogy perhaps would be sufficient. Entrepreneurs are like mountaineers who rely on guts, energy, and excitement to reach the summit. Perhaps a manager or leader analyses the route and weather and dispatches a chopper. Both strategies have issues, opportunities, costs, and rewards. However, an entrepreneur is an inventor and takes calculated risks.

Entrepreneur vs professional: 3 significant differences

Factor	Entrepreneur	Professional
Competence	Entrepreneurial core knowledge to establish a firm	Generic knowledge applicable across firms
Passion	Following one's own natural logic, whether others agree or not	Following a system-compliant strategic strategy
Gumption or High return, no risk	High-reward, high-risk	Driven by rewards, not hazards

(Bhaktavatsala, 2019)

Types of Entrepreneurs

Entrepreneurs can be classified into various types as follows:

Arthur H. Cole Classification: Arthur H. Cole classifies entrepreneurs as

Empirical: He's a conservative entrepreneur who rarely innovates.

Rationale: The rational entrepreneur knows the economy well and makes revolutionary changes.

Cognitive: Cognitive entrepreneur uses expert advice and business services.

Pioneering industrial entrepreneur

Entrepreneurs commercialise the most innovative technologies first. Biologics, genetics, digital, and artifical intelligence are current trends with promising futures. Lean structure, risk-taking, and rapid development make the entrepreneurial model ideal for exploring new technology's industrial applications. Entrepreneurs buy economically and technologically viable innovations or businesses. Entrepreneurs act as industrial pioneers, entering interesting sectors that inhibit investment, for instance, exploring Mars. Innovative technology and business methods are often praised more than sales or profits.

Economic activist entrepreneur

Entrepreneurs make money by creating original, interesting, excellent, or new goods and services. Successful startups with few resources become mega-enterprises that provide jobs and money. Entrepreneurs are different from ordinary people, managers, government officials, industry leaders, and academic experts. Private and government investments support entrepreneurship, diversifying economic activity.

Entrepreneurial icons

Some entrepreneurs rewrote industrial history by commercialising breakthrough technologies.

Henry Ford (Ford Motor), Konosuke Matsushita (Panasonic), Akio Morita (Sony), Bill Gates (Microsoft), Steve Jobs (Apple), Larry Page (Google), Sergey Brin (Google), Mark Zuckerberg (Facebook), Elon Musk (Tesla), and Jeff Bezos (Amazon).

Some were industry-changers or pioneer rivals: William Durant, in competition with General Motors, Richard Branson in competition with Virgin.

Some created industrial history in hostile environments (pre-independence India under British occupation) or under-regulated regimens (pre-liberalisation): Jamshedji Tata (Tata Steel), Henning Holck-Larsen, and Soren Kristin Toubro (Larsen & Toubro), Dhirubhai Ambani (Reliance).

Classification can be based on

a) Business type

b) Technology use

c) Ownership

d) Gender

e) Enterprise size

A. Based on Business Type

1. **Trading Entrepreneurs**: They buy from manufacturers and sell to customers directly or through retailers. These are the manufacturers' wholesalers, dealers, and retailers.
2. **Manufacturing Entrepreneur**: Manufacturing entrepreneurs manufacture products. They identify customer needs and then explore resources and technology to manufacture products.
3. **Agricultural Entrepreneur**: Agricultural entrepreneurs run farms. They cover farming, marketing, irrigation, mechanisation, and technology.

B. Clarence Danhof Classification

Clarence Danhof identifies four types of entrepreneurs.

1. **Innovative:** Innovative entrepreneurs gather and synthesise information and combine production factors. They are innovative. These entrepreneurs

see new ideas, technology, markets, and organisations as opportunities. Innovative entrepreneurs transform their country's lifestyle.

2. **Imitative/ Adoptive:** Imitative entrepreneur = adoptive entrepreneur. He adopts others' successful innovations. These entrepreneurs copy existing business models. Instead of innovating, they copy others' ideas. These entrepreneurs help less developed countries grow their enterprises and entrepreneurial cultures. By adopting tested technology, they create jobs for the youth and act as economic development agents.
3. **Fabian**: Fabian's businessman is timid. He only imitates other innovations if he's sure it will hurt his business. They are hesitant to adopt or innovate new technology in their company. They aren't adaptable. They prefer to stick to old production methods. They adopt new technology when they realise failure will lead to enterprise loss or collapse.
4. **Drone**: These businesspeople are traditionalists. They don't like to change their traditional business or systems. Even though the environment and society have changed, they still use old-fashioned production methods. Drone entrepreneurs refuse to change. They're laggards because they stick to tradition and resist change. His innovations may be limited. They refuse to change production despite lower returns.

C. Based on the Technology Use

1. **Technical Entrepreneur**: Technical entrepreneurs are technologists. These are business people who use science and technology.
2. **Non-Technical Entrepreneur**: Non-technical entrepreneurs are not technical. They concern themselves with using alternative and imitative marketing and distribution strategies to make their business successful.

D. Based on Ownership

1. **Private Entrepreneur**: Private entrepreneurs start businesses as individuals. He/she owns the business and assumes all risk.
2. **State Entrepreneur**: "State entrepreneur" refers to the State or Government's commercial or industrial venture.
3. **Joint Entrepreneurs**: "Joint entrepreneurs" are private entrepreneurs and the government who run a business together.

E. Based on Gender

1. **Men Entrepreneurs**: When entrepreneurs who own, manage, and control businesses are men.

2. **Women Entrepreneurs**: Women entrepreneurs own and control businesses with at least 51% female ownership and 51% female employment.

New classifications of entrepreneurs have been made in recent years, which are discussed below:

1. **Solo operators**: These entrepreneurs prefer to work alone. These entrepreneurs prefer a solo venture. They run a proprietorship business.
2. **Active partners**: These entrepreneurs pool resources to build a business. They actively manage the business daily. Active partners run more successful businesses.
3. **Inventors**: These entrepreneurs do Research and Development (R and D) activities. They enjoy inventing new products, technologies, and production methods.
4. **Challengers**: These entrepreneurs view business challenges as a sign of success. They keep improving and face obstacles boldly. They use business savvy and talent to turn odds into profit. Life has no charm without challenges, they say. They're bold because of challenges and don't mind taking risks to make money.
5. **Buyers (entrepreneurs)**: These entrepreneurs buy seized or working units. Using their experience, expertise, and business acumen, they fix sick units. By buying these units, they avoid building infrastructures and facilities.

Other types of entrepreneurs

Innovative entrepreneurs- Introduce new products, services, marketing techniques, and business structures.

Replicative entrepreneurs- Enter existing markets with similar offerings and Unique Selling Points.

Opportunity entrepreneurs- Entrepreneurs seek independence and income growth.

Necessity entrepreneurs- When no other work is available.

Social entrepreneurs- Are yet another group of entrepreneurs without explicit economic motive to help social development. Even innovative and replicative innovators can have a social purpose and promote socio-economic development.

Entrepreneurship and Types of Entrepreneurships

Startups create wealth and jobs through entrepreneurship. Entrepreneurs must manage failure risks, and established firms must adopt an entrepreneurial mindset.

Entrepreneurship is the process of planning, launching, and running a new business for profit and wealth. Every firm, big or small, is an entrepreneurial venture. Entrepreneurship is about having the right product or service at the right time. The journey requires expanding an existing market or creating a new one. Scale, scope, and financial muscle help entrepreneurial firms grow, but passion for growth is key. Established firms can also start new businesses with entrepreneurial thinking.

Serial entrepreneurship: Serial entrepreneurs can retain their individual charisma. Successful serial entrepreneurs build their companies to a critical scale and sell them to larger investors or partners, unlocking value and cashing out their stakes to fund future ventures.

This strategy is useful when their core entrepreneurial skills are not industry or technology-specific or when the industry is expanding. Jerry Rao, GR Gopinath, and Meena and Krishnan are Indian serial entrepreneurs. Entrepreneurs who start a basket of ventures in different fields and have a series of exits and entries are like investors who follow the portfolio approach in startups. Serial entrepreneurship is rare in India because founders are emotionally attached to their companies.

Conglomerate entrepreneurship: Tata, Birla, Bajaj, Reliance, Hinduja, Adani, TVS, Murugappa, Apollo, Essar, Dhoot, and other individual or families conglomerates institutionalised Indian entrepreneurship. Fervent entrepreneurs can co-opt other capable entrepreneurs to start and grow strategic business units (SBUs) and firms as future conglomerates. Institutionalising conglomerate entrepreneurship requires professionals with entrepreneurial passion and energy. Why conglomerate entrepreneurship is dominated by entrepreneurial families is an enigma. Entrepreneurs must constantly rethink their self-discovery model as their businesses grow.

Social entrepreneurship: Refers to recognising a social problem and using entrepreneurial/business principles to create a social venture. Social entrepreneurs focus on creating social capital, while business entrepreneurs focus on profit. Social entrepreneurship promotes social goals. Social entrepreneurs are often associated with the non-profit and voluntary sectors, but this isn't always the case (e.g. Grameen Bank in Bangladesh).

Corporate entrepreneurship: Formal and informal process to create new business products or services within an existing organisation to create value and grow revenue. Corporate entrepreneurship (C.E.) is when employees pursue opportunities without regard to their current resources. An entrepreneurial manager links new technical knowledge that can solve a customer problem with market demand and gathers the resources and skills needed to advance the venture. This process often leads to new businesses and company transformation through idea renewal (e.g., e-choupal by ITC).

Corporate Social Entrepreneurship: Organisational transformation to improve society. Corporate Social Entrepreneurship (CSE) is a process that helps businesses develop more advanced and powerful forms of Corporate Social Responsibility (CSR), though the latter often refers to philanthropy; for instance- Starbucks, partnered with Conservation International to promote sustainable coffee farming in Chiapas, Mexico. This entrepreneurial combination of competencies created new production techniques and a supply of organic coffee for Starbucks, which increased farmer income and improved environmental conditions.

Academic entrepreneurship: Which refers to efforts undertaken by universities to promote commercialisation on campus and in surrounding regions of the university. It has changed dramatically in recent years. Two key consequences of this change are that more stakeholders have become involved in academic entrepreneurship and that universities have become more 'strategic' in their approach to this activity. There is an emphasis on university-industry links. This is due to academic entrepreneurship's focus on transferring lab inventions to patents, licences, and startups.

Three Dimensions of Entrepreneurship

Entrepreneurship's delivery aspect has three dimensions:

Entrepreneurship's first dimension: Creativity, passion, and purpose are to help entrepreneurs solve known and unknown problems and issues.

Creativity: Is the ability to turn new, innovative ideas into products or services

Passion: Extreme and irrepressible urge to pursue a mission or goal, coupled with the course-correcting ability

Purpose: A social or economic purpose that guides the entrepreneur's journey.

Entrepreneurship's second dimension: Self-confidence, self-expression, and self-promotion gives entrepreneurs strength, energy, and openness.

Self-confidence: Technical and management strengths reflect a belief that one can deliver on the first core dimension alone or with co-founders.

Self-expression: Strong belief in the ability to deliver on goal and purpose; ability to advocate for entrepreneurship to inspire, attract, and build talent.

Self-promotion: ability to self-promote rationally; entrepreneurship to inspire, attract, and build talent.

Entrepreneurship third dimension

Acceptance, risk, and failure Tolerance help the entrepreneur navigate unanticipated pitfalls.

Rejection tolerance: Willingness to revisit failed premises

Risk tolerance: Risks are inevitable due to novelty and incumbent pushback.

Failure tolerance: Willingness to revisit failed premises and rebuild projects to make them risk- and failure-proof.

Understanding entrepreneurial risks and rewards

Different entrepreneurs experience risk and reward differently, personally and contextually.

Risks: Financial losses, professional/social esteem loss, personal/family distress, shame, and embarrassment.

Rewards: Valuations, acquisitions, licencing, business profits, industrial and social status, personal and family prosperity.

Risk-Reward balance: Some entrepreneurs focus on building the firm to the largest scale possible, with risk-reward oscillation, while others monetise and move on.

When we think of entrepreneurship as a continuum which ranges from Schumpeterian entrepreneurship on one end to its non-Schumpeterian counterpart on the other, while Schumpeterian entrepreneurship is characterised as risk-loving, based on radical innovations and aiming for high corporate growth, non-Schumpeterian entrepreneurship is risk-avoiding and based on imitation, without aiming for corporate growth.

Intrapreneur

Intrapreneurs are organisation-based innovators who introduce new products, ideas, and services. They help their organisation adapt, grow, and succeed in a changing/competitive environment. They drive corporate entrepreneurship.

Differences between Entrepreneurs and Intrapreneurs:

Entrepreneur	Intrapreneur
Independent businessman = entrepreneur	Intrapreneurs rely on corporate promoters/owners.
An entrepreneur raises capital and guarantees investors/creditors a return.	An intrapreneur neither raises nor guarantees capital returns.
Entrepreneurs bear all business risks.	Intrapreneur risk isn't 100%.
An entrepreneur operates from outside	Entrepreneurs work within the firm
A business owner makes money.	Successful innovations reward intrapreneurs.
Entrepreneurs own businesses.	Intrapreneurs help others.
An entrepreneur develops an intrapreneur's ideas	Intrapreneur innovates.
Entrepreneurs need no formal training.	An intrapreneur is hired based on qualifications.

(Surbi, 2017)

Future of Entrepreneurship

Industry	Past/Current	Future
Pharmaceuticals	Chemical molecule-based	Biological cell-based
Automobiles	I.C. Engine	Electric power-pack driven
Internet	Connecting people	Connecting people and devices
Banking	Conventional Ledgers, password protected	Distributed ledgers, blockchains
Analytics and Services	Human Intelligence	Artificial intelligence
Energy	Fossil fuel	Solar energy, wind energy and other
Crop Production	Chemical fertiliser & pesticides	Bio fertiliser and biopesticides.

(Bhaktavatsala, 2019)

Digital Entrepreneurship

The use of digital and cutting-edge technology to encourage entrepreneurship has expanded in the previous decade, enabling digitally-enabled entrepreneurship. These technologies boost entrepreneurship by redefining business and strategy and competitiveness while navigating turbulent, uncertain environments. New digital and cutting-edge technologies provide new contexts, challenges, and opportunities, making existing innovation obsolete and increasing uncertainty and firms' costs. Additive manufacturing, blockchain, robotics, cloud computing, and big data analytics are vital to digital entrepreneurship.

In a digital context, one business success factor is the adoption of digital and emerging/cutting-edge technologies such as digital business. Firms rely heavily on their own knowledge, resources, and capabilities to gain a competitive edge and achieve high growth. Constant advancements in digital technologies (know-why) like responsible artificial intelligence complicate entrepreneurial processes.

Thus, adopting digital and emerging/cutting-edge technologies is a key strategy for digital entrepreneurship, a process by which Small and Medium Enterprises (SMEs) create new opportunities, innovative strategies, and digital solutions.

Assessing Entrepreneurial Personality Traits

There are a number of psychometric tools that can be used to figure out a person's personality type. Some of these tools are designed to test for entrepreneurs. The more advanced tests, such as the *Myers-Briggs Type Indicator (MBTI),* are licenced tests that have been given to millions of people. However, there are several alternative tests that may be found online for example *BDC* which contains 50 questions.

Even if there is not a widespread agreement that psychometric tests accurately reflect actual managerial effectiveness, these exams nonetheless have the potential to operate as guideposts to some extent. Some of the online tests use straightforward frameworks to measure an individual's motivations, aptitudes, and attitudes, while others, like the MBTI, use frameworks that are more specific and intricate.

Below are the BDC and MBTI frameworks, with credit given to the companies that made them and for assessments directly follow the companies websites.

BDC entrepreneurial potential self-assessment

S.No.	Factor	Sub-factor	Scores		
			Minimum	**Average**	**Maximum**
1.	**Motivations**	Need for achievement/success	5	17	20
		Power/ control appeal	5	17	20
		Need for challenges/ambition	5	17	20
		Self-sufficiency/freedom	4	12	16
		Sub-Total	19	62	76
2.	**Aptitudes**	Perseverance/determination	4	14	16
		Self-confidence/enthusiasm	4	13	16
		Tolerance towards ambiguity/ resistance to change	6	19	24
		Creativity/Imagination	6	21	24
		Sub-Total	20	67	80
3.	**Attitudes**	Perception to act upon one's destiny	6	20	24
		Action oriented	5	17	20
		Sub-Total	11	37	44
		ALL TOTAL	50	166	200

Source: https://www.bdc.ca/en/articles-tools/entrepreneur-toolkit/business-assessments/pages/entrepreneurial- potential-self-assessment.aspx

Types of entrepreneurs in the Myers-Briggs Type Indicator (MBTI)

Trait : A personality typology that looks at 16 different types of people. Each person was given a score based on the four pairs of opposite personality traits.

Personality types

- *"Extraversion" or "Introversion", with E and I respectively*
- *"Sensing" or "Intuition", with S or N, respectively*
- *"Thinking" or "Feeling", with T or F, respectively*
- *"Judging" or "Perceiving", with J or P, respectively*
- The most common unique personality types are ESFJ and ISFJ. The least common unique personality types are INFJ, ENTJ
- The most successful types of entrepreneurs are ENTPs, ESTJs, ENTJs, INTJs and ISTJs
- All these entrepreneurs are thinkers - a trait highly advantageous for business
- They are more inclined to base decisions on evidence. They are also more capable of making unpopular decisions
- Extraversion covers 60% of the most successful types of entrepreneurs, with Introversion not being far behind

MBTI types of entrepreneurs

S.No.	Code	Label	Characteristics
1.	ENTP	"the inventor"	Create new products; challenge authority
2.	ESTJ	"the supervisor"	Draw out order and structure from chaos amazing aptitude at performing mental tasks Amongst the most successful entrepreneurs
3.	ISTJ	"the inspector"	Make great CFOs and legal counsel Follow the rule-book diligently
4.	ENTJ	"highly effective leader"	The rarest personality type in MBTIMake for great CEOsThink of options in face of obstacles
5.	INTJ	"mastermind"	Same as the above, with introversion

Common characteristic of all the 5 types of entrepreneurs.

- They go with their gut and take calculated, assured risks.
- All of these types of business owners want to win and are competitive.
- They have a lot of self-control and can keep their eyes on the end game.
- They rarely agree to compromises and rarely put feelings first.

(Serban, 2018)

Conclusion

An entrepreneur is a businessperson who seeks to increase profits through the discovery and implementation of new ideas. Entrepreneurs are willing to take risks and organize human efforts to make a difference. For the country's economy to grow, entrepreneurs are essential. Entrepreneurial development has long been recognized as an important part of economic growth.

Business and entrepreneurship go hand in hand. It is an enterprise that is the offshoot of a businessman or woman. Entrepreneurship is the key to its success. The entrepreneurial activity takes place in businesses. Examples of these terms include business, industry, firm, organisation, workplace, agency, franchise, and so on. Startup founders create wealth and jobs. Entrepreneurs must manage failure risk, and firms must be entrepreneurial. There are various types of entrepreneurship, for example, serial entrepreneurship, conglomerate entrepreneurs, Social entrepreneurship, corporate entrepreneurship, corporate social entrepreneurship, academic entrepreneurship and digital entrepreneurship.

References

Azqueta Díaz de Alda, A. (2017). *El concepto de emprendedor: origen, evolución e introducción*. https://idus.us.es/handle/11441/74177#.Yg-gkoK-tLw.mendeley

Beliaeva, T., Ferasso, M., Kraus, S. and Damke, E. J. (2020). Dynamics of digital entrepreneurship and the innovation ecosystem. International Journal of Entrepreneurial Behavior & Research, Vol. 26 No. 2, pp. 266-284.

Cavallo, A., Ghezzi, A., Dell'Era, C. and Pellizzoni, E. (2019). Fostering digital entrepreneurship from startup to scaleup: The role of venture capital funds and angel groups. Technological Forecasting and Social Change, Vol. 145, pp. 24-35.

Carland, J. W., Hoy, F., Boulton, W. R., Ann, J., & Carland, C. (1984). Differentiating Entrepreneurs from Small Business Owners: A Conceptualisation. *Source: The Academy of Management Review*, *9*(2), 354–359.

Cunningham, J., Damij, N. and Modic, D. (2022). An Exploratory Study of High-Performance Computing Technology Adoption over the Stages of Entrepreneurship. International Journal of Entrepreneurial Venturing.

Dilli, S., Elert, N., & Herrmann, A. M. (2018). Varieties of entrepreneurship: exploring the institutional foundations of different entrepreneurship types through 'Varieties-of-Capitalism' arguments. *Small Business Economics*, *51*(2), 293–320. https://doi.org/10.1007/S11187-018-0002-Z/TABLES/12

Dolores Martínez García, M., María Moreno Meneses, J., & Valencia Sandoval, K. (2022). View of Theoretical Review of Entrepreneur and Social Entrepreneurship Concepts. *Journal of Administrative Science*, *3*(6), 19–26. https://repository.uaeh.edu.mx/revistas/index.php/jas/article/view/7687/8332

Dong, J. Q. (2019). Moving a mountain with a teaspoon: Toward a theory of digital entrepreneurship in the regulatory environment, Technological Forecasting and Social Change, Vol. 146, pp. 923-930.

Dwivedi, Y. K., Hughes, L., Ismagilova, E., Aarts, G., Coombs, C., Crick, T., Duan, Y., Dwivedi, R., Edwards, J., Eirug, A., Galanos, V., Ilavarasan, P. V., Janssen, M., Jones, P., Kar, A. K., Kizgin, H., Kronemann, B., Lal, B., Lucini, B., Medaglia, R., Le Meunier-FitzHugh, K., Le Meunier-FitzHugh, L. C., Misra, S., Mogaji, E., Sharma, S. K., Singh, J. B., Raghavan, V., Raman, R., Rana, N. P., Samothrakis, S., Spencer, J., Tamilmani, K., Tubadji, A., Walton, P. and Williams, M. D. (2021). Artificial Intelligence (A.I.): Multidisciplinary perspectives on emerging challenges, opportunities, and agenda for research, practice and policy. International Journal of Information Management, Vol. 57, pp. 101994.

Jawad, M., Naz, M. and Maroof, Z. (2021). Era of the digital revolution: Digital entrepreneurship and digital transformation in emerging economies, Business Strategy & Development, Vol. 4 No. 3, pp. 220-228.

Kaur, H. (n.d.). Understanding The Concept Of Entrepreneur Competency. *Journal of Business Management & Social Sciences Research.* Retrieved February 18, 2022, from www.borjournals.com

Kraus, S., Palmer, C., Kailer, N., Kallinger, F. L. and Spitzer, J. (2018), "Digital entrepreneurship: A research agenda on new business models for the twenty-first century", International Journal of Entrepreneurial Behavior & Research.

Modgil, S., Dwivedi, Y. K., Rana, N. P., Gupta, S. and Kamble, S. (2022). Has Covid-19 accelerated opportunities for digital entrepreneurship? An Indian perspective. Technological Forecasting and Social Change, Vol. 175, pp. 121415.

Nambisan, S. (2017). Digital entrepreneurship: Toward a digital technology perspective of entrepreneurship. Entrepreneurship theory and practice, Vol. 41 No. 6, pp. 1029-1055.

Ngoasong, M. Z. (2018). Digital entrepreneurship in a resource-scarce context, Journal of Small Business and Enterprise Development, Vol. 25 No. 3, pp. 483-500.

Olan, F., Liu, S., Suklan, J., Jayawickrama, U. and Arakpogun, E. O. (2021). The role of Artificial Intelligence networks in sustainable supply chain finance for food and drink industry. International Journal of Production Research, pp. 1-16.

Oyemomi, O., Liu, S., Neaga, I. and Alkhuraiji, A. (2016). How knowledge sharing and business process contribute to organisational performance: Using the fsQCA approach. Journal of Business Research, Vol. 69 No. 11, pp. 5222-5227.

Raine, A. L., & Pandya, M. (2019). Three keys to entrepreneurial success: are curiosity, creativity, and commitment. Entrepreneurship Education 2019 2:3, 2(3), 189–198. https://doi.org/10.1007/S41959-019-00019-Y

Sahut, J.-M., Iandoli, L. and Teulon, F. (2021). The age of digital entrepreneurship. Small Business Economics, Vol. 56 No. 3, pp. 1159-1169.

Schiuma, G., Schettini, E., Santarsiero, F. and Carlucci, D. (2021). The transformative leadership compass: six competencies for digital transformation entrepreneurship, International Journal of Entrepreneurial Behavior & Research, Vol. ahead-of-print No. ahead-of-print. https://doi.org/10.1108/IJEBR-01-2021-0087.

Secundo, G., Rippa, P. and Meoli, M. (2020). Digital transformation in entrepreneurship education centres: preliminary evidence from the Italian Contamination Labs network. International Journal of Entrepreneurial Behavior & Research, Vol. 26 No. 7, pp. 1589-1605.

Serban, R. (2018). 5 Most Successful Types of Entrepreneurs And Personality Testing, available at: https://www.hubgets.com/blog/5-most-successful-types-of-entrepreneurs-personality-testing/ (accessed 16 June 2022).

Siegel, D. S., & Wright, M. (2015). Academic Entrepreneurship: Time for a Rethink? *British Journal of Management*, *26*, 582–595. https://doi.org/10.1111/1467-8551.12116

Steininger, D. M. (2019). Linking information systems and entrepreneurship: A review and agenda for IT associated and digital entrepreneurship research. Information Systems Journal, Vol. 29 No. 2, pp. 363-407.

Tarapuez Chamorro, E., & Botero Villa, J. J. (2007). Algunos aportes de los neoclásicos a la teoría del emprendedor. *Cuadernos de Administración*, *20*(34), 39–63. http://www.scielo.org.co/scielo.php?script=sci_arttext&pid=S0120-35922007000200003&lng=en&nrm=iso&tlng=

Troise, C., Corvello, V., Ghobadian, A., O'Regan, N. (2022). SME's agility in the digital transformation era: antecedents and impact in VUCA environments. Technological Forecasting & Social Change, 174, 121227, https://doi.org/10.1016/j.techfore.2021.121227. Dal 01/01/2020 ad oggi.

Upadhyay, N., Upadhyay, S. and Dwivedi, Y.K. (2021). Theorising artificial intelligence acceptance and digital entrepreneurship model International Journal of Entrepreneurial Behavior & Research, Vol. ahead-of-print No. ahead-of print. https://doi.org/10.1108/IJEBR-01-2021-0052

2

Characteristics of an Entrepreneur

Guneshori Maisnam and Nikita Khoisnam

Department of Agricultural Economics and Extension, School of Agriculture
Lovely Professional University, Phagwara, Punjab

Development of the country build is upon the aspect of the human measures. Imaginative, inventive, truthful and persevering persons head the nation in the virtuous path and guide to all aspects of growth in every field. Entrepreneurs drive nation's growth. Entrepreneurs are familiar for their specific features Acknowledging this reality on growth of entrepreneurship. Entrepreneurship is an ingenious and imaginative reaction to the surrounding. The expression "entrepreneurs" normally mention to person who tackle recently developed capabilities that are imaginative and inventive. Analysis towards the entrepreneurial character has manifest that majority of the successful entrepreneurs share a defined category of personality features. This acquires the peculiarity as to. The existing analysis is an effort to inform the main features of entrepreneurs in food processing enterprises of Assam.

The word "Entrepreneur" is derived from the French verb 'entrepredre'. It means 'to undertake'. In the early 16th century the Frenchmen who organized and led military expeditions were referred as 'Entrepreneurs'. In the early 18th century French economist Richard Cantillon used the term entrepreneur to business. Since that time the word entrepreneur means one who takes the risk of starting a new organization or introducing a new idea, product or service to society. The entrepreneur are persons with definite features helpful in forming, commencing, demonstrating, organizing and directing an enterprise successfully. An individual consequently may be converted not only in terms of duties he or she tackles but also examine individual's lifestyle, attitude, ethics and all-inclusive behaviour which simultaneously assemble the personality of entrepreneur distinct than a normal person.

Keywords

Risk : The circumstance of not knowing the consequence of an activity or commitment.

Creative: The ability to produce or develop original work, theories, techniques, or thoughts.

Innovative: To introduce something new, make changes in anything established.

Motivation: Movement or motion an inner state that energises, activates or moves and direct human behaviour towards goals

Achievement motivation: When individuals are driven, inspired or stimulated by success or accomplishments. A desire of brilliance and aspiration for success in participate with the worth set by others as well as set by oneself.

Self Confidence: Ability of doing things and have the capacity to control the pursuit and work of other people.

Leadership: Ability to organise and integrate efforts of team and lead them to predetermined goals.

Networking: Developing a good network of relationships with the persons, agencies, organisations connected with the enterprise.

Orientation towards future goals: Entrepreneurs are very goal oriented. They have an ability to set goals and commitment to work towards them.

Goals setting: An entrepreneur sets goals for himself /herself both in terms of what he/she want to and when.

According to J.B. Say, "An Entrepreneur is the economic agent who unites all means of production, land of one, the labour of another and the capital of yet another and thus produces a product. By selling the product in the market the pays rent of land, wages to labour, interest on capital and what remains is his profit". Thus an Entrepreneur is an organizer who combines various factors of production to produce a socially viable product. An entrepreneur can be regarded as a person who has the initiative skill and motivation to set up a business or enterprise of his own and who always looks for high achievements. He is the catalyst for social change and works for the common good. They looks for opportunities, identifies them and seizes them mainly for economic gains. An action oriented entrepreneur is a highly calculative individual who is always willing to undertake risks in order to achieve their goals. Singh and Rahman (2013) reported fourteen trait variables were considered for measuring the important traits of successful entrepreneurs of Assam. But after factor analysis, the important traits variables leading to the success of entrepreneurs were reduced to five variables. Hence, the important traits variables leading to the success of food processing entrepreneurs in Assam are innovation, futuristic mindset, risk taking ability, adaptability and commitment.

To be successful, an entrepreneur should have the following characteristic features.

1. **Need to achieve**: Entrepreneurs have got strong desire to achieve higher goals. Their inner self motivates their behaviour towards high achievement: most of the people dream of success but do not take any action towards achieving these dreams. Entrepreneurs with high n-Ach factor act continuously to achieve the goal and make their dreams come true. For them, winning is achievement. Papzan et al (2008) found that there was a significant relationship between need for achievement, innovation, internal locus of control, marketing, and lack of bureaucracy and success of entrepreneurs
2. **Independence**: Most of the entrepreneurs start on their own because they dislike to work for others. They prefer to be their own boss and want to be responsible for their own decisions.
3. **Risk-bearing**: Entrepreneurs are the persons who take decisions under uncertainty and thus they are willing to take risk, but they never gamble with the results. They choose moderate risk rather than play wild gamble. They, therefore, undertake calculated risk which is high enough to be exciting, but with a fairly reasonable chance to win. Trait means unique or distinguishing characteristics of somebody (Oxford Advanced Learner dictionary). Successful entrepreneurs often share certain characteristics and the earliest identified entrepreneurial characteristic was risk taking. Carland & Carland (1996) in their study suggests that entrepreneurs are not homogenous. They may well be characterized by need for achievement, preference for innovation and risk taking propensity
4. **Locus of control**: According to Rotter's locus of control theory, an individual perceives the outcome of an event as being either within or beyond his personal control. Entrepreneurs believe in their own ability to control the consequences of their endeavour by influencing their socio-economic environment rather than leave everything to luck. Viral Acharya et al (2004) in a comparative study of Assam and Uttar Pradesh found that success of an entrepreneur was significantly related to self-efficacy and locus of control for both states. Robbin and Judge (2009) examined that entrepreneurs' personality traits to identify traits that have impact on business performance. Personality traits such as internal locus of control and ambiguity tolerance influenced the business success directly and the business process indirectly.
5. **Perseverance**: Entrepreneur has got the quality of sticking to job he decides to undertake. Once committed to a specific goal and course of action, entrepreneurs become absorbed to it. They personally solve the problems

that come across their way while setting up the project. They also work sincerely until the whole project is successfully implemented.

6. **Positive self-concept**: Entrepreneurs are always positive in their action. Being an achiever, he directs his fantasies and dreams towards achievement of worthwhile goals and sets extraordinary standard of excellence in what he is doing. This is based upon his awareness of SWOT analysis, i.e. his strengths, weaknesses, opportunities and threats. He utilizes his positive knowledge to support his thinking. He never exhibits any negative attitude.
7. **Ability to find and explore opportunities**: Entrepreneurs are always alert to opportunities. They are very much quick to see and grab opportunities. They exhibit an innovative turn of mind and convert the problems into viable opportunities. They plan intellectually and anticipate carefully how to achieve their goals in realizing an opportunity.
8. **Hope of success**: Hope of success is a significant quality of entrepreneurial personality. Entrepreneurs set their goals with a hope of success rather than fear of failure. This is because they set their goals on the basis of facts and their ability to maneuver them to their advantage.
9. **Flexibility:** Most of the successful entrepreneurs measure the pros and cons of a decision and tend to change if the situation demands. They never feel reluctant to revise their decisions. They are the persons with open mind without rigidity.
10. **Analytical ability of mind**: Entrepreneurs are unaffected by personal likes and dislikes. They stand beyond these types of prejudices as they are realistic in their approach. At the time of their need they select experts rather than friends and relatives to assist them. They usually avoid emotional and sensitive attitude towards their business or problem.
11. **Sense of efficacy**: Entrepreneurs are always oriented towards action for accomplishment of their goals. Being confident of their abilities, they find themselves as problem solvers rather than problem avoiders. They chalk out their goals for future and make planning to achieve them.
12. **Openness to feedback and learning from experience**: Successful entrepreneurs like to have immediate feedback of their performance. They modify their plans on the basis of the feedback they receive from the environment around them. They learn from their experience and never get discouraged having received unfavourable information. On the contrary, they are stimulated by unfavourable information to involve themselves sincerely in their own tasks to reach their desired goals.

13. **Confronting uncertainty**: Successful entrepreneurs are always optimistic and take every odd as the opportunity. They maneuver their environment in such a way that the works get accomplished rationally. Thus, they win by the application of their extraordinary insight and skill.

14. **Interpersonal skills**: Entrepreneurs are always comfortable while dealing with people at all levels. They interact with raw material suppliers, customers, bankers, etc.. for different activities. As successful entrepreneurs, they should be persons who like working with others possessing the much needed quality of interpersonal skill to deal with people.

15. **Need to influence others**: Once the entrepreneurs set their goals, they have to play the roles of manager too. For influencing others (n Power), a low need to establish emotional relationship (low n Affiliation), and a high need to discipline one's own self (to inhibit over expression of their personality) are essential.

16. **Stress takers**: Entrepreneurs are capable of working for long hours and solving different complexities at the same time. As the captain of an industry or an enterprise, an entrepreneur faces a number of problems and in right moment he takes right decisions which may involve physical as well as mental stress. He can face these challenges if he has the capability to work for long hours and keep himself cool under monotony.

17. **Time orientation**: Entrepreneurs anticipate future trends basing upon their past experience and exposure. They stick to the time pragmatically while doing their jobs. 18. Innovators: Successful entrepreneurs are innovators. They constantly put their efforts in introducing new products, new method of production, opening new markets and recognizing the enterprise.

19. **Communication skill:** Ability to communicate help in maintaining good relationship with people around , having good communication in any form is an important skills for effective running of an enterprise.

20. **Leadership**: Entrepreneurs should possess the quality of leadership. Leadership is the ability to exert interpersonal influence by means of communication towards the achievement of goals. Entrepreneurs as the leaders should provide the necessary spark to motivation by guiding, inspiring, assisting and directing the members of the group for achievement of unity of action, efforts and purpose. Hence, entrepreneurs by their own leadership styles and behaviour reduce the problems by proper handling of situations. Good administrative work depends upon effective leadership of the entrepreneur.

22. **Decision making**: Decision-making skill is a fundamental characteristic of an entrepreneur. This implies the function of choosing a particular course of

action at every stage of creation of an enterprise out of several alternative courses for the purpose of achieving specified goals. Hence, decision making is necessary at all times and mostly at conditions of uncertainty and risk.

24. **Ability to mobilize resources**: Entrepreneurs must have the ability to marshal all the inputs to obtain the end product. They have to mobilize 6Ms, i.e., Man, Money, Material, Machinery, Market and Method effectively to realize the final product as entrepreneurship is a function of gap filling and input completing.

25. **Self-confidence**: Entrepreneurs must have self-confidence to accomplish the task effectively and efficiently. They must take decisions on their own in uncertain and risky situation and should stick to it confidently even if there occur initial setbacks.

The success of small enterprises largely depends on the human capital of their owner-manager. There are various factors leading to success of entrepreneurs. Many authors & researchers are of the view that the success of an entrepreneur largely depends on traits of the entrepreneur. More important character required for successful entrepreneurship is passion. Feeling committed to what they are doing and when they care deeply about it, they stand the best chance of being successful at it.Qualities of entrepreneurship are numerous, as opinions are different for different people, but some qualities that are considered indispensable are considered . Desai (2001) revealed the important personality traits leading to the success are emotional stability, personal relations, consideration and tactfulness. An entrepreneur is an opportunity seeker. He is also the organizer and coordinator of the agents of production. He has to execute many a good functions while establishing a small scale enterprise. He not only perceives the business opportunities but also mobilizes the other resources like 5 Ms-man, money, machine, materials and methods. Ehigie and Umoren (2003) in their study considered self-concept, perceived managerial competence, work stress and business commitment are important psychological variables for perceived entrepreneurial success among female entrepreneurs. Melih Bulu (2005) revealed a number of factors including luck, hard work, good idea, and money which led to success. Sammy King-fai Hui et al (2006) observed that Self efficacy, Locus of control, Decision making and Risk attitude were responsible for success of entrepreneurs. Smartness of an individual is also considered as a key for successful entrepreneur. According to Nandram S. & Samsom S. (2007), the main determinants of a successful entrepreneur are found to be- watchful to spot the opportunities, persuasive, goal oriented, self-confidence, creativity, courage, trustworthy, ambitious, capacity for empathy, perseverance & locus of control. Abdullah F. et al (2009) confirmed that eight factors are vital to the success. In order of importance, the factors considered as success of an entrepreneur are drive, oriented towards achievement, commitment, ability to make decision, risk management, grips firmly ,networking, and optimism. Elenurm and Alas (2009) in a study reported that courage to risk, openness to new information, flexibility, creativity and determination were the features of successful entrepreneurs.

Conclusion

Entrepreneurs play a predominant role in accelerating the socio-economic development of a country. They are regarded as the nation builders and wealth creators. They are the change agents who initiate economic activities to create wealth. They undertake the business initiative, employ themselves in that business and open up employment avenues for others. Therefore, the role of entrepreneur is of fundamental importance to a country like India where the twin problems of poverty and unemployment coexist. Entrepreneur does not belong to a particular region, community,sex, educational level, age or income level. The free market model emphasises minimal government intervention in the economy as the best way to maintain incentives for entrepreneurial behaviour. The issue of unemployment can be overcome by promoting entrepreneur. Government has been promoting increase importance to the development of entrepreneur. So many initiatives focussing on different section of society including promotion of women entrepreneur. Recommendation of small scale industries and product and process-oriented courses for enabling women in entrepreneur. Challenge and a great opportunity comes together in the path of an entrepreneur, and it takes certain qualities to be successful. There's no right or wrong way to be an entrepreneur. As long as individual possess the zeal to achieve something, ability to seize opportunities, it's easy to overcome challenges throughout your journey.

Case studies

It's vital to realise first what an entrepreneur is. Schumpeter described an entrepreneur "as a dynamic agent of change or the catalyst who converted more and more physical, and human resources, into corresponding manufacturing possibilities. Entrepreneurs are people who start, organise, manipulate, and manage the affairs of a commercial business unit that combines manufacturing aspects to supply things and services, whether or not the commercial enterprise relates to agriculture, industry, change, or profession. Entrepreneur and entrepreneurship are used interchangeably. However, the phrases are different. The entrepreneur is the person that undertakes entrepreneurial sports, while entrepreneurship is the method of venture an enterprise. Kirzner said that marketers are the ones who start balancing changes, bringing together things that don't go together because the market was not understood before.

To him, the most important aspect of entrepreneurship is "the ability to detect new opportunities that others have not yet noticed." Entrepreneurship, according to Johnson, "involves capturing ideas, transforming them into products and services, and then establishing a venture to bring the product to market." Finally, the European Communities Commission defined entrepreneurship as "the mindset and process of creating and developing economic activity through the combination of risk-taking, creativity, and innovation with competent management, inside a new or existing organisation." Therefore, the entrepreneur is the person, and entrepreneurship is the process.

Women entrepreneurship is defined by the Government of India (A National level standing committee on Women Entrepreneurs constituted by the Ministry of Industries, India) "as an enterprise owned and administered by a woman and having a minimum financial interest of 51% of the share capital and has at least 50% women employees". Kamala Singh defined woman entrepreneur as "a confident, innovative and creative woman capable of achieving self-economic independence individually or in collaboration, generates employment opportunities for others through initiating, establishing and running an enterprise by keeping pace with her personal, family and social life". So, for the present study, women entrepreneurs are those who start, organise and maintain enterprises under individual ownership and employ employees to carry out entrepreneurial activities. A female entrepreneur is a group of women who start, organise, and run a business. Therefore, entrepreneurs are creative, confident and innovative. The importance of female entrepreneurs is greater because they also create employment opportunities. Women gain financial freedom as entrepreneurs, children become healthier, and the country's overall economic condition improves. Many simultaneous factors create interesting needs for female entrepreneurs.

Economic growth

In most countries, women have less or lower levels of business. Therefore, bringing more female entrepreneurs to the market will make you a more successful company. In addition, women can contribute to economic growth by starting more businesses that serve different niches than men.

Poverty reduction

Female entrepreneurs can help other women who live in poverty. This helps reduce poverty and break down barriers. Earning women play a role in society and advocate independence. The importance of female entrepreneurs is valuable because women are parents and help children in eradicating youth poverty. Women who earn dollars return their income to the local economy. Men do not reinvest at a high rate. That's because they spend on alcohol, cigarettes, and personal consumables. Women spend to buy items for their children and families. Regardless of the reason, the economic purchasing power is increasing, and women support the local economy. This reduces poverty and reinvests the dollar.

Improving Innovation

Female entrepreneurs face double standards. They are innovative, but people don't believe them and are aware of the risk of failure, so investing in their ideas is considered dangerous. However, studies have shown that women-owned businesses do not fail as well as men-owned businesses. Nevertheless, women continue to innovate by finding ways to improve through continuous learning and the acquisition of associated experiences. It can be difficult to balance family and business, but women work hard to navigate their home environment and careers. This innovation score is especially true for those who have benefited from the guidance of a business coach. Ambitious female entrepreneurs are looking for female business coaches to improve their knowledge, skills and attitudes as confident and enterprising women. Intelligent women want to talk to professionals who can help them start a good business and realise their great ideas. Lack of technical knowledge, skills, self-confidence and tools can make it difficult to process and implement innovative ideas. However, anything is possible with the proper guidance of a business coach or consultant. Business coaches are experienced entrepreneurs who have worked with different types of people. Business coaches for women can refer to women who are just beginning their entrepreneurial journey. Some women feel self-doubt, hesitation, and embarrassment when running a business, especially when they need to market assertive and innovative ideas. With the help of business coaches, they learn how to master these difficult situations, strengthening inexperienced entrepreneurs. As a result, they welcome innovative ideas and become confident in implementing them.

Case studies of Women Entrepreneurs

Women play a crucial characteristic withinside the boom of India's monetary system. Through the years, Indian girls have made a considerable effect and done fulfilment in the course of the sectors, every inside India and overseas. These days, India boasts almost 1.4 million girls. For girls to be a part of a group of workers, it's critical to promote ability improvement. Skill improvement permits excessive productiveness, increased employment possibilities and higher income. Skill India envisions teaching over four hundred million humans in India through 2022. India has professional rapid boom and development withinside the years in masses of spheres. Gender equality is not one in every one of them. The

Indian development model has but to completely include the crucial function finished through girls for propelling the socio-monetary increase of the country.

As a woman, everyone wants to be excited about themselves. Whether managing a business, a circle of relatives, or the sports world, every aspect of life has a very high record of women's achievements. Most women are born with an entrepreneurial spirit and are diagnosed for that reason. Women are embedded in patience, risk-taking, difficult works of art, etc., and people are the hallmarks of entrepreneurs. The women who became successful entrepreneurs found solutions to their problems after difficult struggles in their living and artistic work environment. Agriculture for smallholders in Manipur has changed significantly over the last few decades. Many of these changes are not just caused by external factors. They are also inspired by farmers constantly looking for better ways to organise their farms, new crops and breeds, better animals, and alternative techniques to diversify production, increase productivity and reduce risk. Smallholders have used a variety of means to develop alternative sources of income. Such income may be somehow related to agriculture (such as marketing and processing of agricultural products) but can also be found outside the direct realm of agriculture. A typical example of this second group is the production of handicrafts or seasonal migration. In this sense, farmers have traditionally been entrepreneurial for quite some time. But there is no doubt that smallholders, if not entirely new, face unique challenges. In many countries, farmers face the major challenge of producing adequate food, feed and fibre in the rapidly growing urban and rural non-agricultural population. Most domestic demand comes from poor people at the lowest possible price. At the same time, they should move the country forward as an entrepreneur.

There are specific sectors where Indian women are the leaders. The amount of their workforce gradually rises in various industries. In India, with government support, female entrepreneurs have undergone remarkable changes, increasing the likelihood of women following such a positive business environment. The myth that women are only good at design, fashion and crafts is evidenced by the entry of women into every industry. However, the government needs to establish commercial activity incubation centres to gain the trust to advance its business further and consider expansion. About 69% of Indian female entrepreneurs start businesses in real estate, technology and fashion. Funds for businesses women are readily available from banks and other financial institutions. Indian manufacturing employs 20% of the total workforce, which is far less than the number of Asian countries. *JCB India* manufactures construction and agricultural equipment, and women's employment is increasing significantly. Currently, India employs more than 110 women trained in the latest technology. In addition, Maruti Suzuki has increased the production group's female worker group from

274 in 2012 to 366 in 2014. Other companies like Kinetic Communications and United Technologies can increasingly hire more women. The latter launched a women's assembly line at the air conditioner manufacturing facility in Gurgaon. Samsung has also opened 18 technical schools in India. The Patna Office is India's first technical training centre for 4,444 women, training more than 5,000 women annually.

Urban India isn't witnessing women's contribution toward social, fitness care and schooling. In India, over a hundred and ten ladies are lively customers of net development for 46%. There are a huge variety of tasks undertaken through rural ladies on the grass-root level, too, in spreading interest for gender equality. Women at village-degree marketers run some Common Service Centres in India. The great instance, which hails from Bihar Vaijanti Devi, began out one such centre supplying online banking offerings for the Aadhar programme and enrolling villagers.

Banking

An extensive variety of Indian banks and economic carrier businesses maintain the reins of ladies. For instance, Arundhati Bhattacharya is a woman to have held the position of Chairperson of the *State Bank of India (SBI)* and additionally named a number of the 50 Most Powerful Women (International).

Pharmaceutical and Healthcare

The sectors pharmaceutical and healthcare have visible enterprising ladies leaders. Swati Piramal was the first female at the helm of a pharmaceutical empire. She seemed as a pioneer who campaigned for cutting-edge drug studies in India and highlighted the importance of medical innovation. Another exemplary female chief, Kiran Mazumdar -Shaw, based at *Biocon*, the sector's leading biotechnology enterprise, has contributed immensely to analysing,

innovation and much less expensive healthcare. Mazumdar-Shaw has been conferred the '2014 distinct Gold Medal and the coveted '2014 Global Economy Prize' for the commercial enterprise through the Germany-based *Kiel Institute* for the sector monetary system.

A Case of Moirangthem Muktabani Devi

Moirangthem Muktabani Devi was born on 15th December 1960 at Kakching Moirangthem Leikai, P.O. & P.S. Kakching and withinside the district of Kakching, Manipur. She is the partner of Kshetrimayum Naran Singh. Presently Moirangthem Muktamani Devi is the founder and proprietor of Mukta Shoes Pvt. Ltd. Kakching, Manipur. She is broadly known for her woollen knitted shoes. She has employed many people in her shoe company and has been promoting this craft with the useful resource of offering training to the young adults of India.

Around 30 years ago, when her daughter's college shoes were torn, she couldn't have sufficient cash to buy a pair of the latest shoes. So she knitted her daughter's torn shoes with antique woollen threads. Her daughter happily wore knitted shoes and went to college. After seeing today's form of shoes, the college teachers began placing orders. It modified then that she struck upon the idea of knitting woollen shoes with woollen threads and rugged soles. She has exported kintted shoes to many distant places as Australia, South Korea, New Zealand, Japan and Dubai. She acquired orders from worldwide places like UK, France and Mexico etc. Muktamani has imparted training to many males and females under Entrepreneurship Development Programme (1993) organised with the useful resource of the usage of North Eastern Industry Consultants Ltd Imphal; Training Programme of Business & Export Management (2002); Short Term Technical training in Knitted Footwear Fabrication at Central Leather Research Institute Chennai (2001-2002); Entrepreneurship Development and Ethnic Design in Leather area at Imphal (2002); Entrepreneurship Skill Development Programme of Woolen shoe making organised with the useful resource of the usage of MSME 2009;6 month Skill Upgradation Training Programme on shoemaking, Manipur 2009; Enterprise Development training Programme for Winner of the Citi Micro Entrepreneur Awards organised at EDI Campus Entrepreneurship Development Institute of Awards and Recognitions:

i) State Award to Master Craftsmen (Consolation Prize) from the Directorate Of Commerce and Industries, Government of Manipur for the 12 months, 1996.

ii) Citi Group Micro Entrepreneurs National Award 2006

iii) National Award (2008) Micro Small & Medium Enterprises.

iv) State Award to Master Craftsmen from the Directorate Of Commerce and Industries, Government of Manipur for the 12 months 2008-2009.

v) Award for the state of Manipur, Vasundhara NE Women Entrepreneurs of the 12 months 2013-14

vi) Vasundhara award for North East Women Entrepreneurs (2013-14)

vii) True Legends awards in 2018 with the aid of using National Insurance and Telegraph

Muktamani who's in her 60s from Moirangthem Leikai of Kakching district, conferred the *Padma Shri* at the event on 73rd Republic Day for her outstanding offerings in Trade and Industry. Unlike everyday footwear, her footwear is all handmade and vegan footwear that is leather-based. The footwear is made using woollen and nylon yarn, gum and rubber. It took kind of 2-3 days to complete the footwear individually. Speaking completely to the Imphal Free Press, Muktamani stated that the footwear she knitted for her daughter was given high-quality comments from her trainer and asked to make an equal for her daughter. "With getting such high-quality comments, a concept caught in my thoughts to set up an enterprise with the aid of making and promoting footwear. Without any put-off, I began making diverse footwear by using sg for the uncooked cloth from Kakhulong marketplace in Imphal," narrated Muktamani.

Discontinuous innovation makes current merchandise and techniques obsolete; it generates vast investments as different businesses are looking to mimic the ideas. Entrepreneurs capitalise on mounted companies' large investments and technological traits to create worthwhile ventures. These big businesses were accountable for each technological improvement and transfer of generation outcomes. Also, in which sources are scarce, entrepreneurial efforts that bring about new manufacturing strategies can cause productiveness consistent with aid units. When marketers marched forward, human beings accompanied them due to their notable individualistic qualities, a state of affairs that speedy gave incipient institutions, essential for the most desirable usage of charisma. The fabric quarter in India is one of the world's largest; it has extra hooked-up spindles to make spun yarn than every other United States of America besides China and has the maximum looms in the area to weave fabric. The Indian fabric Industry contains 3 inter-associated but competing sectors- the prepared mill quarter, the "decentralised" handloom, and the strength loom sectors (Gurrusamy & et al. 2012).

Jaishree Kabra of Kothari Silk Mills

Jayshree's Kothari Silk Mills fall beneath the power loom sector, consequently accountable for sizeable capital formation and activity advent and notably growing nearby widespread of residing of the workforce. Ms Jaishree was born in a small far-off village-*Piparia,* close to Itarsi, Madhya Pradesh, India, in Marwari enterprise's circle of relatives. She studied eighth grade at Burhanpur, Maharashtra. She finished her commencement from *SNDT, Surat in Food and Nutrition.* After marriage, nearly for nine to ten years, she changed into a domestic maker, catering to the family chores and engaging in social life. Her husband dealing in textiles within the Surat marketplace and her brother in a similar associated activity made her dabble within the style segment. Following this situation changed into an urge to do something extra energetic and innovative in preference to being a staid domestic maker. Ms Jahasee has proven her tenacity and bravery. She started a company no longer as means of compulsion or risk but through awareness, preference and pragmatic interest.

She joined her brothers' layout studio *Kothari* Silk Mills, Surat, along with her husband, for a market survey. This company has now grown and blossomed into a company with one hundred professional and unskilled personnel. Women marketers have the first-rate ability to empower and rework society, consequently synthesising social and monetary development. Jayshree's dynamic and adaptive group generates 20 to twenty-five samples daily and churns out 2 to a few catalogues each month, with every catalogue having 12 to 18 designs. They declare that none in their designs are ever repeated.

According to Jaishree, Fashion is like a fresh vegetable. It needs to be innovatively treated and creatively executed. Perpetual development is the key. Fashion repeats cyclically, and the catalogues are prepared and distributed to the intermediaries, primarily located in the Northern India market, as also to export markets such as Bangladesh, Dubai, the UK, etc. Not much marketing activity is undertaken in Surat. The group is fully equipped with updated technological knowledge, which has resulted in its foray into online marketing for the last 12 months, and the response is overwhelming. The online channel now contributes almost 25% of their turnover. On average, 25000 suits are sold daily from this business house, ranging in the price brand of Rs 350 to Rs 700 per suit (wholesale rate), which translates into a price band of Rs 1200 to Rs 2000 per suit at the retail level. Before this design studio was commissioned, only 12 to 15 % of their design requirements could be catered in-house. The rest had to be outsourced. Now almost 90% of their design requirements are fulfilled in-house. The last five years may not have increased the number of daily units sold, but they have moved up the value chain and creativity, and now the market looks up to them as trendsetters. The design studio and the business house do not participate in fashion shows or similar marketing events. The 3500 sq. ft. design studio employing 100 people has given a springboard to their business volumes where they can double their turnover every second year.

Entrepreneurship plays a significant role in the harnessing of knowledge and the conversion of this harnessed power into future goods and services through industrial innovation, an enviable achievement of *Kothari Design Studio.* With the tremendous growth of technology and the demand for their products, the enterprise has started online marketing, resulting in more far-reaching access. The tie-up with a web content developer, where the developer handles the logistics and accounts part of the business, has helped the business house excellently. Jaishree feels that there are no problems in life or business. They are all challenges which need to be addressed. Not having a background of success made her dig in her heels and perseverance. She adroitly handles skilled and unskilled labour issues. She controls and coordinates this issue by keeping a second line a standby and ready. As of now, she has not faced any labour issues. For a trained and skilled workforce, they have employed students from different fashion designing institutes as designers. Each person needs about six months of in-house training before they start delivering. In the initial stages of the growth of the design studio, this skilled workforce moved off to competitors within six months. However, in the last two years, they're more stable, and now almost 60% of their workforce has been with them for five years or more. People are allowed, incentivised and motivated to upgrade themselves in the hierarchy. Formal education, although desirable, lack of education is not a hindrance for an excellent designer to excel. However, despite all these acceptance of challenges, one area where she feels the trust in the society needs to develop in women entrepreneurs is their capabilities to maintain the business financials. Jayshree's finance is managed and handled by her husband and her brother. This is one glass ceiling she would love to break one day.

Jayshree contributes significantly to increased production quality, productivity, marketing effectiveness, and job creation amongst women. Another important aspect of Jaishree is that she has proactively encouraged females to take up employment in her enterprise. Here they feel safe, and there is a family-like atmosphere. Women entrepreneurs bring ethics in business and a human approach to socio-economic relations, as seen in Jaishree's enterprise. Male-owned companies have a workforce that is often more than 85% men. However, women are more likely to employ more gender-balanced personnel, comprising nearly 52% of females and 48% of males. The same is the case in Kothari Design Studio, managed by Jaishree, where she has a workforce of more than 51% females and 49% males. In the male-dominated textile business, females from all social sectors feel safe working with Jaishree.

Practices in the Textile Industry have the flexibility to respond quickly to market changes and opportunities and rapidly absorb innovation and creativity. This has resulted in a systematic department which follows-a motivational programme, TQM, training programs, personal counselling etc., undertaken for the benefit of the employees. There may be no corporate structure or similar employee benefits, but performance appraisal is conducted periodically. Performance review takes place every month, but in crucial times even everyday review is undergone.

The suits are all non-synthetic. Cotton, viscose, silk, etc. Fabrics procured from Benares, Bhiwandi and Surat are used. The further processing, cutting and packing are done in-house. The products address the fashion requirements of the mass market, and the target is to double the turnover every year.

Ms Jaishree has a fantastic ability to multitask and balance personal and professional life with her focused and goal-oriented approach and future planning. By striking a proper balance between personal and professional life, Kothari design studio is planning the diversification into Garmenting (Kurtis section), which is being seriously pursued. A new team for designing and sampling is being constituted. The manufacturing part of this diversification may be either outsourced or in-house. The business is now co-owned by Ms Jaishree and her brother. Her husband has now taken the liberty of shifting his focus to real estate in Surat and at Jodhpur. This probably is the most satisfying part of the journey of Entrepreneurship taken by Jaishree.

A Case of Yumnam Ongbi Arundayanti

Yumnam Ongbi Arundayanti is a living example of success without much investment and strong family background. However, she possesses a strong will for self-determination and self-confidence. She is a strong icon of Manipuri woman braving all odds and difficulties to keep the kitchen fire burning.

Life background

Naorem Ningol Yumnam Ongbi Arundayanti Devi (50 years), a lady entrepreneur who prepares numerous pickles and sweet merchandise below the logo Arundayanti Food Processing, is many of the hit ladies marketers in Manipur. She presents employment to many ladies of her locality, especially the widowed ladies suffering or poverty-pushed households and kids.

She was married to Yumnam Rajen of Oinam Kangjeibung Mapal, Bishnupur district, Manipur, and she is now a mom of 1 son and a daughter. Her husband is a councillor of Oinam Naga Panchayat, who extends his assistance to his better-half in taking over the enterprise efficiently.

Arundayanti, who finished B. Sc (Zoology), now no longer have a dreamt of proudly owning an enterprise. After marriage, she initiated her vegetable and fruit supplies at Khwairamband Keithel to assist her circle of relatives. The idea of setting up a meal processing enterprise came to her mind when fruits were getting rotten throughout the bandhs. In Manipur, there are hundreds of widowed ladies. These widowed ladies are suffering for their kids and households. "I need to empower them, raise their monetary circumstance", she said.

She began her entrepreneurial adventure compelled with the aid of using her ardour for imparting jobs to many jobless while putting a meal processing enterprise of her very own. Arundayanti commenced her project on meal processing in 2012 and did not use formal schooling or skill. With only Rs 500, she started making processed meals like pickles and sweets at her tiny domestic at Oinam. In due course of time, as she felt the want of present formal schooling, she joined a one-month meals processing training by countrywide meals processing venture held at a Food processing centre, Porompat. After training in meal processing, her enterprise received momentum efficiently by using the best merchandise and advertising strategy. With preliminary capital funding on trial and error, she started her business *Arundayanti Food Processing* with six nearby ladies workers.

Products and employment

She has been able to employ around 15 local women who are engaged in the work of processing and packaging the various pickle and candy items. Arundayanti and her team prepare varied pickle items such as fish, chicken, pork,beef,ngari,thumyakpi and khajing for non-vegetarian groups and soibum, umorok, mushroom, hawaijar akangba, garlic, turmeric, heiribop, mango, hangam (mustard), olive, heimang makeup, heitup, heiku, mange heining, morok atekpa (fresh chilly), heikru (gooseberry) for vegetarian groups.

She is planning to expand the business with the target of exporting. The lady entrepreneur feels that economy of the state can be developed if the state government focuses on growing the food processing sector in priority. However, due to financial constraints, her willingness to expand the business cannot be materialised to date.

The products of Arundayanti have been showcased in the food festival held at Bishnupur organised by Khadi and Village Industries Board, the MSME food expo at Hapta Kangjeibung and Sangai festival. She had also joined the honey festival at Kangla organised by the Horticulture department.

Her farm sells honey too

No doubt, the lady entrepreneur is also a bee farmer. She also keeps around ten bee boxes at home and sells honey-packed bottles. She also collects honey from her locality at a wholesale rate. Her younger brother is the leading supplier of honey.

Appeal to the government to encourage genuine entrepreneurs

Expressing concern over the increasing malpractices in selecting beneficiaries for financial grants or loans, she said the government needs to identify the genuine entrepreneurs while selecting beneficiaries for schemes. Selection of beneficiaries by corrupt practices will waste the public money, and the desired target of the schemes cannot be achieved. Many fake entrepreneurs raise their heads when the government issues notice regarding providing loans/grants. Such fake entrepreneurs misused the loan money to buy luxury cars instead of using the money in the proper way it should be.

Conclusion

It is the need of the hour to assist women in scaling new heights in their entrepreneurial journey. The right kind of assistance from the family, society and government can make these Women Entrepreneurs a part of the mainstream Indian economy. "Woman is the full circle, within her is the power to create, nurture and transform"; therefore, empowering women entrepreneurs is essential for achieving the country's sustainable development goals. There has been a stable enhancement in the participation of women enterprises, indicating the potential for entrepreneurial development among them. India women enterprises made a significant contribution towards the generation of employment, gross output, asset creation and exports. And it additionally indicates that own circle of relatives performs a vital position in helping and inspiring girls to begin their enterprises-the Importance of Women's Economic Independence. A middle circumstance to ladies' safety is to quit their dependence and helplessness, whose key element is to invest ladies with energy: at the man or woman level, to aid the advent in their autonomy and economic independence, and on the social level, to sell their identical get entry to political, social energy and the power enabling the forming of opinion. The creator might ultimately like to speak of the woman entrepreneurship activity, which affords women with profits received of their right, on the same time, confirms their capacity to prosper independently, reduces their lack of confidence concerning the power of looking after their kids, hence encouraging different ladies as nicely to attempt to anticipate their autonomy in personal, monetary, even political sense, to make unbiased decisions, to rise for themselves and their surroundings.

References

Abdullah F. (2009). Developing a framework of success of Bumiputera entrepreneurs, Journal of Enterprising Communities, Vol. 3 No. 1, 2009 pp. 8-24

Adoram, G. (2011). "Gender differences and their impact on Entrepreneurial Ventures", Advances in Management, Vol 4 (2), pp. 13-18

Ayadurai, D. (1987). The Employer, the Employee and the Law in Malaysia, Butterworths: London.

Carland, J.W., Hoy, F., Boulton, W.R., and Carland, J.C. (1996). Differentiating entrepreneurs from small business owners: A conceptualization,' Academy of Management Review, Vol. 9(2). pp. 354-359.

David Z. and Edward B. (2011). Personal characteristics and strategic orientation: entrepreneurs in Canadian manufacturing companies, International Journal of Entrepreneurial Behaviour & Research, Vol. 17 No. 1, 2011, pp. 82-103 |

Desai, V. (2001). Dynamics of Entrepreneurial Development and Management, Himalaya Publishing House, New Delhi.

Ehigie, B.O. and Umoren, U. E. (2003). Psychological factors influencing perceived entrepreneurial success among Nigerian women in small-scale businesses. Journal of International Women's Studies, Vol. 5(1), pp. 78-95. |

Elenurm, T.(2001). "Development needs of Estonian entrepreneurs and managers for international business", 4th McGill Conference on International Entrepreneurship, Vol. 1, |

Evens, George Herberton (1949). "Entrepreneur and Economic Theory," American Economic Review, p.338.

https://www.statista.com/statistics/1047327/india-reliance-industries-exchequer-contribution/

Kala, S., Singal, S. and Gover, I. (2002). Economics of stitching enterprises run by tribal

Kanungo, Rabindra N. (Ed.) (1998). Entrepreneurship & Innovation: Models for Development, New Delhi, Sage Publications.

Kirzner, I. (1973), Competition and entrepreneurship, Chicago, Chicago University Press.

Lalitha Rani, D. (1996). Women entrepreneurs, APH Publishing Corporation, New Delhi. p. 9.

Melih Bulu (2005). The Characteristics Of Turkish Entrepreneurs, Global Business And Technology Association

Nandapurkar, G.G. (1982). Small farmers – A study on their entrepreneurial behaviour Metropolitan Book Co. (Pvt. Ltd.) New Delhi pp. 1-2.

Nandram S. and Karel Samsom (2007). Entrepreneurial Behaviour, NRG Working Paper no. 07-04

Noor H. et al (2009). Is entrepreneurial competency and business success relationship contingent upon business environment? A study of Malaysian SMEs, International Journal of Entrepreneurial Behaviour & Research, Vol. 16 No. 3, 2010, pp. 182-203

Papzan et al (2008). Determining factors influencing rural entrepreneurs' success, African Journal of Agricultural Research Vol. 3 (9), pp. 597-600. Robbins, S.P. and Judge, T.A. (2009), Organizational Behaviour. Pearson education, New York.

Sammy King-fai Hui et al (2006). International Journal of Entrepreneurial Behaviour & Research, Factors involved in the success of Hong Kong construction and property entrepreneurs , Vol. 12 No. 4, 2006 , pp. 228-245

Simeon Djankov et al (2007). What Makes a Successful Entrepreneur? Evidence from Brazil. Timmons, J.A. (1994). New Venture Creation, Entrepreneurship for the 21st Century, 4th Edition, Irwin. University of Strathclyde, Glasgow, pp. 384-407.

Viral acharya et al (2004). what determines entrepreneurial Success, www.ifmr.ac.in/pdf/drishtee.pdf women entrepreneurs- case study of Bihar. Maharashtra J. Extension Edu., 21 (1): 71-74.

3

SWOT Analysis

Roop Kumar and Sharad Sachan

Department of Agricultural Economics and Extension, School of Agriculture Lovely Professional University, Phagwara, Punjab

Introduction

Strategic planning is how an organisation determines how to allocate its resources to pursue its strategy or direction. Based on an assessment of the internal and external environments within which an organisation operates, strategic management is concerned with developing and implementing an organisation's long-term goals for its stakeholders.

When it comes to strategic planning and management, the SWOT analysis (or SWOT matrix) is a tool that can be used to determine a company's competitive advantage by analysing its strengths, weaknesses, opportunities, and threats. Situational assessment or situational analysis is another name. TOWS and WOTS-UP are two other acronyms based on the same components.

Keywords

SWOT analysis: Analysis of external and internal environment together is called SWOT analysis.

Strength: It is the primary asset of an organisation that would provide a competitive advantage for its growth and development.

Weakness: It is an organisation's liability that creates a state of time and situation-specific disadvantage for its growth and development.

Opportunities: The organisation can grow and achieve its specific objective in each situation

Threats: It is a situation that blocks the abilities of the organisation to grow and develop to reach its goal.

SWOT is a planning tool used to understand the Strengths, Weaknesses, Opportunities, & Threats involved in a project/business. A strategy that allows a group or individual to shift from everyday problems and standard approaches to a new perspective. SWOT analysis examines your company's strengths and weaknesses, as well as the opportunities and dangers it faces. This Technique is credited to **Albert Humphrey** who led a research project at Stanford University in the **1960s and 1970s.** It is used as a framework for organising and utilising data and information gleaned from internal and external environment scenario analyses.

A SWOT analysis is a scientific method for evaluating a company's prospects for survival and success. The SWOT analysis provides insight into the organisation's strengths and weaknesses. This method's greatest benefit is that it alerts management to potential threats before they arise. Aside from organisations, this concept is also applicable to businesses and programmes.

An organisation's SWOT analysis looks at its strengths, weaknesses, opportunities, and threats. As part of strategic planning, a SWOT analysis is a quality review of industrial business and any profit and non-profit organisations management and institutions by scanning the internal and external environments. Using SWOT analysis, a situational analysis can be used to provide a list of possible strategy options. It can be used at both the corporate and unitary levels. The SWOT framework can be constructed in the following manner in its simplest form.

Internal attributes: The company has some untapped potential that must be discovered and put to good use if it is to grow. The organisation has its strengths and weaknesses.

External attributes: These are the external factors that have an impact on the company. Obtaining the assistance of external organisations is one way to improve the organisation's status. These are the company's strengths and weaknesses.

Definition

It refers to identifying the strengths, weaknesses, opportunities, and threats of an organisation

The SWOT Analysis framework is in marketing management and other business applications, this is a significant and valuable tool.

- Essential and helpful tool that may be used in the management of marketing and various other company applications.
- Students majoring in business are expected to have a solid comprehension of the SWOT analysis.

- Performing a thorough SWOT analysis on the company and the environment in which it operates, looking for opportunities, threats, strengths, and weaknesses in each of these categories.

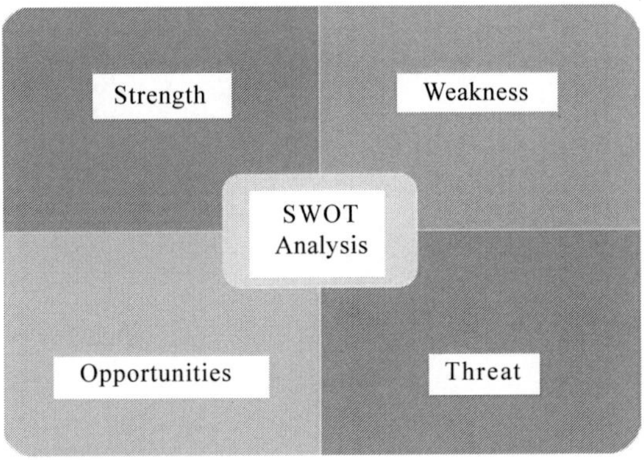

Figure 1. SWOT matrix

SWOT Analysis

1. Strengths

An organisation's mission, aims, and objectives can be achieved if there are good internal influences. A company's core strength is what gives it a competitive advantage in the marketplace and enables it to grow and flourish. An organisation's internal strength can be judged by looking at the environment in which it operates. Positive tangible and intangible attributes, internal to an organisation. Strengths are the company's core competencies, and include proprietary technology, skills, resources, market position, patents, and others strengths are within the control of the entrepreneur and they occur at present. Some of the strengths of an organisation are:

1. Infrastructure is readily available
2. Highly-trained workers
3. Production capacity must be sufficient.
4. Quality assurance and quality control in manufacturing
5. Low manufacturing costs
6. A sufficient light source,
7. Widespread availability
8. Motivated employees.
9. Streamlined operations

10. A good name in the community,
11. The building of a good institution (Rules, regulations, procedures),
12. The practise of fostering cooperation among members of a group,
13. Strong evaluation and monitoring system.
14. Product features (utility, durability, etc.)
15. Good network with customers
16. Superior technology
17. Packaging
18. Managerial experience

Organisational assets include highly trained and committed employees as well as an enthused management team. The appropriate programmes that have been implemented thus far may have produced a favourable environment for the organisation's growth.

2. Weaknesses

Negative internal influences impede the achievement of an organisation's mission, goals, and objectives. An organisation's weakness is a liability that can put it at a disadvantage at any given time and in any given situation. It's possible that the organisation has flaws that make it impossible to move forward. Some of the weaknesses of an organisation are;

1. Escalating operating expenses,
2. A lack of employee enthusiasm
3. The inability to obtain raw resources;
4. A lack of funds
5. Insufficient skilled technicians
6. Ineffective communication and lack of coordination
7. Incompetent leadership,
8. A poor distribution system
9. Lack of adaptability in the workplace.
10. Comparatively high price
11. Lack of promotion experience
12. Limited product life
13. Technological obsolescence

14. Poor design of product
15. Low level of stocks in times of peak sales
16. Lack technical expertise of owner
17. Problem of underutilization of capacity
18. Poor project planning
19. Unorganised nature of operations

It's possible that some staff members may have outdated notions, because of the low pay scale, the time it takes to appoint new employees, and the absence of employee amenities. The organisation's flaws must be addressed if it is to progress.

3. Opportunities

In order to achieve its mission, goals, and objectives, a company can utilise positive external variables. Having an opportunity to expand and achieve its specific goals in a given environment is a benefit to the company. The organisation has to utilise the opportunities or opportunities of an organisation are:

1. The location is excellent.
2. Income that can be spent on other things,
3. The availability of the right technology, if necessary
4. Possibility of varied work environments like market information, distribution channels and media; Favourable government legislation;
5. Predictors of a good cultural context,
6. Common fundamental infrastructural facilities are available
7. The customer group is a responsible and responsive community or society.

In order to generate excitement about the establishment of a new institution, these could be merged with well-known local institutions. The ability to broaden the range of services offered by expanding the competence of the workforce. These are a few instances of how to re-energise an already-existing company.

4. Threats

In order to achieve its aims, the organisation is hampered by negative external forces. A threat is an external circumstance that hinders the organisation's ability to expand and improve in order to achieve its ultimate aim. It is a worry of the organisation's demise. The organisation will suffer if the threats are not dealt with appropriately. Some of the threats of an organisation are;

1. Lack of electricity, water, and fuel
2. The market's rejection of your product,
3. Competition is fierce.
4. Fiscal policy that results in higher taxes, duties, import reservations, licencing, and so on
5. A piece of technology that is out of date.
6. Resources are limited.
7. A shift in the preferences and knowledge of the target audience,
8. There is a great deal of volatility in the economy.
9. Prolonged economic downturns, recurrent natural disasters, and other such events
10. Reversing the direction of government policy.
11. Rising raw materials costs
12. Too much competition
13. Restive labour force
14. Piracy of skilled labour
15. Graft and corruption
16. Poor infrastructure
17. Resources crunch (Chole et al 2012; Mondal 2019)

An organisation's identity, strengths, and reputation may be jeopardised. There's a chance that valuable employees may be left behind, and the culture of the competing business will take hold. These threats must be detected and dealt with in order for the organisation to survive. Regardless of the type of business, SWOT analysis is critical in management science while trying to decipher management issues at various stages. When making decisions about an organisation's development in a specific operational environment, the notion is useful. In addition to trade, commerce, industry, and so on, SWOT analysis is now widely used in agriculture and related fields. (Visual Paradigms, n.d.)

Aim of SWOT analysis

- To help decision-makers share and compare ideas.
- To bring a clearer-common purpose and understanding of factors for success.
- To organise the significant aspects associated with business success and failure.

- To offer linearity to the decision-making process, allowing for the orderly presentation of complicated ideas.

Who needs SWOT analysis?

SWOT analysis has been utilised at various levels of analysis in numerous industries, and also by non-profit making organisations. Non-profits, government agencies, and individuals are all good examples.

SWOT analysis is needed by job holders who work in government or private jobs , business units and company.

- Its require for the job holder when supervisor has issue with work output; assigned to a new job; New financial year fresh targets; Jobholders seeks to improve performance on the job.
- Business unit requires SWOT analysis in situations where the team has not achieved its goals; Customer service can be better; Launching the new business units to pursue a new business; new team leader is appointed.
- Company requires SWOT analysis when revenue costs and expense targets are not being achieved; market share is declining; Industry conditions are unfavourable; and during launching a new business venture.(Indian Council of Agricultural Research, 2020)

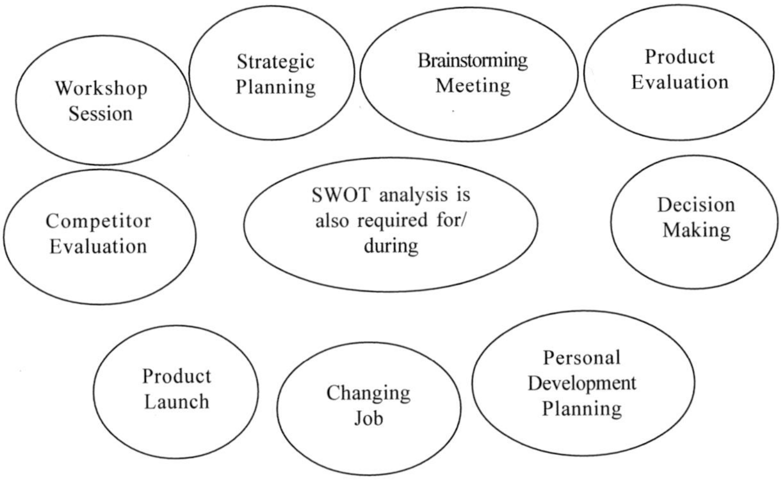

Figure 2. Who needs SWOT analysis

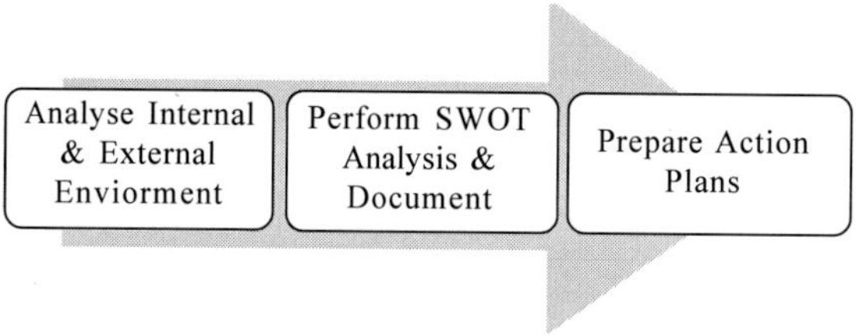

Figure 3. How to conduct SWOT analysis

How to conduct SWOT analysis

i) **Analyse internal & external environment-** This can be done by situation analysis. Situation analysis for internal environment requires to assess weakness and strength. External analysis requires assessing the opportunity and threats available in the environment.

ii) **Perform SWOT Analysis & Document**

1. **Establish the objective-** Purpose of conducting a SWOT may be wide/narrow, general/specific.
2. **Select Contributors-** Expert opinion may be required for SWOT.
3. **Allocate research & information gathering tasks-** Background preparation can be carried out in two stages-Exploratory & Detailed. Information on strengths and weakness should focus on the internal factors.
4. **Create a workshop environment-** Encourage an atmosphere conducive to the free flow of information.
5. **Evaluate listed ideas against objective-** With the lists compiled, sort and group facts and ideas in relation to the objective.
6. **List Strengths, weaknesses opportunities & threats**
7. **Carry your findings forward-** SWOT analysis is used in subsequent planning, revisit your findings at suitable time interval.

iii) **Prepare Action Plan**

After doing the SWOT analysis, you should label each point with one of the following:

- Things that must be addressed immediately
- Things that are currently manageable
- Things that warrant further investigation
- Things need additional research

Shortcoming of SWOT Analysis

- Often highly subjective. Rarely do two individuals arrive at the same final version of a SWOT analysis.
- Use the information as a guide, not as a prescription.
- Causes organisations to regard a situation as extremely simple, resulting in the overlooking of a crucial strategic contact.
- Due to the high level of unpredictability in the market, it may be subjective to classify aspects as strengths, weaknesses, opportunities, and threats.
- For SWOT to be effective, it must be completed frequently. The rate of change makes it challenging to foresee future events.
- The analysis's results may be based on suppositions that ultimately prove to be false (good & bad).
- It lacks detailed structure, so key element may get missed.

Tips for SWOT analysis

Do's

- Be analytical and specific.
- Record all thoughts and ideas.
- Be selective in the final evaluation.
- Choose the right people for the exercise.
- Choose a suitable SWOT leader or facilitator.
- Think out of the box.
- Be open to change.

Dont's

- Attempt to mask your weakness.
- Simply list errors and oversights
- Let yourself become oblivious to outside influences and trends.
- Ignore the influences and trends coming from the outside world.
- Ignore the results of the planning step at later stages of the procedure.

Conclusion

It is essential to either maintain, expand, or capitalise on strengths that have been established. It is imperative to either find solutions to the issues or put an end to the failures. It is essential to organise one's priorities and seize chances when they present themselves. It is essential to organise one's priorities and make the most of one's available opportunities.

Case study- SWOT analysis of Nestle

The case study is based on the (Shen Y, 2022) report.

Nestle is one of the world's most well-known foods and drinks companies. Since it was founded in 1866, Nestle has set up shops or offices in more than 186 countries, giving it a large market share. They have a wide range of products that meet almost all of the needs of customers of all ages, but as the company grows, they ignore some things that hurt Nestle's reputation and image. Since the 1980s, Nestle's reputation has been damaged. The problems include but are not limited to using child labour by companies further down the supply chain, incorrect or missing nutritional product identification, and bad press about its newborn formula. One of their main concerns is how to win back the trust of the market and customers. Even though Nestle is now one of the top 100 companies in the world (it was ranked 39th on Forbes' global brand value list in 2021), the company is still worried about how its customers see it. So, Nestle's social giving has gotten a lot better. Nestle should set up a fund to help people in the third world solve fundamental problems like fetching water, protecting forests, and getting health care and medical help. Also, healthy and nutritious products are at the heart of a competitive market, so Nestle needs to put a lot of effort into research and development and come out with new products to meet the needs of a wide range of customers.

Situation Analysis

Mr Henry Nestle started Nestle in 1867, and its headquarters are in the Swiss city of Vevey. Nestle is the biggest food company in the world. It has more than 500 factories all over the world. "Good food, good life" is Nestle's slogan. Because of this, Nestle's purpose and goal are to give its customers the best food possible. Nestle began by making food for babies, but its chocolate bars and instant coffee are what people know it for. But Nestle hasn't had a good reputation or a lot of customers coming back in the last few years. The first problem is that children are forced to work. Because of this problem, Nestle's reputation has taken a big hit. Because this situation was brought to light, Nestle had to sign a cocoa agreement to protect its reputation. Nestle, however, has used several cruel methods and actions over the past ten years. This gives Nestle a lousy reputation in society.

Another problem is that people are misled, and Henry Nestle's idea of "Nestle's parenting courage" from the 1860s is the first example of this. Then, this product became a big hit. Then, Nestle's marketing said that its way of raising children was slightly better than breastfeeding. As a result, many people are using this product instead of nursing. But this is not true. Also, Nestle's advertising of its raw materials is a good example. The food industry doesn't have any well-known ways to figure out which products are better. Some companies use documents that show their private standards as a way to advertise. Nestle is an excellent example of this. Some regulators think Nestle only shows the parts that can improve its products. It doesn't show the wrong things with its products, like the fact that they contain harmful ingredients. Because of these two things, people and businesses no longer trust Nestle. The last question concerns Nestle's weakness, which is how it interacts with the outside social environment. Nestle uses a lot of plastics that don't break down in the environment to package its products, like the famous Pol Spring bottled water brand. Also, the whole production process wastes a lot of water, but the company has no technology or plan to fix this. In 2015, there was a terrible drought in California. Even though these two worries seem to have nothing to do with each other, Nestle's actions continue to make people worried and angry.

Strengths

- Nestle is one of the essential food and drinks companies in the world. It has been around for a long time and does well in more than 186 countries.
- Many kinds of products exist, including the most well-known and popular brands. Its subsidiaries are better than its competitors in some ways. People are familiar with Nestle's products & have been using them for many years.
- In 2020, the country's natural growth rate will be 3.6%, the highest it has been in the last five years. This shows that the government has a solid financial capacity.
- Nestle has built strong relationships with well-known retailers and suppliers in several countries.
- The strong R&D department is dedicated to making products that protect the environment. As a result, pollution-free status has been reached by up to 293 factories. At the same time, the environmental protection strategy says that for every tonne of goods made in 2018, greenhouse gas emissions will go down by 2.6%.
- A strong marketing department

Weakness

- Some items have issues with production and advertising reputation. For example, some infant milk powder in China contains excessive arsenic. In addition, a California corporation is suspected of illegal water use and anti-union sentiment, and some developing-country suppliers use child labour. These have resulted in negative public criticism, indicating that the legal department has flaws in failing to take proper action.
- Highly reliant on advertising to advertise their products and compete with competitors, resulting in high marketing costs.
- Mislabelling products in the past has resulted in people losing trust in Nestle's products and essential market shares, such as those in India and China.
- Inadequate visibility as a responsible and ecologically conscious corporation.
- Some products have excessive sugar and sodium, which contradicts the company's health image.

Opportunity

- With the advent of digital media, e-commerce sales accounted for 8.5 per cent of total sales in 2019, with an 18.5 per cent growth rate.

  Despite having the lowest overall turnover, Zone Asia, Oceania, and Sub-Saharan Africa have significant potential and a high number of rising economies. Nestle can increase its market penetration and reclaim people's trust in AOA countries.
- Form cooperation with strategic ecological companies such as NGO protection international to promote Nestle's new face and participate in environmental sustainability.
- People are now more likely to choose pre-packaged food and functional food because they work longer hours. As a result, overall sales in this category moved steadily from fifth in 2018 to fourth in 2020.
- Get closer to retailers to encourage them to sell healthy food.
- New trends: caring about the environment and other people.

Threats

- People are paying more attention to what's in things because of the new healthy lifestyle. However, this could hurt Nestle's sales because most products are made with artificial ingredients.

- A lot of stores are making their goods. So Nestle has new competitors in how they price their products and position themselves in stores.
- People are spending less time at home because of changes in how they work. This means there is less time for people to buy certain Nestle products.
- The prices of raw materials, like coffee beans, are rising.
- Customers are becoming less loyal, and people care more about price than brand. In the last few years, some Nestle products have become less popular because there is so much competition, especially in the dairy products market.

Conclusion

Customers are becoming less loyal, and people are choosing price over brand. In recent years, some Nestle products have become less popular because there is so much competition, especially in the dairy products market. By putting a positive transformation strategy into place, Nestle can turn its opportunities and problems into benefits. Its marketing department is a competitive advantage in getting this project off the ground. This move will help Nestle's reputation and bring back the market they lost. Nestle will show that it needs to change its old image by working on environmental and social projects and making healthier products. The marketing department needs to promote these efforts to be seen. This may take a long time, but the results will last.

References

Chole, R.R., Kapse, P.S. and Deshmukh. (2012). Entrepreneurship development and Business Communication Skills. Scientific Publishers.

Indian Council of Agricultural Research. (2020). Handbook of agricultural extension. Indian Council of Agricultural Research. Directorate of Knowledge Management in Agriculture.

Kenton, W. (2017). Strength, Weakness, Opportunity, and Threat (SWOT) Analysis Definition. https://www.investopedia.com/terms/s/swot.asp.

Madsen, Dag Divind (2016). "SWOT analysis: a management fashion perspective". International Journal of Business Research. 16 (1): 39–56.

MindTools. (n.d.). SWOT Analysis Model and Examples - Business Strategy Skills. Retrieved May 23, 2022, from https://www.mindtools.com/pages/article/newTMC_05.htm

MANAGE. (2013). Agri-business and Entrepreneurship Development. https://www.manage.gov.in/moocs/structure.asp

Mondal, Sagar. (2019). Fundamentals of Agricultural Extension Education. Kalyani Publications. India

Nag, R.; Hambrick, D. C.; Chen, M.-J (2007). What is strategic management, really? Inductive derivation of a consensus definition of the field. Strategic Management Journal. 28 (9): 935–955. CiteSeerX 10.1.1.491.7592. doi:10.1002/smj.615.qn|date=June 2018

SWOT analysis of an entrepreneur in Basics of Entrepreneurship Development in Agriculture. (2022). https://www.agmoocs.in/beda/#/home

Sevier, Robert A. (2001). Not SWOT, but OTSW. Thinking outside the box: some (fairly) radical thoughts on how colleges and universities should think, act, and communicate in a very busy marketplace. Hiawatha, Iowa: Strategy Pub. p. 46. ISBN 0971059705. OCLC 48165005

Shen, Y. (2022). *SWOT Analysis and Strategy Selection of Nestle Based On 2018-2020 Annual Report.*

Weihrich, Heinz (April 1982). The TOWS matrix-a tool for situational analysis. Long Range Planning. 15 (2): 54–66. doi:10.1016/0024-6301(82)90120-0.

Visual Paradigms. (n.d.). What is SWOT Analysis? Retrieved May 23, 2022, from https://www.visual-paradigm.com/guide/strategic-analysis/what-is-swot-analysis/

4

Achievement Motivation

Nidhi Thakur

Department of Agricultural Economics and Extension, School of Agriculture Lovely Professional University, Phagwara, Punjab

"Only those who attempt the absurd can achieve the impossible."

- ***Albert* Einstein**

Motivation– An inner state of need or desire that activates an individual to do something that will satisfy that need or desire.

The processes that are responsible for an individual's intensity, direction and persistence of effort toward attaining a goal.

Key Elements

1. **Intensity**: how hard a person tries
2. **Direction**: toward the beneficial goal
3. **Persistence**: how long a person tries

Motivation in Organizations

- If you want to influence/motivate people, first think about their needs.
- Knowing this, the following is the formula for finding out what people's needs are?

  P = f (A X M X O)

  Where:

  P - Performance

  A - Ability

  M - Motivation

  O - Opportunity

Types of motivation

Extrinsic motivation is an example of an extrinsic type of motivation. It is a way of behaving that is motivated by things outside of oneself, such as rewards, money, appreciation, celebrity, grades, and acclaim. This kind of drive originates from sources other than the individual.

The presence of another person is not a prerequisite for extrinsic motivation to exist; rather, it refers to any external demand, obligation, or reward that necessitates the accomplishment of a certain objective.

Intrinsic motivation is an internal form of motivation. It refers to behaviour that is driven by internal factors such as striving or desire towards a goal for personal mental peace/satisfaction or accomplishment.

Achievement – A thing that has been effectively accomplished via the application of work, skill, or daring.

Achievement motivation- Achievement motivation can be defined as the need for success or the attainment of excellence. Individuals will satisfy their needs in different ways. People are motivated to achieve their goals for a variety of reasons, both internal and external to themselves. All of our activities are driven, first and foremost, by our motivation.

What is achievement motivation?

Motive is the driving force behind everyone's actions based on emotions and achievement-related goals. Achievement motivation is a social psychological term; it describes when individuals are driven, inspired or stimulated by successes or accomplishments.

In the workplace, achievement motivation leads people to be high performers who desire success and fear failure. They focus on responsibilities that they are capable of completing well while avoiding jobs or responsibilities that could cause them to fail. The desire to succeed is another factor that motivates people to keep working hard, putting in long hours, and focusing on goals they are confident they can achieve. They have a strong desire to find positions in which they may achieve success, be given feedback, and have a sense of accomplishment in their work. To put it another way, people who are motivated prefer to take on challenging activities with a modest level of risk so that they can succeed and feel capable. They avoid jobs that are difficult because they run the risk of failing at them and ones that are simple because they don't feel satisfied when they finish them.

History

The achievement was initially recognized by the American psychologist Henry Murray as an important source of human motivation in the late 1930s. Although Murray identified achievement motivation as important to the behaviour of many people, it was the American psychologists David McClelland and John Atkinson who devised a way of measuring differences in achievement motivation. They used Murray's Thematic Appreciation Test (TAT), a 20 cards presented in a series which had ambiguous pictures and individuals were asked to write stories (as it helps to determine personality traits) to measure disparity in achievement motivation. By using a content analysis method, the stories were scored for achievement imagery.

Managing a group of people with diverse personalities is not easy. It is essential to know what motivates people, how they respond to feedback and praise and what tasks fit them when you are leading or managing a group/team. Achievement motivation theory gives you a way of identifying an individual's motivating drivers. This can assist you as a leader or manager in giving praise and feedback effectively, assigning appropriate tasks and keeping them motivated.

McClelland's Need Theory

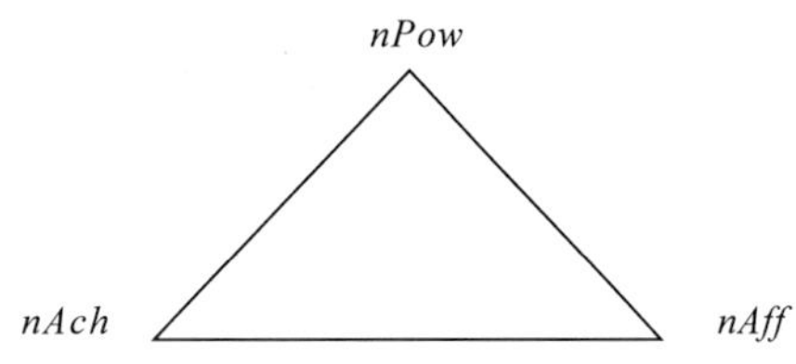

Figure 1. Three types of needs

In the early 1940s, Abraham Maslow stated the theory of needs. In this theory, he identified the basic needs of human beings in accordance with their importance: physiological needs, safety needs, needs for belonging, self-esteem and self-actualization. This idea was expanded upon by David McClelland in his book "The Achieving Society," which was published in 1961. He felt that we all have a need for achievement, a need for affiliation, and a need for power. He categorized these as the three primary drivers of human behaviour. People's primary drivers of behaviour will influence the characteristics they exhibit to varying degrees. People will exhibit a variety of various qualities depending on the primary force that drives them. According to McClelland, we all have three different motivating drivers, and one of them will be our primary motivating driver no matter who we are, where we come from, or how old we are. This is true regardless of gender, culture, or age. This major motivation is largely influenced by our culture as well as our experiences throughout life.

Three types of needs

1. Need for Achievement

In the context of the Acquired Needs hypothesis, "need for achievement" refers to the desire of an individual to do something significant in their lifetime. This is the kind of need that will propel a person to work hard, endure hardship, and eventually achieve their goals. This individual's professional goal is to stand out as a notable figure in his field. Some people have a strong desire to accomplish a lot, and those people are the ones who are always coming up with new ideas and striving to be the best at everything.

One of the most typical illustrations of the urge to succeed is the son of an actor who, to avoid being identified as his father's offspring, strives even more diligently to establish a reputation for himself in the entertainment industry. His ambition to carve out a name for himself in the world drives him to excel in his endeavours and achieve goals that a typical human could not ever be able to imagine achieving.The persons who are focused on the desire for achievement, according to the need for achievement theory, are reluctant to put themselves in risky situations. They do not favour low-risk scenarios because they do not consider it tough enough to warrant the effort, and they do not favour high-risk situations because they believe that their success depends more on chance than on their own abilities. They would rather accept a risk that is moderate or calculated.

People that have a strong desire to accomplish things will place a premium on receiving consistent and timely feedback on their accomplishments and progress. This will allow them to continue to grow, make adjustments, and get better on a consistent basis. They will have a better understanding of how close they are to achieving their goals as a result of this.

2. Need for Power

The need for power is the second need, according to the Three Needs Theory developed by David McClelland. It is the unquenchable desire that an individual has to exercise complete dominion over other individuals. This control is a reflection of the specific desires for personal power, and it demonstrates a desire to modify the decision of another individual so that it better suits the individual's wants and needs. They are willing to incur significant risks in the pursuit of personal glory.People who have a strong need for power are constantly motivated to improve themselves in terms of their reputation and self-esteem, and this serves as the primary impetus for each and every one of their choices. These are people who crave power and would constantly give priority to their own thoughts and perspectives while also wishing that other people would embrace their perspective as superior to their own.

It is an undeniable reality that those individuals who have a strong desire for power are the ones that excel in positions of leadership and management. They can readily demonstrate their capabilities by rising to the ranks of powerful leaders. Collaboration is not their strong suit, but they enjoy a good challenge, especially one that requires them to compete dirty for personal status no matter the cost.

There are two types of persons with a high need for power

The first is the one who is part of a personal power motivator group. He will never stop attempting to exert his authority over others and will never stop seeking recognition and position. He is driven to perform at a higher level by the competition and the difficulties he faces. He is driven to perform at a higher level by the competitive environment and the difficulties he faces.The second classification of people is those who are members of institutional power motivator groups. He has a great level of self-control and will steer the members of his team toward the accomplishment of the goals and aims that have been established.

3. Need for Affiliation

According to David, a psychologist, the term "need for affiliation" refers to the strong desire that an individual has to have close personal relationships as well as social connections with other people. This is the third need that he identifies in his Learned Needs Theory, and it places the emphasis not on achievement, which is where performance is the primary motivation, but rather on social approval.

People who have a strong desire to belong to a community are the ones who dislike working alone and would much rather interact and work in groups than do it alone. People who fit this description are always more interested in working together than taking on a problem. They are members of the team who enjoy maintaining social relationships and participating in social activities. People have an insatiable want to be liked and accepted by others, which is the driving force behind the formation of enduring and amicable relationships. These high achievers are driven by their affiliations; therefore, they stick to the rules and don't see a need for change. They frequently favour maintaining the status quo because they are anxious about being rejected. They struggle to adapt well to frequent change. People who are motivated by the need for connection will avoid uncertain as well as high-risk situations, according to this need hypothesis, which states that such individuals will take precautions. They conduct themselves in a manner that is consistent with the policies and norms that have been established in the workplace. They take an extremely cautious approach, and they abhor both ambiguity and taking excessive chances.

A person who has a strong need for connection performs best in jobs that are intimately associated with the social groups they must serve, such as customer service or occupations that need them to interact with other people's customers.

These dominant motivators and characteristics are as follows

1. Achievement
    - Takes moderate/calculated risks to achieve their goals.
    - Likes to get regular feedback on progress and achievements.
    - Usually likes to do work alone.
    - High self-control, confidence, and energy
    - Assume responsibility for resolving issues.
    - They have a goal-oriented mindset and establish reasonable, realistic, and attainable objectives.
    - They are goal-oriented and set reasonable, attainable objectives.
    - Obtaining entrepreneurial-type roles is a common occurrence.
2. Affiliation
    - Wants to be liked, and usually, they go along with whatever the rest of the group likes to do.
    - Promotes collaboration over competition.
    - Doesn't like uncertainty or high risk in a relationship.
    - Seeking close relationships with others.
    - Wants to be liked by others.
    - Enjoying a lot of social activities.
    - Seeking to belong to the group with which they joined and associated.
3. Power
    - Wants to be dominant and influence others.
    - Cherish to win arguments.
    - They like being in a race where they can win (they don't want to lose).
    - Willingness to confront others
    - Seeking positions of leadership and prestige.
    - Typically ambitious and less dependent on association.

Implications

McClelland's theory of need can help you to determine the leading motivators of people on your team. You can utilize this information to influence people at your workplace on how you can set goals and provide feedback and how you can motivate and reward them. You can also utilize these motivators to craft or design the job around your team members to ensure a better fit.

How to use achievement motivation in the workplace

Understanding achievement motivation can aid in professional success. Follow these methods to effectively employ accomplishment motivation in the workplace:

1. Set goals

Consider choosing specific and measurable goals that you can control over goals affected by factors beyond your control. For instance, requesting a raise necessitates the agreement of your boss and budgetary space within your firm. However, goals such as generating at least ten sales call each day and going to the gym four times per week are under your control. These objectives also have particular success metrics.

Setting daily as well as long-term objectives will increase your sense of accomplishment at work, so boosting your motivation. Setting daily as well as long-term objectives may make you feel like you are making progress at work, which will increase your drive.

2. Get feedback and improve

When supervisors provide extensive feedback, employees with a high need for achievement typically flourish. The level of challenge and learning you need to perform well at work and feel accomplished can be provided by feedback.

Feedback can offer you the necessary amount of challenge and learning to perform well at work and feel successful. At these meetings, request that your manager offer you challenging, novel, or engaging tasks.

During these sessions, you should request that your manager provide you with challenging or novel work. At these meetings, you should request that your manager offer you new or challenging work.

3. Seek out new projects

If your day-to-day responsibilities at work are not difficult enough, or if your boss is unable to provide you with challenging work, you should seek out new initiatives that will challenge you more. If the day-to-day duties you have at work aren't challenging you enough or if your manager is unwilling to give you work that will fulfil you, you should look for new initiatives that will push you further. Make a list of all the new skills and experiences you will have while working on a new project before you start working on the project. This will help keep you motivated and excited about the new job you will be doing. You are in charge of how much you study, and the more you accomplish, the more satisfied you will feel.

4. Start each day, week and month with a plan

Providing yourself with a schedule for the day, the week, and the month can serve as a powerful motivator in assisting you to attain your intermediate goals. You may assist inspire yourself to attain your intermediate goals by creating a schedule for the day, the week, and the month. You can either write down your objectives in a diary or planner that you create, or you can utilize organizing software to keep tabs on them. This exercise will help you prioritize the several chores you have throughout the day by providing you with immediate goals that can be measured.

Start the morning of each Monday and the first day of each month with a similar goal-setting exercise. At the end of each day, week, and month, make a checkmark next to the items on your list that you have successfully completed and add one more item. If you use this planning technique, it will be much easier for you to leave the office each day with a sense of accomplishment and to come into work the next day feeling just as driven as you were the day before.

"Don't let others tell you what you can't do. Don't let the limitations of others limit your vision. If you can remove your self-doubt and believe in yourself, you can achieve what you never thought possible".

– Roy T. Bennett

References

Atkinson, J. W., & Feather, N. T. (1966). *A theory of achievement motivation*. New York: Wiley.

McClelland, D. C. (1961). *The achieving society*. Princeton: Van Nostrand.

McClelland, D. C. (1985). *Human motivation*. Glenview: Scott Foresman.

McClelland, D. C., Atkinson, J. W., Clark, R. A., & Lowell, E. L. (1953). *The achievement motive*. New York: Appleton.

McClelland, D. C., Koestner, R., & Weinberger, J. (1989). How do self-attributed and implicit motives differ? *Psychological Review, 96*, 690–702.

Murray, H. A. (1938). *Explorations in personality*. New York: Oxford University Press.

5

Role of Government in Entrepreneurship Development

Arnab Roy and Priyanka Lal

Department of Agricultural Economics and Extension
Lovely Professional University, Phagwara, Punjab

Introduction

Entrepreneurship assimilates a very decisive dynamic dimension in a modified form through the globalisation progression into the Indian economic system. The core strength of economic development and economic growth in all underdeveloped and developing nations around the world is only due to the presence of entrepreneurial activity. A successful entrepreneurial approach plays a crucial role in the progress of industrial, manufacturing and service sectors and the development of agriculture. The government of most developing countries have invested much effort and resources in the past to enrich entrepreneurship (Oni and Daniya, 2012). According to a recent study, Saudi Arabia has been attempting to build a ten-year innovation and efforts entrepreneurship programme starting the year 2010. Similarly, in Malaysia, the government guided to set up of several technologies through the growth of technological know-how in entrepreneurship.

Role of Entrepreneurship in Economic Growth and Development

Entrepreneurship is one of the significant inputs in the economic progress and development of the country. The entrepreneur, a business pioneer, searches for novel concepts and then implements those concepts in ways that boost any nation's economic growth and overall standard of living. The significant role played by the entrepreneurs in economic expansion differs from economy to economy, subject to industrial climate and resources. Through path-breaking contributions by entrepreneurs, new employment opportunities often produce a virtuous circle in the economy. Active and enthusiastic entrepreneurs can only find out the potentiality of resources is a widely accepted concept. Wickham (2006) envisaged the key role of the entrepreneur as the key figure in the economic development of any nation because of its role in familiarising innovations. Parson and Helms (2013) illustrated entrepreneurship with the two essential conditions, i.e. risk-taking and innovativeness for economic advancement and development. The key roles played by an entrepreneur in the development of the economy are discussed in an orderly and systematic manner as follows.

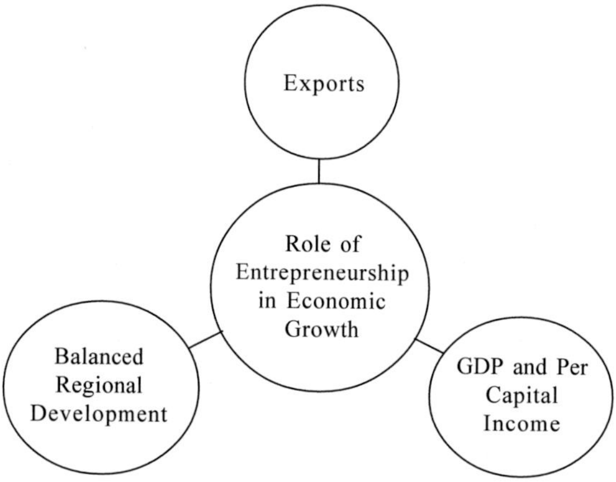

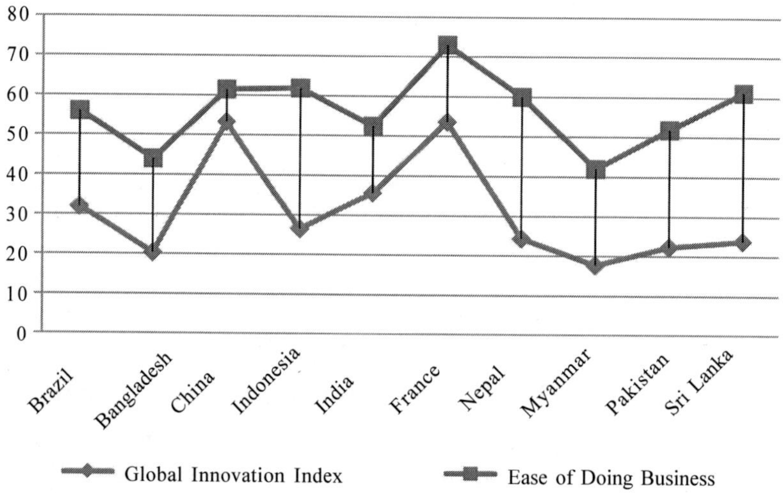

Figure 1. Global Innovation Index vis-à-vis Ease of doing business

Creates Employment Opportunities

By nature and definition, entrepreneurs are job architects and job providers. In other words, when an individual becomes an entrepreneur, there is one more job seeker and one more job provider in the economy. Entrepreneurship offers significant scale employment to the unemployed in an underdeveloped economy, a long-lasting problem in underdeveloped countries. Though India's innovation journey is strictly restricted to particular provinces that have been fortunate with a legacy of industrialisation, it is a potent tool for all the states in their combined journey to make India an innovation-driven nation.

Promotes Balanced Regional Development

Setting up new ventures and business units by entrepreneurs helps with regional development through locating in remote and backward areas. The growth of business units and unique experiences in these remote areas leads to improvements in physical and social infrastructure like transportation, electricity, educational establishments, health institutions, and other public and private services that would not be available. Moreover, setting up business industries in the country leads to more improvement in backward provinces, and the auxiliary jobs in other industries enlarge regional economic productivity.

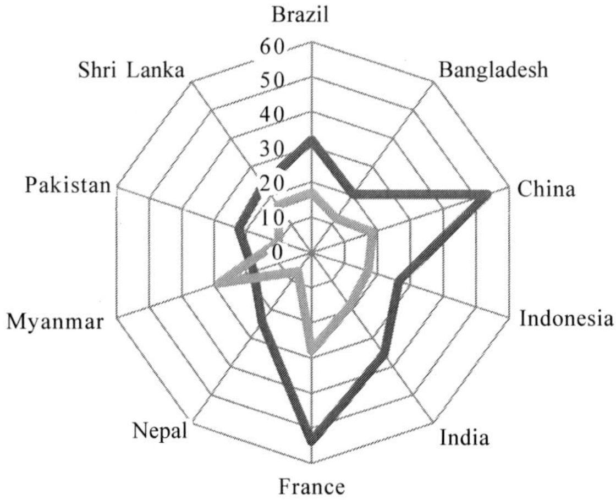

Global Innovation Index — Exports of goods and services (% of GDP)

Figure 2. Relationship between innovativeness and export performance of different countries

Increasing Gross National Product and Per Capita Income

MSME sector is the second largest employment providing sector in India after agriculture. It employs 80 million people, accounting for almost 37% of the country's GDP. The emphasis on entrepreneurial activity in business industries has always been an important part of India's economy. Every developed or developing country needs entrepreneurs to improve their Per Capita Income (PCI).

Promotes Country's Export Trade

India's merchandise export from industrial sector has increased significantly. Small scale industries hold enormous potential for exports in the post-globalisation period. In addition, the entrepreneurial skill in various levels of SSIs has registered positive growth in exports.

Entrepreneurial Scenario in India- Ministry of Micro, Small, and Medium Enterprises

The importance of micro, small, and medium enterprises (MSME) has always been an essential part of India's built-up strategy. Irrespective of developed or developing, almost every country needs entrepreneurs. A developing country like India requires entrepreneurship skills in different enterprises to take off the practice of economic development, whereas the developed nations need entrepreneurs to endure it. During the post-independence period, the public investment focused on heavy industries and the setting up of micro, small, and medium enterprises, which provided an ideal atmosphere for entrepreneurship development. An entrepreneurship skill has not only been confined to micro, small, and medium enterprise workers but also expanded in size beyond that. In the present scenario, wherein, on the one hand, the scope of employment-generating opportunities in the public sector is shrinking.

On the other hand, massive prospects arise from globalisation. Therefore, the necessity for entrepreneurship comes up from the entrepreneurial functions to the process of development. MSMEs in India enjoy a distinct position in view of their contribution to the country's socio-economic development.

> Start-up India Scheme: The key objectives of Start-up India are to figure out a strong network for fostering innovation and startups. This scheme explicitly targets to: (i) prompt an entrepreneurial ethos and inculcate entrepreneurial skills in the economy at a large scale and also influence the mindset of people towards entrepreneurial activities, (ii) it also focuses on generating cognisance about the appeals of being an entrepreneur. Finally, (iii) it boosts the dynamic set up by inspiring youth, technologists, scientists and business people to consider entrepreneurship as a preferred and lucrative viable career.

Why should the government promote entrepreneurship?

Since most countries have developed programmes to support entrepreneurship, the significance of entrepreneurship development cannot be overemphasised in several global economies. It is already the fact that entrepreneurship is the utmost constituent of economic growth and job creation. The triumph of revenue generation for rural and urban inhabitants without routine paid jobs enormously depends on entrepreneurial skills (Friedman B.A. 2011). Developed nations have established experience and notable policies to sustain entrepreneurship. At the same time, the developing and underdeveloped countries make basic steps in the development of entrepreneurship which have great importance for the development of the economy.

Recently, many strategic initiatives have been taken by Govt. to promote entrepreneurship in the country. Interest subsidy, Khadi Institutions Registration and Certification Seva (KIRICS), SPIN (Strengthening the Potential of India) etc. In government support, it is expected that the government provides the plentiful financial resources and such resources include an environment favourable for business that will encourage entrepreneurship. Government policy aims to regulate and improve the environment of small and medium enterprises in terms of financial and implementation, also targeting to promote entrepreneurship. Literature from numerous sources has shown that favourable government policy is positively related to entrepreneurship development (Ghani *et al.,* 2019)

Role of Government in Promoting Entrepreneurship

Both the central and state government performs a significant role in the growth of entrepreneurship. The governments have been operating several programmes to promote entrepreneurship in India. These are given below:

I. Prime Minister's Employment Generation Programme

This premier scheme is executed by Khadi and Village Industries Commission (KVIC) as a nodal agency at the country level. In the year 2020-21, this programme has performed very well by supporting almost 75000 candidates for setting up new micro-enterprises through expanding a subsidy of more than two thousand crores and creating employment opportunities for an estimated more than five lakh people.

II. Entrepreneurship and Skill Development Programmes (ESDP)

The programme under the Entrepreneurship and Skill Development Programmes Scheme includes the following components:

1. Entrepreneurship Awareness Programme (One day)
2. Entrepreneurship-cum-Skill Development Programme (Six weeks)

III. Self-Employment and Talent Utilisation (SETU)

The main objective of the mentioned scheme is to organise traditional/desi businesses and artisans. This scheme also helps make the company more competitive and supports their long-run sustained employment and sustainability of products.

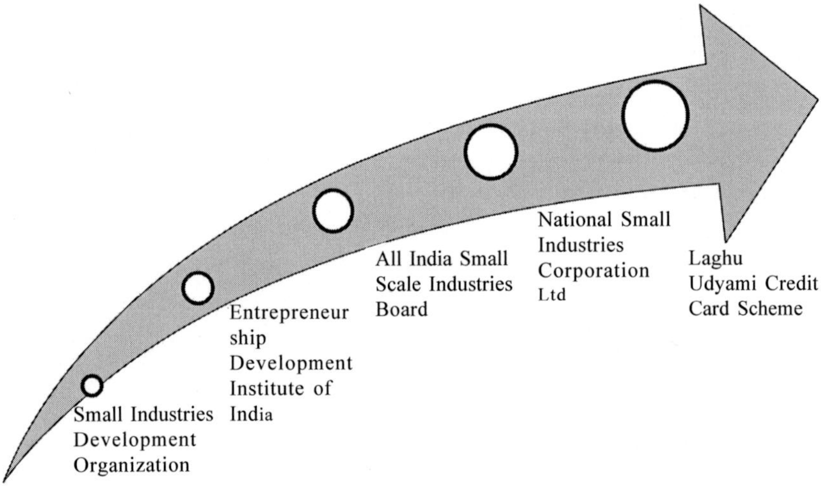

Figure 3. Roadmap of the significant entrepreneurial scheme of MSME

IV. India Aspiration Fund

The India Aspiration Fund (IAF) is envisioned to perform a vibrant role in the financial environment. SIDBI set up India Aspiration Fund (IAF) with assistance from RBI.

V. MSME Champions Scheme

It was urgent to promote a combined, robust, empowered, and technology-driven stand for promoting and supporting the country's micro, Small and Medium Enterprises (MSMEs). Hence, the Ministry of Micro, Small and Medium Enterprises of the government of India has launched the Champions scheme, erstwhile known as CLCS-TUS, for the construction and harmonious application of modern processes.

VI. Mahatma Gandhi Institute for Rural Industrialization (MGIRI)

The scheme is trying to enhance, upgrade, and hasten the process of industrialisation in the country's rural areas to move toward the Gandhian idea of a sustainable village economy for sustainable employment.

Conclusion

Unexpectedly, a large figure of entrepreneurs often leads to severe competition and loss of occupation choices for individuals. With increasing numbers of entrepreneurs, aspirations levels of business people ordinarily rise. Maintaining this inconsistency of accomplishment in entrepreneurial speculations, the situation of having too many businesspersons also may lead to high-income inequalities, In the current international market, the economic scenario in India must embolden to achieve high productivity and efficiencies. The government should be able to safeguard the creativity and resources of the entrepreneurs in the public and private sectors to achieve a versatile and creative sense of self-government.

References

Anonymous. (2021). Annual Report. Government of India, Ministry of Micro, Small and Medium Enterprises, New Delhi.

Baumol, J. W. (1990). Entrepreneurship: Productive, Unproductive and Destructive, Journal of Political Economy, Vol. 98(5): p. 20-25

Friedman, B.A.(2011). The relationship between Governance Effectiveness and Entrepreneurship.

Ghani, E Kerr, W. R. and O'Connell, S. (2019). Spatial Determinants of Entrepreneurship in India," in Entrepreneurship in a Regional Context. International Journal of Humanities and Social Science, 1(17): p. 221-225.

Oni, E.O. and Daniya, A. (2012). Development of Small and Medium Scale Enterprises: The role of Government and other Financial Institutions. Arabian Journal of Business and Management Review, 1(7): p. 16-29.

Pearson C. A. L. and Helms, K. (2013). Indigenous Social Entrepreneurship: The Gumatj Clan Enterprise in East Arnhem Land, J. Entrep.

Wickham, A. P. (2006). Strategic Entrepreneurship. Fourth Edition, Prentice-Hall, Esses, England.

6

Institutions for Entrepreneurship Development

Sapna Jarial, Haobijam James Watt, and Devina Seram*

Department of Agricultural Economics and Extension, School of Agriculture Lovely Professional University, Phagwara, Punjab

**Department of Entomology, School of Agriculture, Lovely Professional University Phagwara, Punjab*

Introduction

Entrepreneurship has a significant impact on the country's economic growth and standard of living. As a start-up founder or small business owner, the person contributes not only towards oneself but also towards the local community, state, region, and country. Starting a new venture requires resources and facilities. Small scale enterprises generally find it difficult to have these resources and facilities of their own. Adequate finance is life and blood to start and run enterprises as it facilitates an entrepreneur to have enough funds to procure land, labour, materials, plant, machinery etc. Recognizing it, the government has come forward to support small entrepreneurs by providing them funds and other needed facilities.

Keywords

Starup India: Startup India is an initiative of the Government of India. Indian Prime Minister Narendra Modi first announced the campaign on 15 August 2015

Skill India: Prime Minister Narendra Modi launched Skill India, or India's National Skills Development Mission, a campaign managed by India's National Skills Development Corporation.

Pradhan Mantri Kaushal Vikas Yojana (PMKY): It's a 2015 initiative for youth to promote skill development in the country by giving free short-term skill training and monetary awards for skill certification.

Make in India: Make in India is an initiative by the Government of India to make and encourage companies to develop, manufacture and assemble products made in India and incentivize dedicated investments into manufacturing.

Standup India: Was launched by the Government of India on 5 April 2016 to support entrepreneurship among women and SC & ST communities.

Institution Support: Institutional support refers to providing an economical and social environment for industry and business.

Institutional support for entrepreneurship development

Institutional support provides an economic and social environment for industry and business. It helps create awareness, capacity building, hand holding, incubation, mentorship, etc., using financial support and policy advice. Institutional support is needed in all the 3 stages of promotion of any entrepreneur: the inception stage, operational stage, and expansion or diversification stage. There are three dimensions of institutional support that are:

a) Central government,

b) State government, and

c) Non-government support system. (Indian Council of Agricultural Research, 2020)

a) **Ministry of Micro, Small and Medium Enterprises** -The ministry is tasked with promoting Micro and Small Enterprises (MSMEs). Different policies and programs are being executed for providing infrastructure and support services to small enterprises through the small industries development organisation (SIDO) and the national small industries corporation limited (NSIC) etc. Central government institutions are providing support for entrepreneurship development

b) **Ministry of Skill Development and Entrepreneurship-** This ministry has been formed to focus on youth employability through skill development and prepare youth for job opportunities in the international market. Pradhan Mantri Kaushal Vikas Yojana (PMKVY) is the ministry's flagship programme for attaining its goals. Major activities and schemes for entrepreneurship development are: educating and equipping early-stage entrepreneurs across India, connecting entrepreneurs to peers, mentors, incubators, supporting entrepreneurship through entrepreneurship hubs (e-hubs), catalysing a culture shift to encourage entrepreneurship, encouraging entrepreneurship among under representative groups like scheduled caste and scheduled tribes, minorities, differently-abled, etc., promoting entrepreneurship amongst women and fostering social entrepreneurship and grassroots innovation.

c) **Organization and institutions at a national level** some of the national level institutes which help in entrepreneurship development through policy support, research and training activities are small scale industries board, National Bank for Agriculture and Rural Development(NABARD), Small Industries Development Organisation (SIDO), National Small Industries Corporation (NSIC), National Institute For Food Technology Entrepreneurship And Management (NIFTEM), Entrepreneurship Development Institute (EDI), ZTM and BPD units of ICR, National Institute of Rural Development and Panchayat Raj (NIRD& PR) etc.

State government institutions providing support for entrepreneurship development: All the states in India have their programs and projects for skill development and entrepreneurship development and centrally sponsored programmes. Some of the institutions which are helping in the implementation of different state-level entrepreneurship development programs are state financial Corporation (SFC), technical consultancy organization (TCO), state small industries Development Corporation (SSIDC), khadi and village industries Commission (KVIC), Small Industries Development Bank of India (SIDBI), District Industries Centre (DIC), State Coir Development Corporation Limited, State Handicrafts Development Corporation, Institutional Setup for Women Entrepreneurship etc.

Non-governmental institutions providing support for entrepreneurship development:

a) **Indian Council of Small Industries (ICSI)** is a non-government Institute with the main focus on information dissemination, consultancy and managerial support, and training and research for entrepreneurship development.

b) **Laghu Udyog Bharti (LUB)** is responsible for undertaking entrepreneurial training, technology up-gradation and marketing services. Other than the above-listed institutions and programs, several other schemes and projects are functioning in our country to promote entrepreneurship development among rural youth, women and would-be entrepreneurs. Agri Clinics and Agribusiness centres (ACABC), central sector scheme jointly managed and implemented by National Institute of Agricultural Extension Management (MANAGE), and National Bank for Agriculture and Rural Development (NARARD), Atal Incubation Centre (AIC) supported by NITI ayog, Rural Self Employment Training Institute (RSETI) managed by banks with active corporation from the Government of India and state government in line of

Rural Development and Self Employment Training Institute(RUDSETI), Rural Technology Park (RTP) of NIRD, Mudra bank established under Pradhan Mantri Mudra Yojana (PMMY), Agriculture Skill Council of India (ASCI), Rural Livelihood Programs under ASPIRE scheme of Ministry Of Micro Small And Medium Enterprises (MSME) etc. are some support schemes and institutions for entrepreneurship development in India. (Indian Council of Agricultural Research, 2020)

c) **Bharatiya Yuva Shakti Trust (BYST):** Lakshmi Venkatesan founded an NPO in 1992 that provides financing, coaching, networking, and marketing to underprivileged micro-entrepreneurs. BYST develops young micro-enterprises to the point where they are self-sufficient and contribute to society by creating wealth and jobs. Since its beginning, BYST has partnered with over 4,000 specialists and professionals, including actors and public celebrities.

Since its establishment, BYST has helped 4200 micro-businesses employ over 175,000 people and trained thousands more. BYST offers rural and urban training in six main Indian areas. The CII provides BYST with infrastructural and administrative assistance. BYST is also connected to worldwide organisations with similar goals. The NPO model is ideal when minimal funding demands and mentorship are essential.(BYST, n.d.)

Further, institutional support to entrepreneurship development can also be broadly classified into three categories:

1. National Level Institutions
2. State-level Institutions
3. Fund based Institutions

1. National Level Institutions: national level institutions supporting entrepreneurs are below

a) Small Scale Industries Board (SSIB)

b) Small Industry Development Organization (SIDO)

c) National Small Industries Corporation Limited (NSIC)

d) The Khadi and Village Industries Commission (KVIC)

e) **National training institutes like the** National Institute of Small Industry Extension Training(NISIET) **NISIET, NISEBUD, and IIE**

a) The Small-Scale Industries Board (SSI Board)

is the apex advisory committee to render recommendations to the Government on any troubles referring to the small-scale area that became constituted in 1954. The Board is reconstituted at every two years interval and is headed by the concerned Minister from the Government of India oversees Small-Scale Industries. The SSI Board consist of other States Industrial Ministers, a few members from the Parliament, Secretaries of numerous Departments of Government of India, monetary institutions, public sector undertakings and various eminent professionals from the associated industry. The Member Secretary is served by the Additional Secretary and Development Commissioner (SSI). The Board is serviced via the Board and Policy Division from the workplace of the DC (SSI). The variety of improvement spread at the small-scale area includes numerous Departments / Ministries and numerous Central / State Governments corporations. Though a non-statutory board, the SSI Board facilitates a helpful platform for knowledgeable debate and helps coordination and inters - institutional linkages. (Source: http://laghu-udyog.gov.in)

b) Small Industries Development Organisation (SIDO)

The Small Industries Development Organization (SIDO) is headed by the Additional Secretary & Development Commissioner (Small Scale Industries), and it was established in 1954. It is one of the apex bodies of the Government of India. Formulating the various policies and programmes, projects, schemes, etc., for the Government and promoting and developing small-scale industries by monitoring and coordinating the programmes, etc., is being assisted by the Ministry of Small-Scale Industries. States and Union Territories (UTs) took the primary responsibility to look after the development and promotion of the small-scale industries. The Central Government assisted and provided aid to the States/UT on this endeavour.

The function of SIDO goes through a network of Small Industries Service Institutes (SISIs), MSME Testing Centres (RTCs), Branch SISIs, Field Testing Station (FTSs) and various autonomous bodies. It renders services such as: -

- Advise the government on policy formulation for the promotion and development of small-scale industries, small-scale service, and business entities (collectively referred to as small enterprises), and their progression to medium-sized enterprises.
- Providing small businesses with techno-economic and managerial consulting, as well as common facilities and extension services.
- Providing facilities for small business technology advancement, modernization, quality improvement, and infrastructure.

- Developing human resources by training and upgrading the skills of small entrepreneurs as well as its workforce.
- Providing economic information to the government and small businesses.
- Maintaining liaison with other Central Ministries, the Planning Commission, state governments, and other organisations concerned with small business development.

SIDO's network of specialised field groups has helped small businesses thrive throughout the years.

- The Small Industries Development Organization (SIDO) is a subordinate office of the Department of SSI & Auxiliary and Rural Industry (ARI).
- It's the leading body and nodal agency for promoting and growing small-scale industries.

SIDO functions include

- Co-ordination
- Industrial development, and
- Extension.

Functions Relating to Co-ordination

a) To develop a national policy for the development of small-scale industries,

b) Coordinate state policies and programmes,

c) Maintain adequate communication with Central Ministries, Planning Commission, State Governments, Financial Institutions, etc.

d) Coordinating industrial estate development.

Functions Relating to Industrial Development

a) To set aside items for small-scale industries production,

b) To collect information about consumer goods that are brought in from other countries and then, with coordinated help, to encourage industrial units to start making these goods.

Function Relating to Extension

a) To make provision to technical services for improving the technical process, production planning, selecting appropriate machinery, and preparing factory layout and design,

b) To provide consultancy and training services to strengthen the competitive ability of small-scale industries.

c) National Small Industries Corporation (NSIC)-

The NSIC was set up in 1955 to promote, aid, and foster the growth of SSIs with a focus on commercial aspects. National Small Industries Corporation (NSIC) is an ISO 9001-2015 licensed Government of India Enterprise under the Ministry of Micro, Small and Medium Enterprises (MSME) control. NSIC has been effectively working to promote, resource, and foster the boom for the country's micro, small and medium companies. NSIC operates via a national community of places of work and Technical Centres in the Country. In addition, NSIC has installation Training cum Incubation Centre controlled via way of means of expert manpower

Mission: "To promote and support Micro, Small & Medium Enterprises (MSMEs) Sector" by providing integrated support services encompassing Marketing, Technology, Finance and other services.

Vision: "To be a premier organization fostering the growth of Micro, Small and Medium Enterprises (MSMEs) Sector".

Schemes of NSIC

NSIC helps Micro, Small and Medium Enterprises with a hard and fast, mainly tailor-made scheme to improve competitiveness. NSIC presents incorporated aid offerings under the Marketing, Technology, Finance, and different Support service.

Marketing Support

Marketing has been recognized as one of the maximum critical devices for business development. NSIC performed to facilitator and provided some schemes to sustain establishments of their advertising and marketing efforts, each domestic and overseas market. These schemes are in brief defined as under:

Consortia and Tender Marketing- Small Enterprises face trouble to procure & execute big orders, which deny them by powerful and large enterprises. NSIC form consortia for Micro and Small production unit to be the identical product, thereby pooling their potential.

Single point Registration for Government Purchase-Those registered units, under the Single Point Registration Scheme of NSIC are eligible to get the settlement for "Public Procurement Policy for Micro & Small Enterprises (MSEs)

Order 2012" as notified through the Government of India, Ministry of Micro Small & Medium Enterprises, New Delhi vide Gazette Notification dated 23.03.2012.

MSME Global Mart Business to Business (B2B) Web Portal for Micro, Small & Medium Enterprises (MSMEs)-With the increase in competition and melting away of international boundaries, the demand for information is reaching new heights. NSIC realizes the required need for MSME. It is provided Infomediary Services, a one-stop, one-window bouquet of aids, an excellent way to offer statistics on technology & business and show the core competence of Indian MSMEs. Business to Business web portal provides the following benefits to the members of infomediary services.

- Interactive database of MSMEs
- Self-web development tool
- National Tenders on email
- Centralized mail system
- Popular Products Section
- Unlimited global Trade Leads
- Trust Seal of NSIC
- MSME Web Store
- Multiple Language Support
- Discussion Board
- Call Centre Support & Live Chat
- Other Value-added Services
- Payment Gateway for membership subscription

Marketing Intelligence-It used to collect and disseminate the market intelligence from both domestic and international for the benefit of MSMEs.

Exhibitions and Technology Fairs-To exhibit the capabilities of Indian SSIs and to seize marketplace opportunities, NSIC participates in choose International and National Exhibitions and Trade Fairs each year.

Buyer-Seller meets- Railways, Communication department, Defense and large companies which use to buy in Bulk and departmental are invited to take part in buyer-seller meets to enhance the small enterprise's knowledge regarding their terms and conditions, standards quality, etc. required through the buyer. These programmes are geared toward seller improvement from MSMEs for most manufacturers.

Credit Support-NSIC helps credit score requirement of small enterprises in the below following areas:

Financing for procurement of Raw Material (Short term)- For purchasing Raw Material from the domestic and international market for the Small Enterprises, NSIC's Raw Material Assistance scheme provides finance for the purchase.

The most important things are:

1. Financial Assistance for procurement of Raw Materials up to **ninety** days.
2. Bulk procuring of basic raw materials at reasonable rates.
3. Scarce raw materials required to be imported facilitated by NSIC.
4. The procedures, documentation & issue of letter of credit in case of imports are provided by NSIC.

Finance through syndication with Banks-NSIC has a strategic tie with various commercial banks to ensure a smooth flow of credit to the small enterprises by providing long term/ working capital financing thought the country. NSIC arranged the loan application forward to the banks and shared the required processing fee.

Technology Support- Various support services for the small enterprises provided by the NSIC through its Technical Services and Extension Centres are as follows.

1. Advice on application of new techniques
2. Material testing facilities through accredited laboratories
3. Product design.
4. The common facility supports machining.
5. Energy and environment services at selected centres.
6. Classroom and practical training for skill up-gradation
   (*Source*: www.nsic.co.in)

d) The Khadi and Village Industries Commission (KVIC)

It is a legal body set up by a law passed by Parliament (No. 61 of 1956, as amended by act no. 12 of 1987 and Act No.10 of 2006). It took over the work of the former All India Khadi and Village Industries Board in April 1957.

The classification of KVIC.

1. Mineral-based industry.
   i) Pottery and
   ii) lime.
2. Agro-based and food processing industry. (ABFPI.)
   i) Pulses and cereals processing industry.
   ii) Gud and khandsari industry.
   iii) Palmgur industry
   iv) Fruit and vegetable processing industry.
   v) Village. Oil industry.
3. Polymer and chemical-based industry. (PCBI)
   i) Leather industry,
   ii) non-edible oils and soap industry.
   iii) Cottage match industry,
   iv) Plastic industry
4. Forest-based industry. FBI
   i) medicinal plants industry.
   ii) Be keeping industry. And.
   iii) Minor forest-based industries.
5. Handmade paper and fiber industry (HMPFI)
   i) Handmade paper industry.
   ii) Fibre industry.
6. Rural engineering and biotechnology industry (REBTI)
   i) Non-conventional energy.
   ii) Carpentry and black Smithy.
   iii) Electronics.
7. SCP or service industry. Coordination.(*Khadi and Village Industries Commission*, n.d.)

Objectives

The broad objectives that the KVIC has set before it is:

- The social objective of providing employment.
- The economic objective of producing saleable articles.
- The broader objective is to create self-reliance amongst the poor and build up a strong rural community spirit.

Functions

For the promotion and development of Khadi and other village industries in the rural areas, KVIC is responsible for planning, organization, promotion and implementation of various programs by coordinating with multiple agencies engaged in the development of the rural area. It also provides the capacity increase for the reserve of raw materials and implements to supply for producers, creation of common service facilities for the process of raw materials as semi-finished goods and provisions of facilities for promoting of Khadi and Village Industries product apart from organization of training of artisans engaged in these industries and encouragement of co-operative efforts amongst them. To increase the sale and promote material and development of village industries or handicrafts, the KVIC could forge linkages with established marketing agencies where possible and necessary. The KVIC also take the responsibility of encouraging and promoting by researching production techniques and instrumentality used in the Khadi and Village Industries sector and providing facilities for the study of the various problems related to it, as well as the utilization of non-conventional energy and electricity with a hope to increasing productivity, eliminating hard labour work and otherwise enhancing their competitive capability and arrangement for dissemination of salient results obtained from such research. Further, the KVIC is entrusted with providing monetary help to establishments and people for the development and operation of khadi and village industries and guiding them through the provision of designs, prototypes and various technical information. By implementing KVIC activities, the KVIC must ensure the authenticity of the product warranty, maintain quality standards, and ensure that the Khadi and village industry products are conventionally at standard.

KVIC can also be directly or by other studies of agencies concerning the problems of the Khadi and village industry and the research or determination of pilot projects for the development of Khadi and Village Industries.KVIC is authorized to establish and maintain separate organizations to conduct any or all of the foregoing business and other business-related to its activities.(*Khadi and Village Industries Commission*, n.d.)

e) Training Institutes

There are three national-level training institutes. These are

1. National Institute of Small Industry Extension Training (NISIET)

It undertakes operations training, consultancy, research, and education, to extension and information services. NISIET has made great strides since its establishment in 1960 by the Government of India to become the leading institution for promoting, developing, and modernization the SME (Small and Medium Enterprises) sector. As an autonomous branch of the Ministry of Small Industry (SSI), the Institute strives to achieve its stated goals through activities ranging from training, consulting, research, and education to advisory and information services. (Source:online.iasri.res.in)

NI-MSME, formerly known as the National Institute of Small Industry Extension Training (NISIET), was prepared in 1960 in New Delhi as a central government department under the Ministry of Trade and Industry and was initially known centrally known Industrial Extension Training Institute (CIETI). The Central Industrial Extension Training Institute (CIETI) was established in New Delhi in 1960 as a Department under the Ministry of Industry and Commerce, along with Micro, Small, and Medium Enterprises (MSMEs). The Institute was renamed Small Industry Extension Training Institute (SIET) in 1962 and shifted to Hyderabad to provide greater autonomy in administration and procedures and play a critical role in promoting MSMEs. In 1984, the UNIDO granted SIET national status and renamed it the National Institute for Small Industries Extension and Training (NISIET) to recognise its outstanding performance under the scheme of Centers of Excellence. The Institute has received national and international recognition for its work in entrepreneurship promotion. The Institute was renamed National Institute for Micro, Small and Medium Enterprises (NI-MSME) with a redesigned innovative focus on inclusive growth under the Ministry of MSME with the Micro, Small and Medium Enterprises Development Act of 2006 (MSME-D).(*Livestock Entrepreneurship: National Institute for Small Industry Extension Training (NISIET)*, n.d.).

Centres of Excellence

The Government of India designated SIET as a national institute to assist in promoting Small Enterprises, primarily by creating a pro-business environment. In 1984, the UNIDO recognised SIET as a meritorious performance institute under its Centres of Excellence Scheme; later that year, it was also granted national status, and SIET Institute became NISET. Since then, the institute has come a long way, carving out a space for itself in entrepreneurship promotion achieving national and international recognition. To deal with the pressures of globalisation, the Government of India enacted the MSMED Bill in Parliament, which went into effect on October 2, 2006. As a result, the Institute was renamed NI-MSME on April 11, 2007, to reflect the expanded focus of its objectives, and its structure and organisation were redesigned. It is an organisation of the Government of India's Ministry of Micro, Small, and Medium Enterprises (M/o MSME) (formerly Ministry of SSI & ARI). The NI-MSME (formerly known as SIET) was established on July 1, 1962, in Hyderabad, Andhra Pradesh, under Public Societies Registration Act I of 1350 Fasli. (Source: www.nimsme.org)

Objective: The primary objective was to be the trainer of trainers.

2. The National Institute for Entrepreneurship and Small Business Development (NIESBUD)

Is a premier Ministry of Skill Development and Entrepreneurship organisation that promotes entrepreneurship and Skill Development through training, consulting research, and other activities. Training of Trainers, Management Development Programmes, Entrepreneurship-cum-Skill Development Programmes, Entrepreneurship Development Programmes, and Cluster Intervention are the Institute's significant activities. Since its inception, NIESBUD has trained 12,37,307 people through 46,837 different training programmes. This includes 5,011 international participants from over 145 countries around the world.

Objective

NIESBUD is an apex organisation that reports to the Ministry of Skill Development and Entrepreneurship, Government of India.

Training of Trainers, Management Development Programmes, Entrepreneurship-cum-Skill Development Programmes, Entrepreneurship Development Programmes, and Cluster Intervention are the Institute's major activities.

The Institute's Core Objectives are as follows:

- To standardize and systemize the selecting, training, supporting, and sustaining potential and existing entrepreneurs.
- To assist and motivate institutions/organizations in carrying out training and other activities related to entrepreneurship development.
- To serve as the apex national level resource institute for accelerating and enhancing entrepreneurship development and assessing the impact of the same across various strata of society.

- Organize research and documentation activities relevant to entrepreneurship and skill development to provide vital information and support to trainers, promoters, and entrepreneurs.
- To provide national/international consulting to promote entrepreneurship and small business development on a national and international scale.
- To provide national/international forums for interaction and idea exchange in the formulation and refinement of policy at various levels.
- To share experience and expertise in entrepreneurship development across national borders to raise national awareness.
- To share international experience and expertise in entrepreneurship development to map its development on a global scale.
- To create a holistic environment in which trainers, promoters, and consultants can be trained in various aspects of entrepreneurship and skill development. (Source: niesbud.nic.in/institute.html)

3. Indian Institute of Entrepreneurship (IIE), Guwahati

The Indian Institute of Entrepreneurship (IIE) is a self-governing organisation that reports to the Ministry of Skill Development and Entrepreneurship. The Institute's main goal is to provide training, research, and consultancy services in Small and Micro Enterprises (SME), emphasising entrepreneurship development. The Indian Institute of Entrepreneurship (IIE), a registered society under the Societies Registration Act of 1860, was founded in 1993 in Guwahati by the then-Ministry of Industry (now the Ministry of Micro, Small, and Medium Enterprises), Government of India. The Institute began operations in April 1994, with the Northeast Council (NEC), the governments of Assam, Arunachal Pradesh, Nagaland, and SIDBI as stakeholders.

On May 22, 2015, IIE was transferred to the Ministry of Skill Development and Entrepreneurship. IIE has its headquarters in Lalmati, Basistha Chariali, 37 NH bypass, Guwahati-781029.

Objectives

1. To encourage and grow entrepreneurship.
2. To conduct research and provide consulting services to develop entrepreneurship.
3. Coordinate and collaborate with other organisations to increase the institute's outreach through training, research, and other activities.

4. To provide MSMEs/potential entrepreneurs with consulting and monitoring services and improve participants' employability.
5. To encourage greater use of information technology in the IIE's activities/ functions.
6. To maintain statutory requirements.

Functions

1. Creating and organising training activities for various target groups and conducting entrepreneurship-related research.
2. Improving the efficiency, effectiveness, and delivery of change agents and development practitioners, such as trainers and support organisations involved in enterprise development, and so on.
3. Provide consulting services to aspiring and established entrepreneurs.
4. Increasing the institute's outreach through collaborative activities and increasing their effectiveness through various information technology tools. (Source:iietraining.org/about.html)

2. State-Level Institutes

State-level institutions supporting entrepreneurs are as follows:

a) State Small Industries Development Corporation (SSIDC)
b) State Directorate of Industries (SDIs)
c) District Industries Centres (DICs)

a) State Small Industries Development Corporation (SSIDC)

SSIDC were set up in different states as wholly-owned companies for promoting industrial development in their respective states and were incorporated under the Companies Act 1956. The functions of SSIDC are as follows:

1. To provide term finance to all the small, medium, and large industrial enterprises set up in the state.
2. To contribute to the shares and guarantee the debentures of business corporations available in the state.
3. To engage in marketplace surveys, prepare feasibility studies, and motivate private entrepreneurs to start their business ventures in the state.
4. To collaborate with private entrepreneurs for starting business ventures in joint and assisted sectors.

5. To implement the schemes of the Industrial Development Bank of India (IDBI)of seed capital in the state.

b) State Directorate of Industries (SDIs)

6. The Constitution of India regards the promotion and development of small-scale industries as a state subject. The directorate of industries in each state has the primary responsibility for implementing policies and programmes of assistance. SDIs functions under the supervision of SIDO and concerned central institutions. It performs the regulatory and developmental functions through a network of district industries offices, industries and extension officers at district sub-division and block-level, respectively. The following are the functions of SDIs:
   - Registration of small-scale units
   - Provision of financial assistance
   - Supply of indigenous raw materials to industrial units
   - Granting essentiality certificate for import of raw material
   - Establishment of industrial Estates and industrial cooperative
   - Development of industrial infrastructure
   - Undertaking industrial service and collecting information
   - Arrangement of concessions and incentives for industries
   - Overall management of village and small scale industries
   - Maintaining liaison with other agencies for industrial development

c) District Industries Centres (DICs)

District Industry Centre programs were launched on May 8, 1978, to effectively promote cottage and small-scale industries widely dispersed in rural areas and small towns. These centres are the focal points providing all the services and support required by small scale and village entrepreneurs, which comes under one **umbrella**. The functioning of DICs is at the district level and serves as an integrated administrative framework for industrial development.

Functions of DICs

1. Conduct surveys to know the industrial potential of a district keeping in view the availability of raw materials, human skills, demand, etc.
2. Formulate a strategic plan for industrial development.

3. Review various investment plans received from different entrepreneurs.
4. Guide and assist entrepreneurs in buying appropriate machinery, equipment, and raw material.
5. Suggest appropriate marketing strategies to entrepreneurs.
6. Promote and maintain ties with research institutes for industrial training, quality improvement, technology up-gradation, etc.
7. Conduct training for entrepreneurs, including artisans
8. Allocate responsibilities and self-employment to educated unemployed youths

3. Fund Based Institutions

a) Small Industries Development Bank of India (SIDBI)

b) Commercial banks

c) State Financial Corporations (SFCs)

a) Small Industrial Development Bank of India (SIDBI)

The SIDBI was set up on 2nd April 1990 under an Act of the Indian Parliament. It acts as the Principal Financial Institution to promote, finance, and develop the Micro, Small and Medium Enterprises (MSME) and maintain co-ordinations between various institutions engaged in allied activities. SIDBI's mission is to assist and support MSMEs' credit flow and state the developmental and financial gaps in MSME operations.

The role of SIDBI includes serving as the Principal Financial Institution for implementing the three strategies of MSME, i.e. promotion, financing and development through co-ordination of different institutions involved in allied activities. The ultimate vision of SIDBI is to emerge as one frame for achieving the monetary and developmental requirements of the MSME sector to form a strong and globally competitive enterprise. Improvement of the share-holders wealth, its corporate values through recent modern technologies, and making itself the most sought after and customer-friendly institution.

The Bank executes its mandate through the following plans

Direct Lending: Serves to fill the prevailing credit gaps in the MSME sector, which is carried out through demonstrative and innovative credit products that can be further expanded through the credit delivery ecosystem.

Indirect Lending: This allows lending based on the multiplier effect, greater extent in financing the MSME sector and is carried out by Banks, SFBs, NBFCs, MFIs and New Age Fintechs.

Fund of Funds–Boosts the entrepreneurship culture by supporting emerging start-ups through the Fund of Funds channel.

Development and Promotion: Encourages new entrepreneurship and assists aspiring businesses in the MSME sector's holistic growth through credit-plus initiatives.

Facilitator: Plays the role of facilitator for MSME oriented schemes started by the Government, similar to the Nodal Agency (Source: www.sidbi.in)

b) Commercial Banks

A commercial bank is a type of financial institution that lets people put money in and take it out of their accounts, as well as get loans for investment purposes. These banks are for-profit businesses that are only in business to make money. Lending and borrowing are the two main things they do. The bank takes deposits and gives the money to different projects in order to earn interest (profit).The borrowing rate is the rate of interest that a bank offers to depositors, while the lending rate is the rate at which the bank lends money.

Credit requirement of small-scale industries (SSIs) is basically of 2 types, i.e. long, term loans and working capital. Commercial banks with an extensive network of nationwide branches are the channels for the working capital requirement. Banks must ensure that a defined percentage (currently 40%) of their overall lending is made to priority sectors classified by the RBI. Some of these sectors include small industries, export-import, agriculture, etc. The inclusion of small enterprises in the list makes them eligible for this earmarked credit. With the liberalisation of the Indian economy, there was a greater emphasis on meeting the credit needs of SSIs.

- Credit for the small sector has been earmarked within overall lending to small industries. To ensure that credit is available to all segments of the SSI sector, RBI has issued instructions that out of the funds ordinarily open to the SSI sector,40% is given to the units with investment in plant and machinery up to rupees 5 lakhs, 20percent for units with investment between Rs.5 lakhs to Rs.25 lakhs and remaining 40% for other units.
- Public sector banks have been advised to operationalize more specialized SSI branches at centres with the potential for financing many SSI borrowers.
- A single window scheme was extended to all districts to meet SSIs' financial requirements(term loan and working capital).

Functions of Commercial Banks

Commercial banks have two major functions as follows:

a) Primary functions

- **Acceptance of deposits** - The bank accepts savings, current accounts, and fixed deposits. Surplus balances collected from firms and individuals are lent to commercial transactions for the short term.
- **Provision of loans and advances** - Another critical function of this bank is to offer loans and advances to entrepreneurs and businesspeople and collect interest. In this process, a bank holds a small number of deposits as a reserve and offers (lends) the remainder to borrowers in demand loans, overdrafts, cash credit, and short-term loans, among other things. It is the primary source of profit for every bank.
- **Provision of credit cards** - When a customer gets a loan or credit, they don't get cash in hand. First, a bank account is set up for the customer, and then money is moved into the account. Through this process, a bank can make money.

b) Secondary functions

- **Discounting exchange bills** - A written agreement acknowledges the amount of money to be paid against the goods purchased at a future point in time. The amount can also be cleared using a commercial bank's discounting method before the quoted time.
- **Facility for an overdraft** - A loan is given to a customer in exchange for allowing the customer's current account to overdraw up to a specific limit.
- **Purchase and sale of securities** - The bank provides the option of selling and buying securities.
- **Provision of locker facilities** - Customers can use the lockers provided by the bank to store their valuable belongings or documents safely. For this service, banks charge a minimum of an annual fee.
- **Payment of credit** employs various instruments such as promissory notes, cheques, and bills of exchange.

Types of Commercial Banks

a) **Public Bank** - This type of bank has been nationalised, and the government owns a significant portion of it. Banks such as Bank of Baroda, State Bank of India (SBI), Dena Bank, Corporation Bank, and Punjab National Bank are some of the examples. The following are the three different types of commercial banks:

b) **Private Bank** –In this type of commercial bank, most of the stocks are owned by private individuals and businesses. Banks such as Housing Development Finance Corporation (HDFC) Bank, Industrial Credit, Investment Corporation of India (ICICI) Bank, and Yes Bank are a few examples. All private banks are registered as limited liability companies.

c) **Foreign Bank** –This type of bank is headquartered in other countries and have different branches in other parts of the world. American Express Bank, Hong Kong, and Shanghai Banking Corporation (HSBC), Standard & Chartered Bank, and Citibank are a few examples (*Functions of Commercial Banks: Meaning, Functions, Types, Example*, n.d.)

c) State Financial Corporations (SFCs)

The Industrial Financial Corporation of India (IFCI) was set up in 1948 to provide financial assistance to only large industrial undertakings. To cater to the financial requirements of many small-scale units, the state financial Corporation act (SFC)was passed. The SFC Act 1951 was brought into force to enable all the state Governments to set up State Financial Corporations as regional development banks. The first SFC was set up in Punjab in 1953.

Functions of State Financial Corporations (SFCs) in India

- SFCs are established in various states under the State Financial Corporation Act, 1952, to provide term finance to medium and small-scale industries.
- In Delhi and seventeen other states, there are 18 SFCs (including the Tamil Nadu Industrial Investment Corporation Ltd.) The State Government and the IDBI have diarchic control over the SFCs.
- SFCs perform similar functions to that of IFCI. They have the authority to make financial loans and advances, subscribe to shares and debentures, underwrite new issues, and guarantee loans. In practice, however, they have primarily focused on loans and advances. As a result, there is a need to reorient their loan policy.
- One distinguishing feature of SFC is that a large portion of their assistance has gone to small-scale industries and backward regions in recent years.
- However, it has been observed that the development of industries with the assistance of SFCs has been uneven in different states and regions. As a result, the SFCs have failed to achieve regionally balanced growth of industries in the proper order. They have also favoured many large-scale industries over small and medium-sized businesses.

- As a result, it is suggested that they take greater care in the distribution of industries in rural and backward areas. They should also encourage self-employment and provide prospective entrepreneurs with composite finance (fixed plus working capital).(Chand, n.d.)

Other Institutions Providing Support for Entrepreneurship

a) Entrepreneurship Development Institute of India (EDI)

b) Centre for Entrepreneurship Development (CED)

c) Agri-clinics and Agribusiness Centres (ACABC)

a) Entrepreneurship Development Institute of India (EDI)

EDI is India's leading institute for managing small and medium-sized businesses. It is a non-profit organisation founded in 1983 with corporate partners such as the State Bank of India and IBDI Bank Ltd, as well as significant involvement with the Indian Industry Development Commission and the United Nations Industry Development Organization. It has two major functions:

i) To provide knowledge and social impact of advanced entrepreneurial procedures and strategies to graduate-level students.

ii) To encourage the promotion and development of specific industries with high employment potential for India's developing economy through consultation with the Central Government. (Source: www.ediindia.org)

b) Centre for Entrepreneurship Development (CED)

CED is a premier Government of Gujarat organisation providing Entrepreneurship Development Training since 1979 and Skill Development since 2009. The concept behind CED is to develop entrepreneurs in the state's urban and rural areas who can establish their Enterprise (Trading/Service/Manufacturing), which aids in the state's economic growth and creates employment opportunities for others. The vision and mission for CED are to encourage the people of Gujarat by imparting knowledge on Entrepreneurship and Skill Development; to carry out Entrepreneurship Development Programs for second-generation entrepreneurs throughout the state.

The objectives of CED are as follows:

- Organization of Entrepreneurship Awareness Programs in Colleges and ITI/Diploma Engineering College/Degree Engineering College.
- Conduction of Achievement Motivation Training programmes at various levels for existing faculties, staff, and employees.

- Creation of Industry Responsive Skill Manpower (including Up-skilling) on an annual basis, in addition to skill assessment and placement.
- Establish modern Skill Development Centres with the active participation of industries/industry associations.
- Provision of a unique approach to women's empowerment through skill and entrepreneurship.
- Carry out a particular counselling cell for ST/SC/Women for Hand Hold Support for their new enterprise/venture.
- Provision of handholding support to CED Trainees.
- Establish and manage EDP Cells in various educational institutes/colleges/ universities throughout Gujarat. (Source: www.ced.gujarat.gov.in)

c) Agri-clinics and Agribusiness Centres (ACABC)

The Government of India's Ministry of Agriculture, in collaboration with NABARD, has launched a one-of-a-kind programme to bring better farming methods to every farmer in the country. The program's goal is to tap into the expertise of the large pool of Agriculture Graduates. Irrespective of whether he or she is a fresh graduate or not, or whether he or she is currently employed, one can set up his/her Agri-clinics and Agribusiness Centres (ACABC) to offer extension services to farmers.

As part of this programme, the government is now offering start-up training to graduates in agriculture or related fields such as horticulture, sericulture, veterinary sciences, forestry, dairy, poultry farming, and fisheries. Graduates who have completed the training can apply for a loan under special venture start-ups. The following are some of the ACABC ventures offered by the Government:

i) **Become a consultant to farmers to earn money and prestige**-In this, agribusiness centres would offer paid services to farmers to increase agricultural production and income. Farmers would need to be advised on crop selection, best farming practices, post-harvest value-added options, key agricultural information (including possibly an Internet-based weather forecast), price trends, market news, risk mitigation and crop insurance, credit, and input access, as well as critical sanitary and phytosanitary considerations.

ii) **Setting up ACABC to provide free trainings** - Agriculture graduates interested in establishing such a centre will receive specialized training as part of this nationwide initiative. The course, initiated by SFAC and coordinated by MANAGE, consists of Entrepreneurship and Business Management modules and skill improvement modules in your chosen areas of activity. The 2-month training course will be provided free of charge by select institutes.

iii) **Provision of bank loans for setting up ACABC** -For an individual project, the project cost ceiling for the subsidy has been raised to Rs.20 lakhs (Rs.25 lakhs for exceptionally successful individual projects) and Rs.100 lakhs for a group project. ACABC Loans can be repaid in 5 to 10 years, depending on the type of venture the graduate wants to start, with a moratorium of up to 2 years. The respective banks will determine the interest rate, margin, and security on loans by the RBI guidelines. Depending on the eligibility, the graduate may even be able to apply for margin money assistance.

The objectives of ACABC are as follows

- To enhance the efforts of the government extension system.
- To provide additional sources of input supply and services to needy farmers.
- To provide agricultural graduates with gainful employment in new emerging areas of the agricultural sector.

The graduates can also apply their indents to set up agri-clinics / agribusiness centres to NABARD. The loans can be repaid within 5-10 years, where the respective bank will determine the interest rate, margin and security on loans by RBI guidelines. These graduates are envisaged to provide expert services and advice to farmers on cropping practices, technology dissemination, crop protection from pests and diseases, market trends and prices of various crops in markets, and clinical services for animal health to increase crop/animal productivity. ACABCs are expected to offer input supply, farm equipment rental, and other services. Along with the Agri-clinics/ Agribusiness Centres, agriculture graduates may also take up allied sectors apart from agriculture to enhance the viability of the ventures.

Eligibility criteria for the start-up of ACABC

- This scheme is open to agricultural graduates /graduates in subjects allied to agriculture like horticulture, animal husbandry, forestry, dairy, veterinary and other allied activities. Agricultural graduates can take up the project either individually or on a collaborative / group basis.
- The group may normally be of 5 members, of whom one could be a management graduate with experience in business development and management.

- The maximum cost of the project for an individual is set at Rs.20.00 lakhs, and the full cost for a group is Rs. 100.00 lakhs.

Training programmes under ACABC

- The eligible graduates are given almost free of cost training for two months at selected training centres by paying the nominal registration fee.
- It was initiated by SFAC (Small Farmers Agribusiness Consortium), coordinated by MANAGE. The training course comprises Entrepreneurship and Business Management and skill improvement modules in the chosen area by the unemployed graduate.

Project Activities under ACABC

- Laboratories for soil and water quality testing
- Services for pest surveillance, diagnosis, and control
- Seed processing plants
- Establishing vermin-culture units, as well as the production of bio-fertilizers, bio-pesticides, and bio-control agents
- Provision of livestock health insurance, the establishment of veterinary dispensaries and services
- Establishment of Information Technology Kiosks in rural areas to provide access to various agricultural portals
- Feed processing and testing facilities
- Value-added centres
- Implementation of the Cool Chain from the farm level onwards
- Retail marketing outlets for agri-products that have been processed
- Rural marketing dealerships of farm inputs and output
- Provision of extension consultancy services
- Setting up Beekeeping and honeybee products
- Hatcheries

Selection of Borrowers

Repayment - The repayment period may include a grace period (to be decided by the financing bank as per the individual scheme) of a maximum of 2 years. The loan period will range from 5 to 10 years, depending on the activity.

Advantages of ACABC

- Multi-sourced extension services. The input supply and support services are provided on a competitive basis.
- Location-specific specialized crop advice is provided.
- Field level staff are adequately qualified and trained for extension work.
- Provision of specialized agri-services like agricultural insurance, technology information, maintenance, repairs etc.
- It serves as a source of incentive to graduates by affording them to various viable business opportunities. (*ACABC*, n.d.)

Training of Trainers (ToTs)

a) National Academy of Agricultural Research Management (NAARM)

The Indian Council of Agricultural Research (ICAR) established the National Academy of Agricultural Research Management (NAARM) in Hyderabad in 1976. The major mandate of the Academy is to build capacity in agricultural research, education and extension education systems and provide policy advocacy for the National Agricultural Research and Education System (NARES).To carry out these mandates, the Academy organises various capacity-building programmes for NARES researchers, academicians, extension personnel, scholars, and other stakeholders. The Academy works to increase NARES's individual and institutional capacity for innovation. Given the strategic importance of agricultural research to the country's food security and economic growth, leadership, governance, and innovation are emerging as prerequisites for transforming NARES into a more pluralistic innovation system. With this in mind, the Academy created its vision, mission, and mandate.

Vision, Mission and Mandates of NAARM

i) The vision for NAARM is to provide a global knowledge institution that enables the National Agricultural Research and Education System (NARES) to adapt to change by fostering continuous innovation. Whereas the mission of NAARM is to strengthen the National Agricultural Research and Education System's (NARES) leadership, governance, and innovation capacities through capacity building, education, research, consulting, and policy support. The mandates of NAARM include the following:

ii) To improve the individual and institutional competencies in innovation management through capacity development, research, and policy advocacy.

iii) To serve as a think tank for the National Agricultural Research and Education System, facilitating strategic human capital management.

b) MANAGE- National Institute of Agricultural Extension Management

The Ministry of Agriculture & Farmers Welfare, Government of India, established MANAGE in 1987 as the National Centre for Management of Agricultural Extension in Hyderabad as an autonomous Institute, from which its acronym 'MANAGE' is derived. In 1992, its status was elevated to that of a National Institute in recognition of its significance and expansion of activities throughout the country, later renamed the National Institute of Agricultural Extension Management. MANAGE takes up different challenges of India's extension systems in a rapidly growing and diverse agriculture sector. The economy's liberalization and globalization policies and the sophistication and complexity of agricultural technology necessitated major initiatives to reorient and modernise the agricultural extension system. Effective ways of managing the extension system needed to be evolved, and extension organizations were enabled to transform the existing set-up through professional guidance and training of critical manpower.

Mission of MANAGE

The mission of MANAGE is to facilitate the acquisition of managerial and technical skills by Extension Officers, Managers, Scientists, and Administrators in all sectors of the agricultural economy for them to provide farmers and fishermen with the most effective support and facilities for practising sustainable agriculture systems.

Professional Services

MANAGE offers its services in the following five streams viz.,

- Management Training
- Consultancy
- Management Education
- Research
- Information Services

MANAGE's mandate entrusts the institute with the responsibility to work in the following areas:

- Establishing relationships with prominent state, regional, national, and international institutions involved in agricultural extension management.

- Establishing collaborative relationships with national and international institutions to share faculty resources
- Creating and promoting modern management tools to increase the effectiveness of agricultural extension organisations.
- Organizing need-based training for senior and middle-level agricultural extension functionaries; conducting problem-oriented studies on agricultural extension management; and serving as an international documentation centre for collecting, storing, processing, and disseminating information on agricultural management-related subjects.

Core Values

1. User-friendliness
2. Client-centred process consulting
3. A farmer-centric approach to all our professional services
4. Methodology for interactive and experiential learning.

Programmes Promoting Entrepreneurship in the country

#startupindia	Skill India कौशल भारत-कुशल भारत	PMKVY	MAKE IN INDIA	STAND UP India

Start-Up India

Startup India is a government of India initiative. During his speech on August 15, 2015, Indian Prime Minister Narendra Modi first announced the campaign (TNN, 2015).

The action plan of this initiative focuses on three areas:

1. Simplification and Handholding.
2. Funding Support and Incentives.
3. Industry-Academia Partnership and Incubation.

Another aspect of this initiative is eliminating restrictive State Government policies in this domain, such as License Raj, Land Permits, Foreign Investment Proposals, and Environmental Clearances. The Department for the Promotion of Industry and Internal Trade organised it. (Express News Service, 2015) .

A startup is defined as an entity headquartered in India that was founded less than ten years ago and had annual revenue of fewer than 100 crores (US$13 million)(Express News Service, 2015). "India will celebrate January 16 as 'National Start-up Day,'" the Indian Prime Minister recently announced (Zeebiz, 2022). (Gazette Notification, 2019).

The Startup notifications for February 2019 were updated. The Indian government values entrepreneurship. Entrepreneurship and start-ups boost the economy by increasing technical competitiveness creating jobs and wealth. A start-up is defined as a private limited company, partnership firm, or limited liability partnership that has been in existence for at least ten years and has not exceeded Rs. 100 crore in any year, is engaged in "innovation, development, or improvement of products or services," or is a scalable business model with high potential for job creation or wealth creation. The government offers targeted tax incentives for up to 10 years for biotechnology enterprises and seven years for non-biotechnology firms. (Bhaktavatsala, 2019).

Skill India

Skill India, also known as India's National Skills Development Mission, is a Prime Minister Narendra Modi-launched campaign. The National Skills Development Corporation of India is in charge of it. Prime Minister Narendra Modi launched the Skill India campaign on July 15, 2015, to train over 30 crore people in various skills by 2022.

Initiatives

Various initiatives under this campaign are (Cabral & Dhar, 2019)

- National Skill Development Mission
- National Policy for Skill Development and Entrepreneurship, 2015
- Pradhan Mantri Kaushal Vikas Yojana (PMKVY)
- Skill Loan scheme
- Rural India Skill

Partnership

Under the Skill India programme, the United Kingdom has formed a partnership with India. Virtual partnerships will be established at the school level to allow young people from these countries to experience the other country's school system and understand its culture, traditions, and social and family systems. A commitment was made to achieve mutual recognition of UK and Indian qualifications. (Srivastava, 2016)

Skill India Developments

A recent systematic literature review identified the significance of skill development, wherein implementing such schemes mitigates poverty, utilises demographic dividend, socio-economic empowerment of underprivileged sectors, achieves economic growth, reduces social challenges, and promotes economic inclusion. In terms of institutional mechanisms, the National Skill Development Corporation (NSDC), the Ministry of Skill Development and Entrepreneurship, and Prime Minister Kaushal Vikas Yojana (PMKVY) have yielded significant but not expected results outcomes. The study argues that skill development is necessary to achieve technology adoption and women's empowerment in the country.(Cabral & Dhar, 2019)

On February 12, 2016, Oracle announced that it would build a new 2.8 million-square-foot campus in Bengaluru, India, which will be the company's most significant outside of its headquarters in Redwood Shores, California. Oracle Academy will expand its partnerships to 2,700 institutions in India, up from 1,800 now, to train more than 500,000 students each year in computer science skills (Srivastava, 2016)

The private sector in Japan plans to establish six manufacturing institutes to train 30,000 people in Japanese-style manufacturing skills and practises over ten years, primarily in rural areas. Japan-India Institute of Manufacturing (JIM) and Japanese Endowed Courses (JEC) in engineering colleges designated by Japanese companies in India would be established to collaborate between the public and private sectors. In the summer of 2017, the first three institutes would be found in Gujarat, Karnataka, and Rajasthan(PTI, 2016c).

Every year, at least ten million Indian youth enter the labour force. Still, employment creation in India has not been able to keep up with this influx, making rising unemployment a severe issue. The government of India has decided to set aside 17,000 crores in the fiscal year 2017-18 budget, the highest ever allocation to this sector, to boost the Skill India Mission. The government intends to use this allocation to create jobs and provide a living for the millions of young Indians who enter the labour force each year.

The government has invested Rs. 4000 crore in the launch of SANKALP (Skill Acquisition and Knowledge Awareness for Livelihood Promotion Programme), another major initiative of the Skill India Mission. It hopes to achieve this by providing 350 million young Indians with market-relevant training. Aside from that, the government plans to establish 100 India International Skills Centres, which will offer advanced foreign language courses to help young people prepare for jobs abroad. It gives opportunities to India's youth(ET Bureau, 2017)

Pradhan Mantri Kaushal Vikas Yojana (PMKVY)

Pradhan Mantri Kaushal Vikas Yojana (PMKVY) is the flagship scheme of the Ministry of Skill Development and Entrepreneurship (MSDE) implemented by the National Skill Development Corporation (NSDC). The objective of this Skill Certification Scheme is to enable Indian youth to take up industry-relevant skill training that will help them secure a better livelihood. (*PMKVY*, n.d.)

The PMKVY scheme's goal is to encourage aptitude toward employable skills and to increase the working efficiency of potential and existing daily wage earners by providing monetary awards and rewards as well as quality training. The scheme has a target distribution of 15 billion (US$200 million) in the first year. The average award amount per person has been maintained at 8,000 (US$110). Wage-earners who already have a standard skill level will be recognised under the scheme, with an average award amount of $2,000 to $2,500. Qualification plans and quality plans have been developed by various Sector Skill Councils (SSC) formed with industry participation. Training programmes have been designed based on National Occupational Standards (NOS), and qualification packs are explicitly developed for various skill sectors. The National Skill Development Council (NSDC) has been designated as the coordinating and driving agency for the initiative(PTI, 2016a).

The cabinet has approved a budget of 120 billion (US$1.6 billion) for this project. [5] From 2016 to 2020, the scheme aims to train one crore Indian youth. As of July 18, 2016, 17.93 lakh candidates had been trained out of the 18 lakh enrolled in the scheme (PTI, 2016a).

Make in India is a government initiative to encourage companies to develop, manufacture, and assemble products made in India and incentivize dedicated investments in manufacturing (Chowdhary, 2014). The policy approach was to foster an investment-friendly environment, build modern and efficient infrastructure, and open new sectors to foreign capital. The initiative aimed to "transform India into a global design and manufacturing export hub" by focusing on 25 economic sectors for job creation and skill enhancement(IBEF, 2022); (Ministry Of Heavy Industries & Public Enterprises, 2014).

"Make in India" had three stated objectives:

1. To increase the manufacturing sector's annual growth rate to 12-14 per cent.
2. To add 100 million new manufacturing jobs to the economy by 2022 and
3. To increase the manufacturing sector's contribution to GDP to 25 per cent by 2022. (Later revised to 2025).(Babu, 2020)

Between September 2014 and February 2016, India received investment commitments totalling 16.40 lakh crore (US$220 billion) and investment inquiries totalling 1.5 lakh crore (US$20 billion). (PTI, 2016d) (Mukherjee, 2016). As a result, India surpassed the United States and China as the top global destination for foreign direct investment (FDI) in 2015, with US$60.1 billion in FDI. (PTI, 2016b) Japan and India also announced a US$12 billion fund called the "Japan-India Make-in-India Special Finance Facility" to encourage investment (Chaudhary, 2015).

Standup India

Stand Up India encourages women and people from reserved castes and tribes to start businesses. The plan is backed by the Indian Ministry of Finance's Financial Services Department.

The Stand-Up India Scheme provides bank loans between Rs 10 lakh and Rs 1 crore to at least one SC or ST borrower and one woman every bank branch to start a new business. This company might be in manufacturing, services, or trading. In non-individual firms, a SC/ST or female entrepreneur must own at least 51% of the shares and run the company.(Vikaspedia, n.d.)

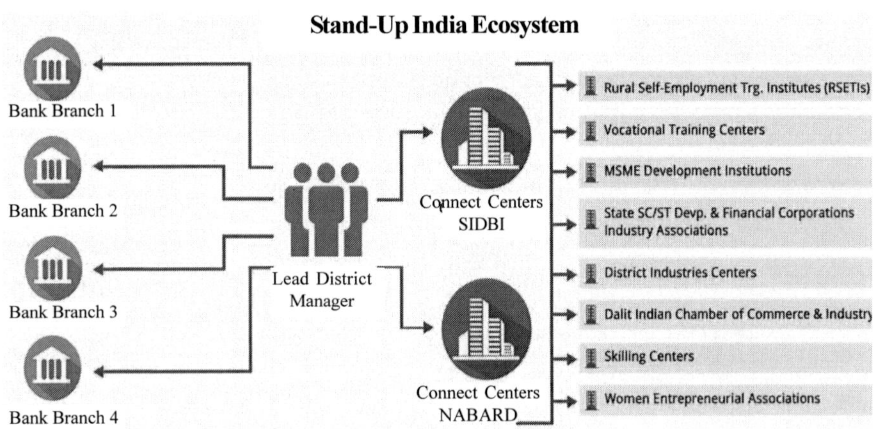

Figure 1. Standup India Ec osystem *Source*: (Vikaspedia, n.d.)

Conclusion

Central, state governments and non-government support and promote small businesses and support their self-sustained growth. A new business requires resources and infrastructure. Small businesses often lack these resources and facilities. Finance is vital to starting and running a business since it allows an entrepreneur to purchase property, labour, materials, equipment, and other resources. The government provides services through specialised organisations/ institutions to encourage entrepreneurs to create businesses and prosper.

References

ACABC. (n.d.). Retrieved March 6, 2022, from http://www.agriclinics.net/scheme-home.htm Agriclinics available at: http://www.agriclinics.net/ACABC Guidelines 2018.pdf

Babu, M. S. (2020). *Why 'Make in India' has failed - The Hindu*. https://www. thehindu.com/opinion/op-ed/why-make-in-india-has-failed/article30601269.ece

Cabral, C., & Dhar, R. L. (2019). Skill development research in India: a systematic literature review and future research agenda. *Benchmarking*, *26*(7), 2242–2266. https://doi.org/10.1108/BIJ-07-2018-0211/FULL/XML Ced available at: https://ced.gujarat.gov.in/vision-and-mission

Chand, S. (n.d.). *The function of State Financial Corporation (SFCs) in India*. Retrieved March 19, 2022, from https://www.yourarticlelibrary.com/banking/function-of-state-financial-corporations-sfcs-in-india/24817

Chand, S. (n.d.). *Function of State Financial Corporation's (SFCs) in India*. Retrieved March 19, 2022, from https://www.yourarticlelibrary.com/banking/function-of-state-financial-corporations-sfcs-in-india/24817

Chaudhary, R. D. (2015). *Japan's $12 billion "Make in India" fund to push investments - The Economic Times*. https://economictimes.indiatimes.com/news/economy/finance/japans-12-billion-make-in-india-fund-to-push-investments/articleshow/50154789.cms

Chole, R.R., Kapse, P.S., and Deshmukh. (2012). Entrepreneurship development and Business Communication Skills. Scientific Publishers.

Chowdhary, G. (2014). *Live coverage: Launch of Modi's Make in India campaign - Hindustan Times*.https://web.archive.org/web/20140925055526/http://www.hindustantimes.com/business-news/live-coverage-launch-of-modi-s-make-in-india-campaign/article1-1268119.aspx

Clement, C and Dhar, R. L. (2019). Skill development research in India: a systematic literature review and future research agenda. Benchmarking: An International Journal. 26(7): 2242-2266. doi:10.1108/BIJ-07-2018-0211. ISSN 1463-5771

Cullen, M., Calitz, A., and Chandler, L. (2014). Business Incubation in the Eastern Cape: A Case Study. International Journal for Innovation Education and Research, 2(05): p. 76-89.

EDII available at: https://www.ediindia.org/ ET Bureau. (2017). *To boost Skill India Mission, Govt sets aside Rs 17,000 crore in Budget - The Economic Times*. https://economictimes.indiatimes.com/news/economy/policy/to-boost-skill-india-mission-govt-sets-aside-rs-17000-crore-in-budget/articleshow/56944089.cms

Etzkowitz, H. (2002). Incubation of Incubators: Innovation as a Triple Helix of University-Industry Government Networks. Science and Public Policy, 29(2): p. 115-128.

Express News Service. (2015). *Start-Up India plan on Jan 16: Modi on Mann ki Baat | India News, The Indian Express*. https://indianexpress.com/article/india/india-news-india/action-plan-on-startup-india-to-be-unveiled-on-jan-16-pm-modi/

Functions of Commercial Banks: meaning, functions, types, example. (n.d.). Retrieved March 6, 2022, from https://byjus.com/commerce/functions-of-commercial-banks/

Greene, F., (2012). Should the focus of publicity provided small business assistance be on start-ups or growth businesss? Ministry of Economic Development, New Zealand.

IBEF. (2022). *Make In India Programme, All About The Manufacture in India Initiative*. https://www.ibef.org/economy/make-in-india

Kathewadi, H. (2015). Government to train 40 crore people under Skill India initiative. The Economic Times, Retrieved on March 3, 2022.

Khadi and Village Industries Commission. (n.d.). Retrieved March 6, 2022, from https://www.kvic.gov.in/kvicres/aboutkvic.php

Krishna, P. (2017). PradhanMantriKaushalVikasYojana: Boon Or Bane. Business world.Retrieved on March 3, 2022.

Laghu-Udyog available at: http://www.laghu-udyog.gov.in/righttoinformationact05.doc

Livestock Entrepreneurship: National Institute for Small Industry Extension Training (NISIET). (n.d.). Retrieved March 6, 2022, from http://ecoursesonline.iasri.res.in/mod/page/view.php?id=73731

Micro Small Scale Industries Board India | Micro SSI Board Meeting India |Micro Small & Medium Enterprises India. (n.d.). Retrieved March 6, 2022, from http://laghu-udyog.gov.in/msme-do/sidoboard.htm

Micro, Small and Medium Enterprises available at: http://laghu-udyog.gov.in/msme-do/sidoboard.htm#:~:text=The%20Small%20Scale%20Industries%20Board,in%20the%20Government%20of%20India.

Ministry Of Heavy Industries & Public Enterprises. (2014). *Focus on Make In India | Business Standard News*. https://www.business-standard.com/article/government-press-release/focus-on-make-in-india-114092501206_1.html

Mukherjee, P. (2016). *Modi's "Make In India" racks up $222 billion in investment pledges | Reuters*. https://www.reuters.com/article/modi-make-in-india-investment-pledge-idINKCN0VR1S0?edition-redirect=in NAARM available at: https://naarm.org.in/announcements/careers/

National Institute for Small Industry Extension Training (NISIET) available at: http://ecoursesonline.iasri.res.in/mod/page/view.php?id=73731

National Skill Development Corporation. (2015). Scheme Document of PradhanMantriKaushalVikas Yojana. http://www.pmkvyofficial.org/App_Documents/News/PMKVY_Scheme-Document_v1.1.pdf

NIMSME available at: https://www.nimsme.org/ NSIC available at: https://www.nsic.co.in/Corporate/AboutUs

Pals, S. (2006). Factors Determining Success/Failure in Business Incubators: A Literature Review of 17 Countries. Worcester Polytechnic Institute.

PMKVY. (n.d.). Retrieved March 19, 2022, from https://www.pmkvyofficial.org/home-page

PTI. (2016a). *17.93 lakh candidates trained under PMKVY as on July 18 | Business Standard News*. https://www.business-standard.com/article/pti-stories/17-93-lakh-candidates-trained-under-pmkvy-as-on-july-18-116072100579_1.html

PTI. (2016b). *India replaces China as top FDI destination in 2015: Report - The Economic Times*. https://economictimes.indiatimes.com/news/economy/finance/india-replaces-china-as-top-fdi-destination-in-2015-report/articleshow/51932057.cms

PTI. (2016c). *Japan to set up skill development institutes in Gujarat, Karnataka and Rajasthan - The Economic Times*. https://economictimes.indiatimes.com/news/politics-and-nation/japan-to-set-up-skill-development-institutes-in-gujarat-karnataka-and-rajasthan/articleshow/55377055.cms

PTI. (2016d). *"Make in India Week" gets Rs 15.2 lakh crore investment commitments - The Economic Times*. https://economictimes.indiatimes.com/news/economy/policy/make-in-india-week-gets-rs-15-2-lakh-crore-investment-commitments/articleshow/51040369.cms

Salem, M.I (2014). The Role Of Business Incubators In The Economic Development of Saudi Arabia. International Business & Economics Research Journal (IBER), 13(4): p. 853-860.

SIDBI available at: https://www.sidbi.in/en/about-sidbi#overview

Srivastava, M. (2016). *After Digital India, Oracle seeks to participate in Make in India, Start-up India*. https://www.livemint.com/Industry/NIK7XM3p7ochGKFtDruhUL/After-Digital-India-Oracle-seeks-to-participate-in-Make-in.html

TNN. (2015). *PM Modi in Mann Ki Baat: "Start Up India, Stand Up India" action plan on January 16 | India News - Times of India*. https://timesofindia.indiatimes.com/india/PM-Modi-in-Mann-Ki-Baat-Start-Up-India-Stand-Up-India-action-plan-on-January-16/articleshow/50340724.cms

Zeebiz. (2022). *LIVE: National Startup Day 2022: How entrepreneurs are applauding PM Narendra Modi's decision - Quotes | Who said what | Zee Business*. https://www.zeebiz.com/small-business/news-live-national-startup-day-2022-how-entrepreneurs-are-applauding-pm-narendra-modis-decision-quotes-who-said-what-176273

7

Entrepreneurial Development

Abhilash Singh Maurya, Ayush Mishra* and Sonia**

Department of Agricultural Economics and Extension, School of Agriculture Lovely Professional University, Phagwara, Punjab

**Department of Extension Education, CCS Haryana Agricultural University Hisar, Haryana*

***Department of Agricultural Economics, CCS Haryana Agricultural University Hisar, Haryana*

Introduction

Entrepreneurship refers to the capability and willingness to develop, establish and run an enterprise and manage uncertainties to profit. It can also be defined as a process concerned with the creation and extraction of economic value. Entrepreneurship is more than just starting a business purely to make money. The person who bears the risk of starting a new enterprise is an entrepreneur. In this chapter, we will discuss entrepreneurship and its development in detail.

Entrepreneurship development is a process involving several phases and steps. The process has been viewed at the level of individual-developing entrepreneurial quality in an individual and the group of community-creating an environment in which entrepreneurship activities can grow.

Keywords

Entrepreneurship development: Entrepreneurship development has many stages. The process is considered at two levels: individual (developing entrepreneurial qualities) and community (building an entrepreneurial environment).

Stimulating phase: The stimulatory activities help emerging entrepreneurs in society.

Support Phase: Support activities give entrepreneurs infrastructure, resources, skills, and competencies for founding and managing businesses.

Sustaining Phase: Sustaining phase operations include expansion, modernisation, diversification, technological upgrades, and rehabilitation of sick units.

Phases of Entrepreneurship Development

Entrepreneurship has three stages:

1. **Income generation** is the first stage of entrepreneurship where one tries to make profits. This can be done either part-time or casual, e.g., a person with some spare money may put his money in a Fixed Deposit account in a bank or a mutual fund to earn some interest on this money.
2. **Self-employment** is the second stage where an individual has permanent involvement in his occupation, e.g., a person starts a mobile shop and remains wholly involved in it out of satisfaction.
3. **Entrepreneurship** it is the third stage where an entrepreneur looks to diversify and grow his enterprise after setting up a venture. He is continuously looking for new challenges and is innovative and creative. A small businessman may close or change his business if they anticipate losses, but an entrepreneur will analyse the situation and try again. Accepting challenges and risk-taking behaviour are chief characteristics of an entrepreneur.

Differences between income generation, self-employment, and entrepreneurship

S. No.	Income-generating activities	Self-employment	Entrepreneurship
1.	Supplementary income	Income from one's input	Profit
2.	Partial employment	Full-time employment	Full-time employment
3.	Usually, collective	Usually not collective	Individual, partners, group
4.	Managed by NGOs/SHGs	Sometimes part of SHGs	Managed by owners, partners, etc.
5.	Most common development activity	Fairly common development activity	Uncommon development activity
6.	Programs stop at skill training	Mainly artisan skills used own occupation	Needs more complex skills-Business skills
7.	Programmes generally under schemes	Programmes generally schematic	Programmes focused on economic viability
8.	Target (number) oriented	Target (number) oriented	Employs more than one person
9.	Group employment	Employment for self only	Employs more than one person
10.	Seldom result in actual income generation	Employment for self only	Economic growth-oriented through value addition
11.	Last as long as the grant	It lasts longer but limited	Once started, it is a continuous process
12.	Low investment	Low investment	Investment may be high or low
13.	Useful employment-oriented	Traditional occupation oriented	Investment may be increased or low
14.	No risk	Almost less or no risk	High risk

There are some similarities between an entrepreneur and a self-employed individual in that both own and run a business. Still, self-employment means working for oneself as an independent owner of the business rather than working for someone else. A vast majority of small business owners fall under this category. They commence with a particular set of skills and find an opportunity to make money. On the other hand, an entrepreneur is a self-employed individual who undertakes challenges and possesses risk-taking behaviour to attain their goals. He organises and runs a business, taking an extraordinary risk in his endeavour and have a growth-oriented mindset. Entrepreneurship is all about taking risks and cherishing rewards, thinking outside the box to succeed and moving on to some next venture. While the businesses and financial tips might interest an entrepreneur, it is the passion for taking on a new challenge and motivation that drives him to go this extra mile. (ICAR, 2020)

Entrepreneurship Development Cycle, Process and Stage of Establishing Enterprise stages in establishment of enterprise

There are four stages of enterprise establishment

1. **Entrepreneurial stimulation** : This stage targets the individual sphere of a potential entrepreneur interested in setting up an enterprise. This stage of enterprise establishment is also called the motivational stage.
2. **Enterprise launching:** This stage involves all the preparations needed to unveil the enterprise, i.e., market survey, product identification, report preparation, analysis of finances, availability of subsidies, certifications and other legal requirements for initiation of the enterprise.
3. **Enterprise sustenance** : This stage is the actual running stage of the enterprise involving administration and long term procedures for running the enterprise. Major activities of this stage of enterprise sustenance involve Financial, marketing and label management, client or customer relations, growth orientation, etc.
4. **Social responsibility** : The entrepreneurs have some duties to the society that endorses and supports them in the endeavour. As a result, they must be willing to pay some social costs. Government and other institutional investors also expect something in return. Entrepreneurs must understand this and exhibit a sense of responsibility towards societies. Successful entrepreneurs must form and oblige to a few self-made rules like credibility in repayment, appropriate responses to tax and statutory requirements, humanitarian or broadminded outlook towards workers and above all, care for the environment and natural resources.

Entrepreneurship Development Cycle

There are three phases in the Entrepreneurship development process. These are the Stimulatory phase, Support phase, and Sustaining phase.

I. **Stimulatory phase:** Stimulatory activities help in the appearance of entrepreneurs in society. They prepare the background where entrepreneurship can sprout. People start looking for entrepreneurial pursuits. These generate the initial entrepreneurial motivation, help people see incentives, and offer the chance to acquire relevant information and skills. All these, taken together, help arouse entrepreneurship in society. This initial phase would include all such activities that stimulate efforts such as:

   1. Generating entrepreneurial consciousness in the community through well-planned publicity
   2. Identifying and choosing potential entrepreneurs.
   3. Helping them through training to increase their motivational level.
   4. Refining their skills in contemporary management methods
   5. Developing technical competence
   6. Helping them to develop project reports.
   7. Making available techno-economic information and project profiles.
   8. Helping entrepreneurs select new products.
   9. Developing a data bank on new products and processes available to the target group.
   10. Creating opportunities for entrepreneurs to discuss their mutual problems and success.
   11. Evolving new products and procedures are available to the homegrown situation.
   12. Public acknowledgement of entrepreneurial excellence

II. **Support Phase**: In this phase, support to entrepreneurs such as infrastructure facilities, resources, abilities and skills are provided to help them in enterprise initiation and management. These activities offer much-needed support and help the already stimulated entrepreneur move ahead to accomplish his goal. This comprises all such actions that help entrepreneurs in founding and running their enterprises. The activities in this phase include:

   1. Registering the unit.
   2. Arranging finance, i.e., fixed capital and working capital.
   3. Helping in the acquisition of plant and equipment.

4. Providing land, power, water supply, etc., for establishing the unit.
5. Direction for choosing and gaining plant and machinery
6. Issue of licenses for rare raw materials.
7. Granting tax relief and other types of incentives
8. Offering consultancy for management
9. Support in marketing of produce either through booking or assigning government quota purchase etc.
10. Providing information associated with the industries

III. **Sustaining Phase**: Sustaining phase refers to all those activities that enable progress and steadiness through expansion, diversification and up gradation of technology in the enterprise and restoration of the sick units. This is a phase in which entrepreneurs are supported to continue their enterprise well-organised and profitable. The activities in this phase include:

1. Helping in modernisation/product replacement.
2. Additional funding for full capacity utilisation.
3. Deferring repayment/interest depending on the situation.
4. Help and supervision in diagnosing the cause of the failure or low production.
5. Alteration or change in legislation/policy affecting units
6. Product reservation/creation of new avenues for marketing
7. Quality testing and quality improvement at low cost.
8. Creating common facilities which are not viable in a single unit but are desired by the team both in the production and marketing group

Life Cycle of Entrepreneurial Setup

a) **Birth stage** - Fighting for existence in survival happens. Establishing the firm, getting customers, and finding the money is crucial here.

b) **Breakthrough stage** - Coping with growth and take off happens at this stage. Working on finances, becoming profitable, and growing are some steps.

c) **Maturity stage** - Investing wisely and staying flexible is a must at this stage. In addition, redefining the strategy, continuing growth and managing for success are required.

Theories of Entrepreneurship Development

Entrepreneurial behaviour has been explained in several ways by different scholars. The theories of entrepreneurship have been classified as follows :

a) The Economic Theory
b) The Sociological Theory
c) Entrepreneurship Innovation Theory
d) Psychological Theory
e) Theory of Achievement Motivation/Achievement Theory The Kakinada Experiment
f) Status Withdrawal Theory
g) Theory of Social Change
h) Theory of Social Behaviour
i) Theory of Leadership
j) Theory of Model Personality
k) Theory of Systematic Innovation

a) The Economic Theory

Entrepreneurship and economic growth occur when economic conditions are favourable. Therefore, economic encouragements (incentives) are the primary motivators.

These incentives generally deal with the taxation policy, industrial policy, sources of Investment and inputs, infrastructure development, marketing opportunities, access to information, market conditions, technology etc.

- An Irish French Economist, Richard Cantillon, viewed entrepreneurs as agents who buy production factors at specific prices to combine them to sell them at uncertain prices in the future. He illustrated the farmer as an entrepreneur who pays out contractual incomes to the landlords and labourers, specifically while selling his crops at an uncertain price.
- Entrepreneur as a Risk Taker.

Critical Evaluation

- William J. Baumol criticised the economic theory. According to him, this theory has failed to provide an acceptable study of entrepreneurship's role or its supply.

- The traditional model treated the entrepreneurial function like a managerial occupation.

b) The Sociological Theory

- Entrepreneurship is likely to get an enhancement in a particular social culture. This is because the entrepreneurial behaviour of individuals in a society is influenced by: Society's values, beliefs, Customs, Taboos, etc.
- The entrepreneur merely performs a role as per society's potential. As per Jean Baptiste, an aristocratic capitalist. Entrepreneur combines land of one, a labour of another and the capital of yet another to produce a product. By selling the product, he pays interest on the money, rent on land and wages to labourers, and his profit remains.

c) Entrepreneurship Innovation Theory

Joseph Schumpeter promoted this theory. Entrepreneurship is Innovation. This theory disregards earlier two aptitudes, which were till then considered key for an entrepreneur:

1. Organising Abilities
2. Risk-Taking Abilities

- Joseph Schumpeter was a 20th-century Austrian Economist. He stated- "An entrepreneur is a person who is willing and able to convert a new idea or invention into a successful innovation." Entrepreneurship resulted in novel industries, even though it entailed combining the existing inputs differently. An example of one such innovation was combining a steam engine with a wagon- cart to build the horseless carriage. In this case, the innovation, i.e., the car, was transformational as it didn't require the development of new technology. Instead, just applying an already existing technology differently was entrepreneurial.

Critical Evaluation

- The distinction between innovator and inventor was made
- Development requires fundamental changes, and entrepreneurs do that change
- Limitations: This theory ignores certain aspects related to entrepreneurship such as innovative functions, risk-taking, organising aspect, active type of enterprise, and individuals operating established business and assume entrepreneurs as a large scale businessman, which may not be the case.

d) Psychological Theory

- Entrepreneurship is enhanced when society has an adequate supply of persons with the necessary psychological characteristics.
- These psychological characteristics include:
  - Need for achievement,
  - A vision Foresight,
  - Ability to face opposition.

According to this theory, these entrepreneurial characteristics are formed during the individual's upbringing- by high standards of excellence, self-reliance, and low father dominance.

e) Theory of Achievement Motivation/Achievement Theory

David McClelland gave this theory. He identified three motivations responsible for entrepreneurship. These are:

- Need for achievement
- Need for affiliation
- Need for achievement
- McClelland emphasised the importance of achievement motivation through which entrepreneurs fulfil economic and social development. The Need for Achievement was highest among entrepreneurs through an experiment.

The Kakinada Experiment

- Conducted by McClelland in America, Mexico and India (Kakinada)
- Young adults were selected and put through 3 months of training to induce achievement motivation.
- In the course content:
  - Trainees were asked to control their thinking and be positive
  - Trainees imagined themselves in need of challenges and success and set achievable goals, imitating their role models
  - Results showed- Positive impact on performance,
  - Traditional beliefs do not inhibit entrepreneurial spirit.
- McClelland identified two characteristics of entrepreneurship. These are: doing things in a new and better way and decision making under uncertainty

- He further stressed that people with a high achievement orientation (need to succeed) are more likely to become entrepreneurs. These people are not influenced by money or external incentives. Profits are only a measure of success and competency.

Critical Evaluation

High achievement orientation ensures the success of entrepreneurs. It is necessary to make an environment to enable children to grow to become individuals with high n-achievement. It is possible to improve the performance of existing entrepreneurs by imparting proper training and education.

f) Status Withdrawal Theory

- This theory states that a class that lost its prestige or a minority group shows an aggressive entrepreneurial drive.
- If a group feels that their ideals and position are not respected by society, they turn to innovation to get respect from society.
- Status withdrawal theory says that entrepreneurship is a function of status withdrawal.

Four events which can produce status withdrawal :

- Displacement of a traditional elite group by some physical force.
- Defamation of values and symbols due to change in the attitude of superior class
- Inconsistency of still symbol due to a change in economic power
- Non-acceptance of their expected status on migration to a new culture

Critical Evaluation

- Distinguish between entrepreneurship and intrapreneurship.
- Various factors motivate executives and professionals to do innovative behaviour not administered by status withdrawal.
- Presupposes long term standpoint for entrepreneurial growth, but it does not happen in India.

g) Theory of Social Change

This theory was given by Max Weber. As per him, the Ethical value system protestant ethic and the spirit of capitalism. Religion and its impact on entrepreneurial culture. Weber preached that spirit of rapid industrial growth depends upon

- Modernised technology
- Attainment of money
- Rational use of funds for productivity
- Multiplication of money

These fundamentals depend upon the explicit value orientation of individuals created by ethical values.

Critical Evaluation

Invalid assumptions: This theory does not hold in Hinduism's single system of values. Indian community internalised those values and translated them into their daily life, and these values remained immune to and insulated against external pressures and change. Further, several studies showed that Hinduism is not opposed to the essence of capitalism and adventurous spirit.

h) Theory of Social Behaviour

This theory was based on **Kunkel's** theory of behavioural model. As per this theory, the supply of entrepreneurs is a function of social, political and economic structure. Various activities that individuals perform are either accepted by society or rejected. This theory also highlights the four structures in an organisation: Limitation Structure, Demand Structure, Opportunity Structure and Labour Structure.

Critical Evaluation

This theory assumes ideal structures for the supply of entrepreneurs. However, there is an inconsistency between aims, structures, and entrepreneurs' actual prevalence. Further, entrepreneurship is also governed by specific combinations of conditions which are usually not available in the environment.

i) Theory of Leadership

Hoselitz gave this theory. As per him, entrepreneurship is a function of managerial skill and leadership. Therefore, an entrepreneur should possess the ability to lead and manage. In addition, social conditions should warrant the development of enterprise-driven personalities. Finally, Hoselitz emphasised the role of culturally marginal groups in developing entrepreneurship.

Critical Evaluation

The assumption that marginal men or women enjoy an abstruse cultural and social position due to the lack of bondage to a tradition that inhibits them from entrepreneurial development does not always hold. Economic and political factors also affect and encourage the people towards entrepreneurial behaviour.

j) Theory of Model Personality

The theory **of Cochran** is a sociological theory of entrepreneurial supply. Cochran emphasises cultural values, role expectations and social sanctions as the critical element. According to his theory, entrepreneur performance is influenced by his attitude towards his occupation, role expectations held by sanctioning groups, operational job requirements, and society's values.

Critical Evaluation

- The theory deals with only social factors.
- Profit is an imperative factor for inspiring entrepreneurs to assume risky behaviour.
- The need for achievement starts from the profit-making process.
- An entrepreneur is expected to perform managerial functions, but the theory fails to include all these requirements

k) Theory of Systematic Innovation

Prof Peter Drucker gave this theory. According to him, "Systematic innovation consists of the purposeful and organised search for changes and the systematic analysis of the opportunities such changes might offer for economic or social innovation." Systematic innovation means seven sources for the innovative opportunity. The first four sources lie within the enterprise. These four source areas are 1. The unexpected success, failure or outside event 2. The dichotomy between reality 3. Innovation based on process needs 4-changes in industry or market structure that catch everyone unaware. The second set of sources for the innovative opportunity, a set of three, involves changes outside the industry's enterprise: 1) Demographics, 2) Changes in perception, mood and meaning 3) New knowledge, both scientific and non-scientific. Lines between these seven source areas of innovative opportunities are unclear, and significant intersection occurs between them.

Critical Evaluation

Quite inclusive theory. An entrepreneur must identify diverse sources of change and direct these changes with opportunities available in the environment. Reliability and predictability of seven sources were observed.

Summary of Entrepreneurship Development Theories

The above theories show that entrepreneurship is a multidisciplinary area governed by numerous factors such as continuously changing society and economic, social, and psychological objectives. Hence, the Entrepreneurship Theory is woven into the sociological, cultural, psychological, political, and managerial fibre. The combination of which forms an economical web.

Models of the Entrepreneurship Development

While the theory is aimed at a generalised statement explaining a phenomenon, a model reflects a purposeful illustration of reality. Another way to link the two and point out differences is that a model is frequently used to define an application of a theory. In comparison, several models were developed to explain entrepreneurship and entrepreneurial behaviour. Some of those important models are described below:

1. Psychodynamic model
2. Social development model
3. Social marginality model
4. Kao's model
5. Timmons Models

1. Psychodynamic model

Kets de Vries offered this. As per this model, people tend to be self-employed and become successful because of a "troubled childhood". In troubled childhood, children lack security, are abused, have low self-esteem and lack confidence. Therefore, growing up in such a setting, some people have suppressed wishes towards those in control.

2. Social development model

This model reflects that dealings with a different context in one's life and career shape one's tendency to be self-employed. These factors start in early, middle or late life.

3. Social marginality model

This model observes that those persons who observe a strong level of disparity between their traits and their role in society are motivated to change or recreate their social reality. While some individuals may rebuild their existence by shifting careers or employers, others may choose the path of self-employment. In this model, "Marginal men" are those personalities who are less integrated into their society. This lack of integration into the society allows these marginal men to be free of the restrictions imposed by its value system. Also, having moved out of their community, they are no longer inhibited by its dominant values. This state gives way to the progress of unconventional patterns of behaviours, which increases their tendency to become entrepreneurs.

4. Kao's model

According to Kao's model, entrepreneurship is a consequence of contact between three elements: person, task, and organisational context.

In this model, the individual (i.e., the entrepreneur and team members) is the most vital element as they are the ones who create an enterprise through their efforts. Hence, their personality, skills, and motivation are critical for the endeavour's success. The task includes the activities assumed by the group or association. These are, in turn, influenced by organisational strategy and the external environment. Tasks include noticing opportunities, assembling and allocating resources, and discovering and creating market opportunities. Organisational context refers to the setting in which activities take place. This includes organisational structure, culture, systems, policies, etc. and significantly affects entrepreneurial outcomes. These fundamental elements are entrenched within the outside environment, which is the outside world. It comprises resources, infrastructure, laws and regulations, policies and technology. The setting significantly influences the enterprise and is affected by it in return. A successful entrepreneur is successful in adapting himself to this changing environment.

5. Timmon's model of the entrepreneurial process

In Timmon's model, the important elements are the entrepreneur, the founding team, the opportunity, and the resources assembled to start the novel organisation. According to this model, an entrepreneur, under the right conditions, will deliberately hunt for a chance and, upon discovering it, will shape it so that it has the potential to be a commercial success. The entrepreneur then assembles the resources that are needed to start an enterprise; explicit in the Timmons framework is the notion that the entrepreneur and the provider of capital will be rewarded with profits and that both are commensurate with the risk and effort involved in starting, financing, and building the business. Entrepreneur generally risks their career, personal cash reserves, and some or all of their net worth. In a perfect situation, all this is computed in a business plan before the business is operational.

Conclusion

The conceptual framework presented here identifies several critical components of entrepreneurs, entrepreneurship and entrepreneurial behaviour. The entrepreneurship process starts when the entrepreneur recognises an opportunity in the environment. The entrepreneurship development process goes through identification of enterprise, creation of enterprise, nurturing of enterprise and maturation and expansion of the enterprise. Several theories and models try to predict the actual behaviour of entrepreneurs and the development of entrepreneurship. These theories show that entrepreneurship is a multidisciplinary area governed by numerous factors such as continuously changing society and economic, social, and psychological objectives. Hence, the Entrepreneurship Theory is woven into the sociological, cultural, psychological, political, and managerial fibre. The combination of which forms an economical web.

References

Chole, R.R., Kapse, P.S., and Deshmukh. (2012). Entrepreneurship development and Business Communication Skills. Scientific Publishers.

Indian Council of Agricultural Research. (2020). Handbook of agricultural extension. Indian Council of Agricultural Research. Directorate of Knowledge Management in Agriculture.

MANAGE. (2013). Agri-business and Entrepreneurship Development. https://www.manage.gov.in/moocs/structure.asp

Theories of Entrepreneurship in Basics of entrepreneurship development in agriculture. (2022). https://www.agmoocs.in/beda/#/lecture/819

Models of Entrepreneurship in Basics of entrepreneurship development in agriculture. (2022). https://www.agmoocs.in/beda/#/lecture/824

Mondal, Sagar. (2019). Fundamentals of Agricultural Extension Education. Kalyani Publications. India

8

Impact of Economic Reforms on Agri-enterprises

Priyanka Lal and Arnab Roy

Department of Economics and Extension, Lovely Professional University Phagwara, Punjab

Introduction

India's change in the economic environment and market-oriented economic reforms can be traced back to the 1990s which led to the growth of the country. There was a clear evident change from the condition it was in the 1970s when it was far behind the other Asian countries. The economic reforms brought by LPG (Liberalisation, Privatisation and Globalisation) model have affected not only international trade but also led to an increase in the competitiveness of the industries. But what triggered these economic reforms? Before 1990, India was in a severe economic crisis condition due to repeated policy failures. India was experiencing a huge fiscal and balance of payment deficit, a high inflation rate and a fall in foreign exchange reserves. This led to the sickening of the public sector units whose prime role was to bring a reduction in inequality and poverty. The self-reliance condition in India was not of much help as there was insignificant trade with the rest of the world. The crisis mainly depicted the mismanagement of the resources. In light of this, this chapter discusses the impact of the economic reforms on agri-enterprises.

The vicious circle of poverty can only be broken by inducing credit and this can be done by entrepreneurs. The change in the global economic environment during 1990s affected these entrepreneurs. During the time of early economic reforms, the focus was to increase the investment and especially in the industrial sector because it was believed that it is important for the growth of the country. Though agriculture sector was also given priority as the public investment increased considering it to be the mainstay. The issue that hindered was a less private investment. Though the reforms led to rapid industrialization by investing in the creation of state-owned enterprises, this helped in the trickle-down effect in the agriculture sector (Adhia 2015).

Through the reforms of 1991, the agricultural sector was globalized and an important impact was on the exchange rate and the trade openness. Another important global landmark that happened during this time establishment of the WTO (World Trade Organisation) in the year 1995. Now the Indian market started reacting to the foreign market which had both positive and negative impacts on Indian agriculture. The agribusiness of the country was still in the bud stage and the capping of subsidies according to the regulations of the agreement had worked adversely. But it acted as a catalyst for increasing agricultural exports since the boundaries of the country was open for both output and inputs. India was able to support the farmers with the self-sufficiency of the inputs imported from other countries.

Keywords

Economic reforms: are the steps taken by a government to reduce the government's role in the economy while increasing the role of the private sector. "The goal of the economy is to reform the economy, not the other way around." Reform is merely a means to an end.

Globalization: Integrating economies and societies through information, ideas, technologies, goods, services, capital, finance, and people.

Privatization: It refers to private ownership in public enterprises.

Liberalization: It decreases state-economy traits and increases market-economy traits.

Economic Reforms: The Process

Liberalization

The process of liberalization started in the year 1991 through exposing the Indian agricultural market to the foreign countries. A new EXIM policy was introduced in the year 1992-97 which led to liberalization of the trade. There were three major changes in export and import. Channelizing of the trade was removed and private agents were allowed to enter. Removal of quantitative restrictions and reduction of tariff which have boost to the agricultural exports (Chand 1999). India got a comparative advantage in some products over rest of the world but the fear of destabilization of the prices and fluctuating international prices was prevalent. The infrastructural disadvantage at first suffered by India was redressed and the fruit processing industry having potential for competing was given due attention.

Privatization

In the time back to 1980's there was a huge queue for telephone services but with the advent of the LPG model after 1991 and opening up the sector to private companies and foreign investors, telecom services are no more a hindrance towards growth (Panagariya 2001). Privatization has led to several reforms in agriculture as well. The industrial growth in the agribusiness requires faster privatization because the organized sector only is not enough. With the current consumption preference change and urbanization, people are moving towards more processed foods. The focus of the privatization should not only be in input sector but it should also be in output sector. It has led to increase in the Foreign Direct Investment after 1991 that can be depicted by the following Figure 1.

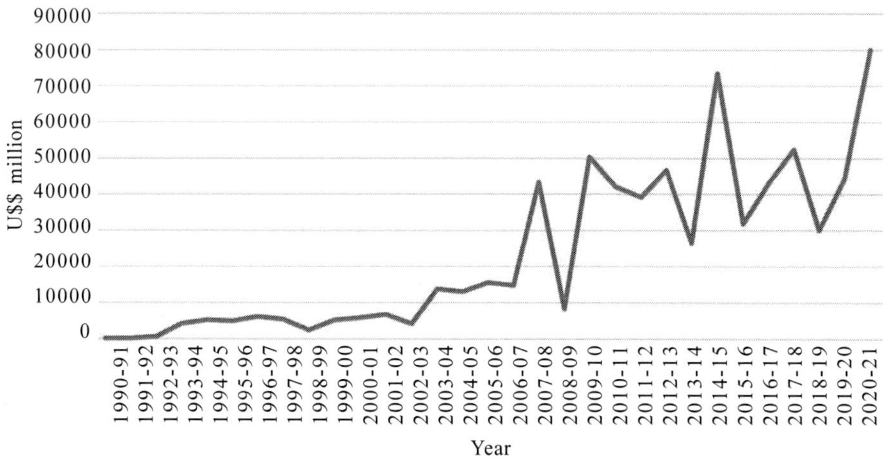

Figure 1. Foreign Direct Investment in India
Source: Various RBI reports

Globalization

Several studies were conducted to evaluate the impact of economic reforms on the agricultural sector. There were many indications showing the positive impact of the economic reforms; like India's share in trade increased from 13% in 1990 to 20% in 2000 which gave a competitive edge through further appropriate economic reforms (Wadhva 1991). Government undertook both macro-economic and well as sectoral economic reforms. On the one hand the fiscal deficit was reduced to 4.8% of GDP under macro-economic management reforms while sector reforms included Industrial policy reforms, trade reforms, fiscal sector reforms, monetary policy reforms, finance sector reforms. India adopted the framework of China's Specific Economic Zone to boost agricultural export by setting up agricultural export zone. This competitiveness led to the increase in quality of the produce and productive efficiency (Siggel and Agrawal 2009).

Privatisation and globalization led to the shift towards high value crops like fruits, plantation crops, etc. This imbibed competition in the market that led to development of various agribusiness and removal of infrastructural disadvantage. The green revolution gave impetus to the growing agribusiness industry.

The1950s: Era of stagnation in agriculture

Low growth in crop and grain production (0.4 and 0.1 percent p.a.)

Foodgrain production of 59.2 MT in 1952–53, with a yield of 579.8 kg/ha

The 1960-1980s: Green Revolution

- High Yield Variety (HYV) of seeds, increased use of fertilizers and irrigation, resulting in a significant spike in production
- Food security and reduced import of food grains
- Subsidies given to the farmers was started

The 1980-2000s: Surplus production and exports

- Expanding cereal production
- LPG model
- India emerged as a net exporter of agricultural products

2000 Onwards: Economic Reforms, Technological Advancements and Disruptive Transformation

- Better technology adoption
- Rise in institutional credit for agriculture
- Schemes like National Horticulture Mission (NHM) and Bringing Green Revolution in Eastern India (BREI) that helped achieve record production.
- Commodity exchanges that helped in fair pricing of commodities
- Atmanirbhar Bharat led to self reliance of agriculture enterprises

Figure 2. Evolution of Agriculture Industry

Reform Measures

Monetary and Financial Sector Reforms: The economic policy made banking sector efficient. The prime measures taken were removing interest rate distortions and restructuring the lending rates. Credit is an important aspect for the development of the sector and credit disbursement became competitive among public, private and foreign banks as the market was liberated. Moreover, the capital market reforms aimed at removing the government control and mobilizing the resources thorough the securities market for which The Securities & Exchange Board of India (SEBI) was set up in 1988. Due to these monetary reforms different schemes were started and also motivated the investors to move towards agribusiness. The Regional Rural Bank Credit Refinance Fund was set up in 2016 with a capital of USD 2.1 billion to disburse short term loan to the small and marginal farmers. In the recent year Rs. 20 lakh crore package was also announced for strengthening agriculture infrastructure like cold storage, post-harvest management, warehouses, etc.

Industrial Policy Reforms: In order to give stimulus to the Indian Industry, government announced New Industrial Policy on 24 July 1991 to bring competitiveness of the domestic industries. Small Farmers Agribusiness Consortium (SFAC) was launched in the year 1994 to create wider linkages and better market opportunities for the Farmer Producer Organization (FPO). The private sector was encouraged and under new policy the area reserved for public sector was reduced to 8. Moreover in the recent years the import duty was scrapped on capital goods and raw materials for export oriented units. In addition to this, for installation of cold storage facilities there was full excise duty exemption.

Trade Policy Reforms: It was aimed to create an environment that will greater openness to the Indian industry. There was subsequent reduction in the degree of regulation and licensing control on foreign trade. Agricultural Export Policy was framed in 2018 for export-oriented production. Mere production will not increase the income of the farmers because of which under this policy, it lifted all restrictions on organic and processed food. The government also allowed 100% FDI in storage and warehouses under automated route.

Agri-reforms in India

Though the farm laws were repelled, but the current scenario of agriculture points out towards serious amendment of APMC laws because without marketing, the production is in vain. The very first remarkable reforms introduced was land reforms and green revolution. Agriculture in India has evolved in a dynamic fashion and appeared in stages described below:

1. Early Stage reforms (1950-2000)

Land Reforms: Post independence, there was abolition of intermediaries, tenancy reforms and redistribution of land ceilings. As there was abolition of zamindari system, the land was redistributed and made the tenants owner of the land (https://www.xcubelabs.com/blog/the evolution-of-indian-agriculture-industry-key-policies-and-reforms/#the1980).

Green Revolution: India was made self-sufficient nation through green revolution. Increase in production was the main focus of the revolution by using improved technologies. There was increased use in fertilizers, pesticides, HYV seeds, etc. Because of green revolution, India became a self-sufficient nation.

2. Governmental schemes during 2000's

During 2000's there was adoption of digital technologies that marked the significant investment in agriculture. Some of them are listed below:

a) Small Farmers Agribusiness Consortium (SFAC) [1994]
b) Horticulture Mission for North East And Himalayan States (HMNEH) [2001-2002]
c) Agricultural Technology Management Agency (ATMA) [2005]
d) National e-Governance Plan in Agriculture (NeGP-A) [2006]
e) National Food Security Mission (NFSM) [2007]
f) Rashtriya Krishi Vikas Yojana (RKVY) [2007]

3. Market and credit linked reforms

a) National Crop Insurance Programme (NCIP) [2013-14]
b) Pradhan Mantri Krishi Sinchai Yojana [2015]
c) Paramparagat Krishi Vikas Yojana (PKVY) [2015]
d) Pradhan Mantri Fasal Bima Yojana (PMFBY) [2016]
e) eNAM [2016]
f) Regional Rural Bank Credit Refinance Fund
g) Contract Farming Law
h) Agriculture Export Policy, 2018
i) Pradhan Mantri Kisan Maan-Dhan Yojana (PMKMY)

4. ICT based reforms in India

One of the important and untapped reform is the Information and Communication Technology (ICT) as surge in digital marketing was seen after LPG was introduced. The second generation reforms as we talk about sustainability and focus on long term implications. One of the initiative in this regard is e-Choupal. The e-Choupal is the re-engineered value chain by ITC which is a private company. It's a model that uses IT to deliver service to the farmer and business enterprise. E-Choupal is not subsidized where ITC is a shareholder and public and private companies participate to deliver benefits to the stakeholders. The social impact of e-Choupal includes providing accessibility of the village to the world. It bridges the information gap that helps in better quality of produce.

Priority Areas for Support

1. Enhancing agricultural productivity, competitiveness, and rural growth
2. Promoting new technologies and reforming agricultural research and extension

3. Improving Water Resources and Irrigation/Drainage Management
4. Promoting high growth commodities
5. Poverty alleviation and community actions
6. Sustaining the environment and future agricultural productivity
7. Dissemination of Agricultural Technology
8. Better delivery of irrigation water

Conclusion

The agricultural sector has seen a significant growth after 1991 reforms despite of the reforms primarily focused on the formal sector. The trickledown effect on agricultural sector led to its growth in production, productivity and exports. Green revolution and increasing population has led to increase in the demand for food. This created a way for attractive opportunities for agri-entrepreneurship especially for high yielding varieties seeds, fertilizers, post-harvest management, etc. The opportunity of trade liberalization was also taken by the foreign firms as they strengthen their roots on the Indian grounds. The LPG model gave boost to the food processing industries, input market, and digitalization of agriculture. Different schemes were also started that focused both on input and output sector after the economic reforms. Since then many strategies have been made to make the international trade a smooth operation. The states need to buckle up and future ready for more such reforms.

References

Adhia, N. (2015). The History of Economic Development in India since Independence. 20 (3): 18–22.

Panagariya, A. (2001). India ' s Economic Reforms What Has Been Accomplished/ ? What Remains to Be Done/ ? no. 2.

Siggel, E. and Pradeep A. (2009). The impact of economic reforms on indian manufacturers/ : evidence from a small sample survey. Eckhard Siggel Institute of Economic Growth.

Wadhva, C. (1991). India trying to liberalise/ : economic reforms since 1991, 259-284.

9

Essential Skills for Entrepreneurship Development

Haobijam James Watt

Department of Agricultural Economics and Extension, School of Agriculture Lovely Professional University Phagwara, Punjab

Introduction

An entrepreneur is someone who starts or runs their own business. By having an equity stake in the company, the entrepreneur can profit greatly if things go well; however, they also take on a great deal of risk-far more than a regular employee of the company. Financial, career, emotional, and overall business risks are all examples of entrepreneurial risk. Because there is so much at stake in starting and growing a successful business, there are very specific skills that an entrepreneur usually requires to be successful. It could be a picture of a talented college dropout or a seasoned business professional with an uncanny ability to predict the next big thing. Replace whoever the persona is with ourselves. A successful entrepreneur does not have a specific demographic or personality profile. We can be entrepreneurs regardless of our age, race, gender, sexual orientation, socioeconomic status, or upbringing if we have dedication, drive, and essential business skills. Unlike personality traits and demographic information, entrepreneurial skills can be learned and practiced. If we want to pursue entrepreneurship, use this list to assess our strengths and weaknesses and determine which skills we need to develop before launching our venture.

Keywords

Equity Stake: An equity stake is the percentage of a company owned by the holder of a certain number of shares of stock in that company. The most common way to acquire an equity stake is through the purchase of equity shares, though smaller businesses may simply create such a stake for an investor through a contract.

Risk: In finance, risk is the probability that an outcome or investment will not yield the expected return.

Dropout: A dropout is someone who leaves school, college, or university without completing a qualification or who lives unusually.

Socio-economic status: is concerned with the differences between groups of people, which are primarily caused by their financial situation.

Venture: A new activity, usually in business, that is fraught with risk or uncertainty.

When we hear the word "entrepreneur," what comes to our mind? While the prospect of becoming your boss and making a fortune is appealing to aspiring entrepreneurs, the potential downside of hanging one's shingle is vast. Income is not guaranteed, employer-sponsored benefits are no longer available, and when your company loses money, your assets and the company's bottom line can suffer. However, adhering to a few tried-and-true principles can go a long way toward mitigating risk.

Being an entrepreneur is comparable to being a mother. To be prepared to deal with most crisis situations, one must be skilled in a variety of areas. Ask any entrepreneur and they will be able to recount a list of skills they have acquired on their journey from a fledgling idea to a full-fledged profitable company. Entrepreneurs are frequently confronted with uncertainty, high stress, and looming deadlines. An entrepreneur's life is fast-paced, scrappy, and ever-changing. It's not for the faint of heart, but it can result in higher rewards for those willing to take a risk.

Entrepreneurs play a crucial position in any economic system due to the fact they have the abilities and initiative to count on desires and convey correct new thoughts to the market. Entrepreneurship that succeeds in taking on the risks of launching a startup is rewarded with profits, fame, and opportunities for continued growth. Entrepreneurship that fails results in losses and less market presence for those involved.

There is no doubt that entrepreneurship has grown in recent years, even during the COVID-19 pandemic. In France, for example, business creation increased sharply in 2020, despite, or perhaps because of, the crisis. In fact, more new businesses were established in France last year than in the previous 20 years combined (EDHEC, 2021). The pandemic may have destroyed large swaths of industry, but it has also fuelled an unprecedented surge in startups and new small businesses as those laid off from affected firms seek new opportunities. According to reports from the United States, Japan, and across Europe, business registrations are at an all-time high. According to U.S. Census Bureau data, new business registrations in July 2020 were 95% higher than in the same period in 2019 (MindTools).

So, if we're thinking about starting our own business, we're not alone. But what are the essential entrepreneurial skills required for the success of your business? What skills do you need to be an entrepreneur? Although some of these abilities may come more naturally to some people than others, many of them can be learned or developed with practice (EDHEC, 2021).

What, does it take to be a successful entrepreneur? Whether you've noticed an exciting gap in the market or are forced to reassess your career after a job loss, this article will go over the skills you'll need to succeed as an entrepreneur. It also directs you to resources that can help you develop the skills needed for success.

Entrepreneurship is a journey that necessitates commitment, determination, and years of hard work. One thing it does not require is that you belong to a certain demographic. Anyone can pursue entrepreneurship if they have financial literacy, networking skills, confidence, the ability to accept feedback and recognize patterns, and a growth mindset. You can position yourself to start your own company successfully if you are willing to put in the time to strengthen your entrepreneurial skills (Cote, C. 2020).

Entrepreneurial Skills

Entrepreneurial skills are those that are typically associated with being an entrepreneur, but they can be developed by anyone.

Entrepreneurial skills are those that are typically associated with being an entrepreneur, but they can be developed by anyone. Entrepreneurship typically entails starting and growing your own successful business, but people with entrepreneurial skills can also thrive within larger organizations. Many researchers have studied entrepreneurial skills but have come up with no conclusive answers (MindTools).

Entrepreneurial skills encompass a wide range of diverse skill sets, including technical skills, leadership and business management abilities, and artistic thinking. As a result, entrepreneurial skills are frequently applied to a wide range of job roles and industries; developing your entrepreneurial abilities will entail learning a wide range of skills (EDHEC, 2021)

While for some, becoming a successful entrepreneur comes naturally, for others, certain essential skills are required to start and lead a business to success. Your entrepreneurial success is determined by these abilities. Successful entrepreneurs have mastered both hard and soft skills. Accounting, marketing, and economic making plans are essential for running and handling a business, even as smooth competencies consisting of communication, problem-solving, and decision-making help you grow your business. Entrepreneur skill mastery necessitates practice and a dedicated learning plan (Anonymous, 2021).

The following are a few characteristics required to be a successful entrepreneur

1. Business management skills

An entrepreneur must-have business management skills to run a business and ensure that all business goals are met. Because they have a thorough understanding of each function, entrepreneurs with this skill set can oversee and manage the operations of various departments. Multitasking, delegating responsibilities and making critical business decisions are all examples of business management skills (Anonymous, 2021).

2. Communication and active listening skills

Communication is the most important component of any organization. In fact, no organization can exist without communication. An organization is a group of people formed to accomplish a specific goal. The achievement of these goals is heavily reliant on the proper coordination and integration of human effort within an organization. People in an organization are interconnected, and their activities are interconnected as well because all activities are performed solely to achieve the organizational objectives. The more effective the communication system, the better the relations between workers and between workers and management.

Communication was derived from the Latin root 'communis,' which means 'common' – Communication also necessitates a degree of commonality between individuals. The goal of communication is to establish common ground. Thus, communication refers to the process of sharing information, feelings, and ideas in such a way that there is a shared understanding of the message's meaning, intent, and use.

Communication is an organization's nervous system. It keeps the organization's members up to date on internal and external events that are relevant to a task and of interest to the organization. It directs the efforts of its members toward the achievement of organizational goals. It is the process of influencing the behaviour of an individual or a group. It is a process of meaningful interaction between humans to initiate, execute, accomplish, or prevent specific actions. As a result, communication is essential to the survival of any organization. Without communication, an organization is lifeless, and its very survival is jeopardized.

3. Willingness to learn

Learning is an ongoing, lifelong process. The majority of people make the mistake of limiting their knowledge development to academic timelines. This rookie error, as well as the attitude of being blasé about furthering one's knowledge to increase one's growth potential, is extremely harmful. Accepting that there are gaps in one's knowledge and correcting them through a strong desire to learn will go a long way toward assisting a person in paving their path to success (Jain, 2019).

4. Basic Finance Skills

Finance skills, such as budgeting and financial statement analysis, are required for business ownership. Making and sticking to a reasonable budget can mean the difference between your venture's success and failure. You can avoid overspending and properly allocate your company's resources if you learn this important finance skill.

It's also critical to understand how to read and prepare financial statements, such as a balance sheets, income statements, and cash flow statements. These documents, in addition to being required for reporting and tax purposes, assist you in tracking performance, making future projections, and managing expenses. They can also be useful to investors and banks who are considering funding your start-up because they show the financial progress of your company (Cote, C. 2020).

5. Networking

One of the most valuable assets is the network. Networking can help you not only meet like-minded professionals but also build your future team and stay on top of industry trends.

Your professional network may include the following individuals:

- Former and current co-workers
- Alumni from your educational institutions
- Former professors and teachers
- Industry leaders and speakers
- Friends and family members
- Business professionals in your geographic area
- Others in your industry with similar interests, responsibilities, and goals

Identify and contact people in your network who can help you navigate your entrepreneurial journey and inform your decision-making. Inquire about their company, how long they've been in business, and what lessons they've learned from successes and failures. Perhaps they've founded several businesses and can provide valuable advice on raising funds, developing products, and building a client base. They might even be able to introduce you to professionals in their networks whose work is similar to yours.

Extend your network in addition to leveraging it. Signing up for networking events in your area or industry is one method. Because of the coronavirus (COVID-19) pandemic, virtual events have recently increased in popularity, and they are often more accessible because no travel is required.

LinkedIn is yet another useful tool for connecting with others. We can find professionals with whom we have shared connections, as well as similar interests and job titles, by using the platform's feed and recommendation algorithm. People on LinkedIn are expected to reach out to one another, so don't be afraid to send a note introducing yourself to a potential new contact (Cote, C. 2020).

6. Speaking Confidently

As an aspiring entrepreneur, the importance of speaking confidently cannot be overstated. Whether you're pitching to investors, communicating with clients, or striking up a conversation at an event, how you talk about your company and its potential can influence how others perceive it. A lack of confidence can deter investors from funding your venture and cause customers to second-guess their decision to purchase from you.

Keep in mind that you are your company's most powerful advocate. Present your company as if it is ready for the market. Back up your points with research and data to demonstrate that you've done your homework to validate your idea. People will have their doubts along the way, but you should never be one of them. When it comes to attracting and retaining customers and investors, confidence can make all the difference (Cote, C. 2020).

7. Accepting and Acting on Feedback

We must be eager to receive and act on feedback if we want to be successful entrepreneurs. This skill necessitates remaining humble and accepting that your vision of the ideal version of your product may not resonate with potential customers.

Conducting customer validation interviews with people from your target market segment is one way to gather feedback. These interviews with potential customers can validate your business idea while also providing constructive criticism about your product, proposed business model, or user assumptions.

Investors, more experienced entrepreneurs, and friends and family may also provide feedback. Some of it may have been uninvited. You are not required to follow all of their recommendations, but it is beneficial to do so. Would their suggestion improve your product's quality, value, or user experience? If the answer is yes, take the necessary steps to make the necessary improvements (Cote, C. 2020).

8. Recognizing Patterns

Pattern recognition in data, market trends, and user behaviour is a skill that many entrepreneurs overlook. Identifying patterns in cash flow statements, for example, can help you forecast future cash flows. When you examine market sales data, you can identify seasonality or other time-related trends that can help you plan for the long term.

Pay attention to how users react to specific elements and what questions arise during use when observing how they interact with your product. Patterns will start to emerge. If your product is an app, you may notice a pattern among adolescent male users who download it and immediately open the chat function. You can use user behaviour trends to learn more about your customers' motivations and improve your product to better meet their needs (Cote, C. 2020).

9. Maintaining a Growth Mindset

It's critical to have a growth mindset as an aspiring entrepreneur. A growth mindset considers intelligence, abilities, and talents to be learnable and malleable, as opposed to a fixed mindset, which considers those same characteristics to be inherently stable and unchangeable over time.

Maggie Robb, vice president of operations at Spire Health, is one professional who exemplifies the growth mindset. Robb knew she had a lot to learn when she moved from a large corporation to a Silicon Valley start-up, so she enrolled in the online Entrepreneurship Essentials course to hone her entrepreneurial skills.

"While I have a strong business background," Robb explains, "I was lacking in several critical aspects of entrepreneurship, such as investment structure, fundraising, and valuation."

Robb says the course helped her recognize the importance of testing and iteration in the entrepreneurial process, in addition to enhancing her knowledge of those topics.

"While it wasn't something I was completely unfamiliar with, I realized the importance of it within a startup," says Robb. "It made me rethink our resource allocation in comparison to conventional businesses with established products."

Robb's story teaches an important lesson: your skills aren't fixed; they're the result of your hard work, practice, and perseverance. You can avoid taking your skills for granted and capitalize on opportunities to grow and improve throughout your career by maintaining a growth mindset (Cote, C. 2020).

10. Risk-taking skills

One of the most important entrepreneur skills to learn is the ability to take calculated and intelligent risks. Employees with an entrepreneur mindset are never afraid to take calculated risks because they understand that calculated risks lead to tremendous success. They understand that risk is a chance to learn and grow a business to the next level. Employers seek candidates who are willing to take risks in the pursuit of potential gains and profit (Anonymous, 2021).

11. Critical thinking skills

Critical thinking is an entrepreneur skill that analyses information objectively and draws a rational conclusion. It assists entrepreneurs in assessing a situation and devising a logical solution. Employers seek candidates who are capable of critical thinking because it aids in problem-solving and the development of business strategies. A critical thinker is typically self-sufficient, competent, and reflective. This skill assists entrepreneurs in connecting ideas logically, scrutinizing information, evaluating arguments, identifying inconsistencies in work, and resolving complex issues. Instead of memorizing information, such candidates apply it to derive meaningful insights (Anonymous, 2021).

12. Problem-solving skills

Entrepreneurs frequently face difficult and unexpected situations. It could be a venture capitalist refusing additional funding or a team member refusing to work within project guidelines; an entrepreneur must be able to handle stressful situations and calmly identify alternate solutions. Their exceptional problem-solving abilities ensure that they meet their business objectives (Anonymous, 2021).

13. Creative thinking skills

In the digital world, creativity is a valuable but underappreciated skill. Creative thinking is the foundation of innovation, and it forces employees to think in new ways. Entrepreneurs with creative thinking skills are never afraid to try solutions that others might overlook for fear of failure. Such individuals think outside the box and constantly seek input from professionals in different fields to comprehend a new perspective. It is one of the most sought-after entrepreneur skills because it enables them to see patterns (even when there are none) and devise novel solutions to business problems (Anonymous, 2021).

14. Customer service skills

Customer service that is of high quality promotes the brand and increases loyalty. Excellent customer service skills are critical for business success in any industry. Customer service skills help entrepreneurs connect with their potential customers, from talking to clients to discussing funding opportunities (Anonymous, 2021).

15. Financial skills

Entrepreneurs must be able to manage resources, assess investments, and calculate ROI. Aside from that, they must be familiar with accounting and budgeting software to keep track of all financial processes. Entrepreneurs can avoid overspending and allocate resources more effectively by learning financial skills (Anonymous, 2021).

16. Leadership skills

Leadership has been defined as "a social influence process in which one person can enlist the aid and support of others in the completion of a common task." The definition of leadership is "organizing a group of people to achieve a common goal."

The leader may or may not be in a position of formal authority. Leadership students have developed theories involving-

i) Traits

ii) Situational interaction, function, behaviour, power, vision and values

iii) Charisma, and intelligence, among others.

- Someone who people look up to someone who guides or directs others. Contact farmers/adarsha raithu/model farmers/extension worker, for example. To be an effective leader, you must understand and cultivate skills for various roles in your group. Several of these abilities are discussed in depth in other chapters. This chapter delves into the theory, styles, and functions of leadership.
- A lack of leadership and other management skills has brought several community-initiated projects to a halt. Many local leaders start projects with the best of intentions to solve environmental problems in their community, only to see them fail due to poor leadership.

- They may have an outdated management philosophy that does not sit well with volunteer members of government and non-government organizations. Leadership ideas have evolved significantly, as have the expectations of groups and communities.
- As people become more educated, they become more articulate and no longer respond to authoritative leadership styles in all situations. There is both a need and a demand for community participation in decision-making. When addressing the complex problems that land and water management groups must solve, participatory management styles are required.
- The majority of members of land and water management groups will need to hone these and other leadership skills. Leaders are responsible for a variety of tasks such as planning and implementing, evaluating, monitoring, controlling, motivating, managing conflicts, organizing task groups, mobilizing human and financial resources, and, most importantly, setting an example for the group.
- Sometimes leadership is viewed as headship, as in a formal position such as chairperson, director, or politician. Even if a person lacks leadership abilities, he or she may be appointed to such a position. If this person does not learn to exercise leadership functions in a way that meets the needs of the group or community, he or she may be replaced by new leaders in due course. While government officers or corporation employees are usually referred to as "managers," and people elected from the community are referred to as "leaders," both positions involve leadership and management functions.
- Leadership has been defined as "the process of influencing an individual's or a group's activities in efforts to achieve goals in a given situation." Influence can come from a formal or informal source. Leaders can emerge from within a group as well as be appointed formally.
- Although we all begin with varying degrees of natural talent, leadership is a learned behavior. The necessary skills can be learned. Leaders are created rather than born.
- Everyone has the potential to be a leader. Natural abilities can be developed through study and practice, just as they can in any other field of endeavours, such as cricket, medicine, or farming. Many of today's prominent rural leaders began as inexperienced members of community groups. Take the initiative in rescuing the future.

Leadership Roles- Each member of a participatory action group will be responsible for one or more leadership roles. These functions are related to the three needs of any group and can be classified as follows:

- Instilling in the group and community a well-informed vision of a better future based on long-term sustainable use of land and water resources.
- Leading by example in what they say and do to help bring that vision to fruition.
- Sifting through various information sources to get a sense of the group's upcoming threats and opportunities, as well as its strengths and weaknesses in dealing with them.
- Creating a comprehensive database to aid the group in participatory decision-making; coordinating the contributions of various government and non-government agencies in leadership roles; initiating action; and clarifying issues.
- Creating a procedural plan with the help of the rest of the group, deciding who does what, when, where, and how through participatory planning methods.
- Motivating group and community members through transactional methods (exchanging benefits) and transformational methods (awareness of new priorities).
- Mobilizing the human and financial resources required for projects monitoring progress.
- Assisting in the resolution of problems and seizing opportunities as they arise

Leaders in participative action groups perform the following functions for group and individual needs maintenance

- Maintaining good working relationships with other group members as well as key individuals and organizations outside the group
- Keeping interpersonal relations pleasant
- Providing encouragement
- Allowing minorities to be heard
- Stimulating self-direction and self-development
- Increasing interdependence among members
- Giving due recognition to people and agencies
- Managing needs and values conflicts

Leaders' social styles must be participative and group-centered. The degree and type of leadership action must be appropriate to the situation and the group's maturity. Self-leadership is a process that takes place within an individual rather than an external act. It represents who we are as individuals.

Time management and organizational skills

This is a necessary soft skill for any entrepreneur who wants to make the most of their time. You've probably heard the phrase "work smarter, not harder," and it all comes down to time management. There are numerous time management tips and tools available, but here are a few to get you started:

It does not exist if it is not on the calendar: Schedule your meetings (even if they're just five-minute catch-ups) just as much as you do your downtime. Allow yourself as much time to disconnect as you do to connect.

- **To-do lists work:** Unfinished goals, according to research, can lead to poor performance unless they are recorded in a to-do list. Set micro and macro goals for yourself. Plan as thoroughly daily as you do every quarter.
- **Make way for morning routines:** Routines are excellent for organising your day so that you can be as productive as possible. Consider breakfast and tea/coffee, meditation, exercise, and general warm-up time for the day.

Time management that is effective increases productivity and organises your workspace. Entrepreneurs with strong time management and organizational skills are aware of various methods for prioritizing tasks and avoiding procrastination. Entrepreneurs analyze their and their team's time, set time limits for each task, complete priority tasks first, delegate work to others, create a to-do list, and use technology to keep the workspace organized to ensure project completion on time.

Technical skills

Technical skills are hard skills acquired through the use of digital tools and software. Entrepreneurs must understand how to use software for planning, marketing, and budgeting. Knowledge of software aids in project management, sales tracking, and allocating a viable budget for the project (Anonymous, 2021).

17. Emotional intelligence skill

In the last two decades, emotional intelligence, or EI, has grown in popularity within positive psychology. It is the ability to recognize and manage emotional situations. This soft skill has a surprising shelf life and, once mastered, can truly assist an entrepreneur in communicating better, dealing with stress, and effectively harnessing emotions for greater workplace performance.

18. Public speaking skills

Giving speeches in front of large crowds is not always considered public speaking. Speaking in public can be as simple as striking up a conversation in the elevator.

It is your level of confidence in your conversation and your ability to engage the listener.

Public speaking classes are available. Joining an improved class, on the other hand, is a more enjoyable way to overcome the anxiety that many people experience when faced with the prospect of speaking in public. After putting yourself out there to improve, you'll soon realize that public speaking is a piece of cake.

19. Consistency skill

Consistency is a critical soft skill for establishing trust with customers, employees, and partners. People will assess your character and business based on your consistency.

Create and stick to your mission statement in the early stages of your business. Allow your values to shine through in your daily actions, and if your company commits to something, show off your efforts to make it a reality.

20. Empathy skill

Empathetic leadership is a quality that will not only help you gain customers but will also assist you in retaining talent. A great leader understands, adapts to, and includes all people and their differences. You will be able to relate to people better and form more genuine business relationships if you lead with empathy.

21. Adaptability

Every start-up must be agile. The year 2020 taught the business world that a person's adaptability can make or break a small business. Along your entrepreneurial journey, you will face numerous challenges; how you overcome them will determine the trajectory of your business.

That being said, there may come a time when a challenge is simply too great to overcome, and it is necessary to pivot, changing course completely. There's no shame in it; adaptability is a trait that often clashes with pride, but if you can harness it, you'll be a better entrepreneur.

22. Data literacy

Data will be one of your most valuable assets as an entrepreneur in its early stages. However, if you can't read your data, no matter how many tracking tools and data collection software you use, your time will be wasted.

The ability to understand numbers and convert them into actionable insights is referred to as data literacy. Google Analytics, Google Search Console, Social Media Analytics, and other tools should be used by small businesses. Reading data with these tools can assist you in building your business on facts rather than feelings.

23. Video editing

Video is expected to account for 82% of all online traffic by 2022. As business people, we understand the value of video. It has had a massive impact on social media and marketing in general. There's no doubt that you'll need to incorporate video into your marketing or personal branding strategy at some point. This isn't to say you have to be an Adobe Premiere Pro expert. A basic understanding of video editing software, on the other hand, will come in handy when you need to get creative and create engaging content on a shoestring budget.

24. Design-UX and UI

Design thinking and basic design knowledge are difficult skills that every entrepreneur should at least dabble in. Strategic user experience efforts can boost conversion rates by up to 400%. Understanding good UX and UI is essential for maintaining a professional brand online and gaining loyal customers. Again, as with video editing, this doesn't mean you have to change your career path to gain a wealth of design knowledge.

Look for novel ways to incorporate simple design-friendly tools into your customer-facing platforms. Consider using Type form for your business forms, lead generation, and early-stage sales orders. To create good UX, you don't have to be a coding expert (Berry, 2020).

25. Sales

Sales soft skills are inextricably linked to the communication skills required for success. As an entrepreneur, this person must be able to sell anything and everything. An entrepreneur must sell the business concept to prospective investors, the product or service to customers, and themselves to employees. When an entrepreneur can communicate effectively, he or she is better able to sell ideas and physical products.

It's natural for entrepreneurs to be the first salespeople at their respective companies in the beginning. These sales abilities are required to demonstrate value to all stakeholders both inside and outside the company.

Some suggestions for improving the entrepreneur skills

Mastering these entrepreneur skills can help you outperform at work and steer your company to success. You can improve your skills by reading books, taking a course, or attending seminars. Here are some steps you should take to improve your entrepreneurship skills.

1. Read business books

Reading books promotes self-improvement and is an excellent source of information on effective business strategies. It boosts your cognitive ability, improves your decision-making, and allows you to learn from the mistakes of others. As a result, read books to succeed as an entrepreneur.

2. Enrol in a course

Enrolling in management, marketing, or finance course is another way to hone your skills. Taking and finishing a professional course can help you improve your business management and financial planning skills.

3. Attend workshops

Attend entrepreneurial workshops and networking events regularly. Many of these workshops may feature speakers who are experienced business owners. It fills a knowledge gap and may provide you with valuable insights into how to run your business successfully. These workshops are a great way to meet industry leaders and build networks.

4. Listen to podcasts

Listening to a podcast of successful entrepreneurs is one of the best ways to consume business-related information on a busy day. Listening to business podcasts can provide you with insights into how various entrepreneurs use technology to accelerate their business growth. It also helps you improve your listening skills.

5. Hire an experienced business mentor

Experienced mentors can assist you in developing the skills you lack. You can either work for a successful business owner for some time to learn how to manage a business. You can also meet with a professional group of like-minded people regularly to discuss various methods of building and marketing a brand. Mentors contribute valuable insights and professional advice that are required for success.

During the hiring process, highlight the entrepreneur's skills.

Because entrepreneur skills can be applied to a variety of job roles, they should be highlighted in your CV and interview. Here are two ways to demonstrate your entrepreneurial abilities.

1. In your CV

Mentioning the most relevant entrepreneur skills required for the job attracts attention to your resume. These skills can be mentioned as a bulleted list under the skills section or briefly described in your employment history. Make sure you write about how these skills influenced the outcome and quantify it whenever possible. Also, use skill words to ensure that your CV is ATS-compliant and is shortlisted.

2. In the interview

Talk about your entrepreneurial streaks and achievements whenever you are asked a personality or behavioural question during the interview. Discuss your strengths and provide examples from previous jobs to demonstrate how you completed various projects. Tell the interviewer how mastering these entrepreneur skills enabled you to form a like-minded team that is always working toward a common business goal. When you demonstrate these abilities, you are telling the interviewer about your ability to build and grow your business.

Conclusion

Becoming a successful Entrepreneur, required understanding and learning the various essential skills of an entrepreneur. They need to improve their skills to match their personality towards creativity to customer requirements and market opportunities. This will help in thinking strategically, excellent communication skills, leadership abilities to lead from the front, and ability to manage crises that arise uncertainly. Identifying and mastering various essential entrepreneurship skills will lead to a chance for a prosperous business. The above various characteristics of essential entrepreneurship skills will undoubtedly be helpful for start-ups or entrepreneurs in grappling toward a successful business.

References

Anonymous (2021). Entrepreneur Skills: Definition and Examples. Retrieved April 10, 2022 from https://in.indeed.com/career-advice/career-development/entrepreneur-skills

Berry, R. S. (2020). *10 essential skills you need as an Entrepreneur.* Retrieved April 10, 2022 from https://hivelife.com/essential-entrepreneurial-skills/

Cote, C. (2020). *Must-have entrepreneurial skills for aspiring business owners*. Retrieved April 10, 2022 from https://online.hbs.edu/blog/post/entrepreneurial-skills

EDHEC (2021). *Entrepreneurial skills: Top 7 skills required for successful entrepreneurship.* Retrieved April 10, 2022 from https://online.edhec.edu/en/blog/skills-needed-to-be-entrepreneur/

Jain, M. (2019): 5 Essential Skills Required to succeed as an Entrepreneur. Retrieved from https://www.entrepreneur.com/article/339531

MindTools (N.A.). Entrepreneurial skills The Skills you need to Start a Great Business. Retrieved from April 10, 2022 from https://www.mindtools.com/pages/article/newCDV_76.htm

Tarver, E. (2021). *5 skill every entrepreneur should have*. Retrieved April 9, 2022 from https://www.investopedia.com/articles/personal-finance/080615/5-skills-every-entrepreneur-needs.asp

10

Entrepreneurial Characteristics

Nikita Khoisnam

Department of Agricultural Economics and Extension, School of Agriculture Lovely Professional University, Phagwara, Punjab

Introduction

Entrepreneurship plays a vital role in ensuring our country's economy as well as social welfare. Entrepreneurs are considered national assets to be motivated, cultivated and remunerated for the greatest possible outcome. It is a fact that our societies today give importance to entrepreneurship and have higher income levels, and are self-reliable. Entrepreneurs have the highest potential to change the way how people work and live on a local and national level. Along with the creation of wealth and entrepreneurial projects, entrepreneurs have the ability to create jobs and employment opportunities which will contribute to the growing economy of India. These reasons it signifies the importance of entrepreneurship. In the current era of science and technology, many youths are not afraid to try out their idea, talents, skills and knowledge to become an entrepreneur. The present entrepreneurs are well established with the recent technologies and are prone to the effects of changes. The majority of society has access to the internet, and the youth are reintegrating their technological powers into their passion for bringing changes into society with entrepreneurship. India is facing a major issue regarding employment generation; however, with its rich, resourceful, distinctive geographic and demographic advantage, it has a major prospective to raise and innovate the entrepreneurs resulting in employment generation and hence contributing to the nation's economy. The Indian government, for the past few years, have launched several support programs and schemes to bring innovation through fostering entrepreneurship across various sectors, from engaging with industries, academic researchers, investors, experts, SMEs, and NGOs to the most deprived and underprivileged parts of society. Now it is of prime concern to develop and bring innovation through expanding entrepreneurship across various sectors. In order to understand entrepreneur traits, it is important to study entrepreneurial behaviour and its characteristics. While entrepreneurship at the initial stage always involves a new startup, there is greater risk and sacrifice for any business. According to Deen (2003) majority of businesses always startup and fail within the first five years. And it was proved that entrepreneurs were not born but made, Ernst & Young, (2008). Here are some important entrepreneurial characteristics identified. Namely, risk-taking tendency, innovativeness, locus of control, need for achievement, general self-efficacy and tolerance for ambiguity.

1. Risk-taking tendency

The risk-taking tendency is considered the ability of an individual to take or avoid risks when faced with terrifying situations. Entrepreneurship may undoubtedly be connected with risk-taking. For example, Cantillon (1755) illustrated that the differentiating factor between employed workers and entrepreneurs is the ability of the latter to assume uncertainty and risk (Entrialgo et al., 2000; Thomas and Mueller, 2000). The difference between entrepreneurs and professional managers is that entrepreneurs take on the risk of profit or loss. Since the entrepreneurs take such kinds of risks and uncertainty, they are associated with financial anxiety, job opportunities, family and other relationships, and psychological well-being. Entrepreneurs have a higher tendency to take risks as compared to other people, so practical judgment skills should not be neglected by the entrepreneurs.

2. Innovativeness

Innovativeness requires a complete description, which includes the desire to create completely new items or provide greater quality using latest manufacturing techniques, developing strategies to access new markets, establishing timely supply sources, or establishing a framework for a new business venture. An entrepreneur should have the characteristics of knowing their customer and also the ability to identify the innovative approaches coming on their way. Anticipation of changes and perceiving the trend are associated with them. Entrepreneurs are required to have the ability to anticipate the future consequences of current situations. It requires the strong willpower of the leader to achieve successful innovation. Innovativeness is considered the most influential attribute among entrepreneurs as they always search for further opportunities (Zacharakis, 1997; Entrialgo et al., 2000). Drucker also stated that innovativeness is an essential trait in an entrepreneur since it allows for a methodical search for market developments that can be met with new ideas and goods. Different studies also concluded that entrepreneurship is characterized by its innovativeness, which differentiates “entrepreneurs” from “professional managers”.

3. Locus of control

The locus of control (LoC) is another attribute that has been broadly studied. It's an identity variable that refers to a man's total aspirations and whether or not he can manage his life circumstances. The people with external LoC believe that events beyond their immediate control, such as luck, destiny, fortune, and other people, have an impact on their ability to execute a variety of jobs. At the same time, people who have internal LoC believe that they have influence over the consequences and events that happen to them. It is highly believed that entrepreneurs who are looking for new business prospects and developing a creative mindset should have the characteristic of an "internal locus of control." The majority of the studies conducted have confirmed this concept (Mueller and Thomas, 2000; Hansemark, 1998; Chye Koh,1996; Utsch and Rauch, 2000). LoC to differentiate between successful and unsuccessful small business owners.

4. Need for achievement

The theory on the need for achievement given by Mc Clelland in 1961 is very much applicable to entrepreneurship as it acts as a stimulus which pushes an individual to struggle until he/she achieves success. People who have a strong desire to achieve are those who want to be problem solvers, target setters and work towards them on their own initiative, who show high execution in difficult jobs, and who are unconventionally innovative when looking for new ways to better their performance. According to McClelland, a highly achievement-oriented person is more inclined to enter the entrepreneurial field in order to gain more achievement pleasure than he might from other employment possibilities (Entrialgo et al., 2000; Stewart et al., 2003).

5. General self-efficacy

Self-efficacy can be defined as "One's own belief in one's own capabilities when posed with some situations which demand mobilizing the motivation, cognition and modus operandi" (Arafat et al., 2018; Wood and Bandura, 1989). Self-efficacy of entrepreneurs is considered an important trait for understanding the entrepreneurial success and impact on the start-up and business growth processes. Self-efficacy is considered as an explanatory factor of the high performance that people should show in entrepreneurship processes. If an individual has desire for a successful outlook on their potential to act then they are more expected to have entrepreneurial spirit as compare to others. Self-efficacy and self-confidence are related but not the same, they have different meanings like self-perceived value and self-image. Self-confidence is often refers to the strength of one's belief whereas self-efficacy refers to the capability to attain the required outcome by an individual.Generally entrepreneurs have higher self-confidence when compared with others as they stand out from the crowd by taking up challenging tasks and successfully completing it.

6. Tolerance of ambiguity

Entrepreneurs are those people who have the potential to take risk. However, the entrepreneurs are often in situations where there is uncertainty of their output. Entrepreneurs are most of the time are confusing, unclear, or open to different interpretations like decisions about pricing, marketing, vendors, and finances that don't have certain outcomes. The way a person reacts to ambiguous and negative events reflects their ability to tolerate ambiguity. When a person accepts contradictory data and believes in himself, his tolerance level rises. People with low tolerance, on the other hand, are more uncomfortable when confronted with ambiguous and unstructured situations, and they prefer to avoid them. Tolerance can be defined as a person's willingness to take risks when making decisions. Because entrepreneurial managers are continually confronted with unstructured, more unpredictable circumstances and are ultimately held accountable for their decisions, they are better at accepting ambiguity than conservative managers. Entrepreneurial behaviour is strongly associated with risk and uncertainty, as entrepreneurs' decisions result in new and unique activities (Cromie, 2000; Teoh and Foo, 1997 and Chye Koh, 1996).

Conclusion

Entrepreneurs are innovators who shape society and play an important role in economic progress. They make good use of their surroundings and are profit-driven. In entrepreneurship, establishing accurate goals is critical. Being open to innovation with team spirit and teamwork, acting bravely, and dreaming are all crucial qualities of entrepreneurship. Most people are prompt to take entrepreneurship due to economic concern. To summarise, an entrepreneur is a self-assured and tenacious individual who is cost-conscious and understands how to make a profit, while solving their problems with an indirect and creative approach, typically through viewing the problem in a new and unusual way which encourage them in innovation. As a result, they come up with fresh ideas and stay focused on the important things. Apart from that, they do not give up in the face of adversity, but instead press on despite setback and adversity, eventually achieving success and changing the world. Thus to be a successful entrepreneur the individual must have those entrepreneurial characteristics.

References

Arafat, M.Y., Saleem, I., Dwivedi, A.K. and Khan, A. (2018). "Determinants of agricultural entrepreneurship: a GEM data based study", International Entrepreneurship and Management Journal, Vol.1,pp.1-26.

Cantillon, R. (1755). "Essay on the nature of general commerce", Henry Higgs, Trans, Macmllan, London.

Cromie, S. (2000). "Assessing entrepreneurial inclinations: some approaches empirical evidence", European Journal of Work and Organizational Psychology, Vol.9 No.1, pp.7-30.

Deen. A Shepherd, Wiklund, J., & Haynie, J. M. (2009). "Moving forward: Balancing the financial and emotional costs of business failure". *Journal of Business Venturing*, 24(2): 134-148.

Entrialgo, M., Fernandez, E. and Vazquez, C. (2000). "Characteristics of managers as determinants of entrepreneurial orientation: some Spanish evidence", *Enterprise and Innovation Management Studies*, Vol.1No.2,pp.187-205.

Ernst & Young (2008), The Global Executive Report (2008). URL: http://www.ey.com/Publication/vwLUAssets/Global_Executive_2008/$FILE/GE_2008_Global_Executive.pdf [Accessed on 18 March 2016].

Mueller, S.L. and Thomas, A.S. (2000), "Culture and entrepreneurial potential: a nine country study of locus of control and innovativeness", Journal of Business Venturing, Vol. 16 No. 1, pp.51-75.

Stewart, W.H., Carland, J.C., Carland, J.W., Watson, W.E. and Sweo, R. (2003). "Entrepreneurial dispositions and goal orientations: a comparative exploration of United States and Russian entrepreneurs", Journal of Small Business Management, Vol.41No.1, pp.27-46.

Teoh, H.Y. and Foo, S.L. (1997). "Moderating effects of tolerance for ambiguity and risk taking propensity on the role conûict-perceived performance relationship: evidence from Singaporean entrepreneurs", Journal of Business Venturing, Vol.12,pp.67-81.

Thomas, A.S. and Mueller, S.L. (2000). "A case for comparative entrepreneurship: assessing the relevance of culture", Journal of International Business Studies,Vol.31No.2,pp.287-301.

Wood, R. and Bandura, A. (1989). "Social cognitive theory of organizational management", Academy of Management Review,Vol.14 No.3,pp.361-384.

Zacharakis, A. (1997). "Entrepreneurial entry into foreign markets", Entrepreneurship: Theory and Practice, Spring, New York, NY, pp.23-40.

11

Roadmap for Business Start-up Project Planning Formulation and Report Preparation

Sapna Jarial, Sharad Sachan, Haobijam James Watt and Devina Seram*

Department of Agricultural Economics and Extension
School of Agriculture Lovely Professional University, Phagwara, Punjab
**Department of Entomology, School of Agriculture*
Lovely Professional University Phagwara, Punjab

Introduction

Entrepreneurial and start-up firms share traits but also differ. It takes courage to start a new business, but not always with the latest technology. Founders of new companies, almost always based on new technology, take risks. Both types of firms must overcome limited resources and talent. Both entrepreneurs and start-ups seek to segment and expand markets. Starting a business involves risks, but start-ups face additional risks of innovation. (Rao, 2018).

The project is the very foundation of any business. As a result, the success or failure of a company is primarily determined by the project. In layman's terms, a project is an idea or plan meant to be carried out. According to the dictionary, a project is a scheme, design, or proposal for something intended or devised to be accomplished. (MANAGE, 2013)

Beginners often wonder where to begin. Some options are obtaining power-water connections, pollution control clearance, approvals of weights and measures/drug control, and registration with sales and income tax departments. But, first, an entrepreneur must set priorities. (IGNOU, 2017).

Keywords

Project: A project is defined as a scientifically evolved work plan devised to achieve a specific goal within a specified time frame.

Quantifiable project: Projects that can be quantified are called quantifiable projects.

Non-quantifiable project: Projects that cannot be quantified are called non-quantifiable projects.

Critical success factors(CSF): CSFs are the components of a project considered the most critical to its achievement or failure.

Project: A project is a scientifically evolved work plan devised to achieve a specific goal within a specified time frame. While projects differ in size, nature, objectives, duration, and complexity, they share the three essential characteristics listed below.:

1. A Course of Action
2. Specific Objectives
3. Define Time Perspective
4. Every project has a starting point, an endpoint with specific objectives

A project can likewise be characterised as a single-use plan to accomplish a particular purpose, for example, presenting something new or changing something and guaranteeing that progress remains focused, by and large, regarding time, cost, and different specialised and quality execution boundaries. Following are the significant parts of a project:

- Starting date
- Specific goals and conditions
- Defined responsibilities
- Budget
- Planning
- Fixed end date
- Parties involved

A project is a single-use plan that ensures progress is kept on track in terms of time, cost, and various technical and quality performance parameters when introducing something new or changing something existing. A project must include the following elements:

- Start date
- Goals and conditions
- Responsibilities
- Budget

- Planning
- End date
- Parties

Project Characteristics

The various characteristics of a project are as follows:

i) Predetermined objectives: When the goals are finalised, the project begins. When the objectives are met, the project is completed.

ii) Projects do not last indefinitely; they must come to an end.

iii) Task completion necessitates collaboration.

iv) Uniqueness: No two projects are alike.

v) Lifecycle: Just as all living things grow in size (definition), projects grow in size (planning) before reaching a peak (implementation) and being terminated.

vi) Made-to-order: The customer specifies the goal and informs the vendor of any restrictions (e.g., time and cost).

Classifications of Projects

Various authorities classify projects. Here are the major project categories:

1. Quantifiable and Non-Quantifiable Projects

Benefits from quantifiable projects can be quantified. Projects in this category include industrial, power, and mineral development. Non-quantifiable projects, on the other hand, can't be quantified. For example, health education and defence projects are not quantifiable.

2. Sectorial Projects

According to this classification, a project can be classified as follows:

i) Agriculture and Allied Sector

ii) Irrigation and Power Sector

iii) Industry and Mining Sector

iv) Transport and Communication Sector

v) Social Services Sector

vi) Miscellaneous Sector

The project classification based on economic sectors can help resource allocation, especially at the macro level.

3. Techno-Economic Projects

Project classification for this category includes technological and economic factors. In addition, this type of classification includes intensity-oriented classification, causation-oriented classification, and magnitude-oriented classification. These are discussed below:

i) **Factor Intensity-Oriented Classification:** Projects can be classified as capital intensive or labour intensive depending on the factor intensity classification. Projects will be labelled as "capital intensive" if significant investments in plants and machinery are made. Labour-intensive projects, on the other hand, will be marked as such.

ii) **Causation-Oriented Classification:** When using causation as a classification basis, projects can be divided into demand-driven or raw-material-driven categories. The availability of certain raw materials, skills, or other inputs causes the project to be demand-based. In contrast, the availability of certain raw materials, skills, or other inputs causes the project to be raw material-based.

iii) **Magnitude-Oriented Classification:** Based on the size of the investment, magnitude-oriented classification divides projects into large-scale, medium-scale, and small-scale projects.

The project classification based on techno-economic characteristics has proven helpful in facilitating the project feasibility assessment process.

Critical success factors or CSF

"Critical success factors" (CSFs) are the components of a project considered most critical to its achievement or failure. For example, the CSFs of an internet layout task would possibly encompass a person's experience in and statistics migration (teamwork).

A critical success factor is something that an organisation, business, or project must achieve to achieve its goal. Essential factors of success assist a team or organisation in determining what to focus on and comparing progress to set goals.

These objectives are frequently referred to as deliverables. Different deliverables will have various critical success factors, and these factors will add up to determine whether the effort was a success or a failure. As a result, if a deliverable is a goal, a critical success factor is required to achieve that goal.

Critical success factors are not a measure of success but the systems that enable a company to succeed. These systems operate in the "background" of operations and projects (Yarbrough, 2021).

If the specific factor is mixed, missing, inadequate, or not adequately taken into account, it can suggest that the project is not feasible or is likely to collapse. The micro screen leads to the SWOT strengths, weaknesses, and threat analysis. Before concluding anything. We should remember that SWOT analysis for any product is not a blanket recommendation but depends on the place. Time in person. So while deciding on the suitability of a product, these things should be kept in mind. A project may be suitable at 1:00 place but not at another location. It may be ideal for one person but not for another individual if the CFS is missing. Is inadequate or not adequately taken into account. It can suggest that the project is not feasible or is likely to collapse (Indian Council of Agricultural Research, 2020).

Selection of Project

Regardless of the growing works on the development of entrepreneurship literature, the selection and identification of projects are still less known. Because of this, suggesting a better selection or identification of a project in any definite manner to an aspiring entrepreneur is difficult to state. However, project selection is not a hazy concept in reality. It's a well-planned game. A specific procedure is followed when selecting a project. In general, project selection is divided into two major steps.

1. Project Identification
2. Project Selection

1. Project Identification

If a question is asked to any aspiring entrepreneur about choosing which type of project they might be choosing, everyone will respond will be "a project with a good market." But on which basis can any aspiring entrepreneur decide and select the best one if they don't know what item they are selling, and how can one discover the market if they don't see the item, i.e. the product? As a result, coming up with ideas for a few projects provides a way out of the above tangle.

The first step in the project selection process is developing a product idea. The entrepreneur must first generate a few potential project ideas to select the most promising project. Project ideas can originate from both internal and external sources. Among these are the following:

a) Knowledge of possible customer requirements
b) Keeping an eye on emerging trends in product demand.
c) Possibility of producing a substitute product
d) Reading professional magazines on electronics, computers, and so on.
e) Achievements of well-known entrepreneurs, friends, or family members.
f) Attending trade shows and exhibitions to see new products and services.
g) Consultation with government agencies,
h) Suggestions from knowledgeable individuals.
i) Knowledge of government policy, concessions, and incentives, as well as a list of items reserved for exclusive production in the small-scale sector
j) Launches a new product by the competitor

These sources consolidated may give a couple of thoughts regarding possible undertakings from which project should be picked. This process is known as "opportunity scanning and identification." For example, assume that you could generate five project ideas due to the initial analysis after the initial process. The following are the five project ideas:

1. Nut and bolt manufacturing (industry)
2. Lakhani Shoes (industry)
3. Photocopying unit (service-based industry)
4. Electro-type writer servicing (service-based industry)
5. Textile and polythene bag industry (ancillary industry)

One good idea must be chosen from the given list above in selecting the project outline from the criteria below.

2. Project Selection

With the Identification of the project ends, project selection thus begins. Following the development of some project ideas, these are assessed in light of current economic conditions, government policy, etc. SWOT analysis, as it is known in the business world, is a tool that is frequently used for this purpose. Next, the aspiring entrepreneur evaluates their strengths and weaknesses and the opportunities/competitive advantages and threats/challenges presented by each project idea. Finally, the best idea is chosen to be developed into a business based on the results of this analysis. The "zeroing in process" refers to selecting a project from several projects.

The preceding analysis indicates a time gap between the project selection and identification. Nevertheless, in some studies, no gap in time was also observed between the two. An example can be used to demonstrate this.

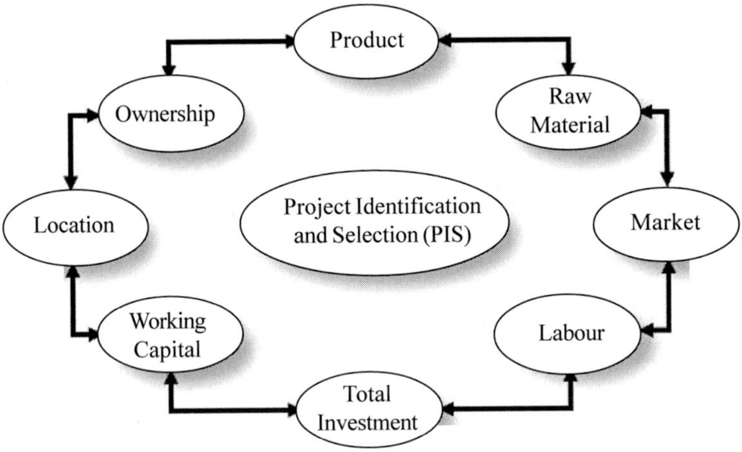

Figure 1. Model of Project Identification and Selection (PIS) Process

The ABC of a business plan:

i) What exactly is a business plan?

ii) Why do a business plan?

iii) Who is responsible for reading the business plan?

iv) How to Write a Business Plan

v) What the investor/lender expects

vi) Different types of business plans

vii) A business plan's format and organisation

viii) Preparation period

ix) A business plan's content and structure (MANAGE, 2013)

Why a Business Plan? A business plan is not required for anyone to start or run a new business. However, some bits of help is provided from it. To raise assets from an investor, you will, without a doubt, require a well-thought-out business plan that includes sound business reasoning.

An extraordinary marketable strategy is the most effective way to convince bankers, venture capitalists, and angel investors that you are worthy of financial assistance. First, make sure your strategy is clear, focused, and achievable. Then show them you have the resources, talent, and team to make it happen.

Like your calling card, your business plan will get you in the door, where you should persuade financial backers and advance officials that you can set your plan in motion. It will fill in as a guide for your business whenever you have raised the assets to begin or extend it. It's anything but a one-time archive that you make and afterwards store. You will refer to it as much time to guarantee that you remain on track, focused and meet achievements. As your business expands, it will change and develop as your organisation develops. (MANAGE, 2013).

Reasons for writing a business plan include

- It helps in a loan application
- Equity funding can be raised
- Establishing and implementing goals to accomplish them
- Create a schedule for normal business reviews and course revisions
- Express a fresh new business plan
- Create arrangements between colleagues
- Assigning out money related worth to a business with the end goal of an offer or judicial procedures
- Assess another product offering, advancement, or extension

What makes a successful business plan?

- A thoroughly examined idea
- Clear and compact composition
- A reasonable and intelligent design
- Demonstration of management's ability to make the company a success.
- Shows benefit

A business plan: It's written in detail about its operations. It is a definite report on an organisation's items or administrations, fabricating methods, markets and clients, promoting procedure, human resources, association, framework, and supply prerequisites. In addition, it covers objectives, systems, deals, showcasing, and monetary projections.

Setting up a business plan is a significant advance while beginning a business since it fills some needs, for example, getting external financing and estimating accomplishments inside your organisation. A business plan is a living record that will help you observe your presentation. It should be refreshed and changed as your business develops. Whether you use it inside or remotely, it should investigate your business. Inability to do so may infer that you and others have ridiculous assumptions about what can and will be achieved. (MANAGE, 2013).

What a business plan should include:

- How you intend to develop your business
- At the point when you will make it happen
- Who will have an impact?
- How you will deal with the funds

Clear information about the funding, finance, or investment should be provided in the business plan if we are looking for it. The most common way of making your arrangement will likewise zero in your brain how your new business should work to find true success. Your technique ought to again include:

- **An executive summary** is critical to provide a high-level outline of the business that needs to be launched. This section of the plan is where many lenders and investors base their decisions on your company.
- **A brief description of the business opportunity**: Who you are, what you intend to sell or offer, why, and whom.
- **Your marketing and sales strategy** - Why do you accept individuals will purchase what you're selling and how you plan to offer it to them.
- **Your management team and personnel** - Your accreditations and individuals you plan to recruit.
- **Your operations** - Your premises, producing offices, the board data frameworks, and information technology
- **Financial forecasts** - In this section, everything you said in the previous sections is translated into numbers. (Chole,2012)

In addition to these sections, a business plan should include a cover, title page, and table of contents. A good business plan's length can range from a few pages to more than 100 pages in the case of an exceptionally detailed plan describing a complex enterprise. A typical business plan is 15 to 20 pages long, but this is not an absolute requirement. The nature of your business will determine a lot. You might be able to express a simple idea in a few words if it is simple. Then again, assuming you're proposing another sort of business or even another industry, it could take some making sense of to convey the idea. Its motivation does not entirely settle the length of your arrangement. To utilise your arrangement to bring a great many dollars up in seed funding to send off a dangerous endeavour, you might need to make sense of and convince many individuals. If you're going to involve your arrangement for internal purposes or deal with a continuous business, a lot more limited rendition should get the job done. (MANAGE, 2013)

Updating your Business Plan: a checklist

The following are seven justifications for why you ought to consider updating your business plan. If even one of these concerns you, it is the ideal opportunity for a redesign.

1. Another financial year is going to start. Assuming your industry is quickly transforming, you might need to update your arrangement on a yearly, quarterly, or even month-to-month premise.
2. You require support or additional financing. Banks and different lenders require a cutting-edge intention to help them pursue funding choices.
3. A critical market shift has happened. Client inclinations, client solidification drifts, and changing administrative conditions can all require plan updates.
4. Your company has to make or will make another product, innovation, administration, or ability. If your company has changed altogether since you composed your arrangement initially, it is the ideal opportunity for an update.
5. There has been an adjustment of the board; new administrators ought to be given refreshed data about your company and its objectives.
6. Your company has arrived at an achievement, for example, moving out of your workspace, arriving at Rs 1 million in deals, or expanding labour.
7. Your previous plan no longer appears to be accurate.

Perhaps you did a poor job the last time, or maybe things simply changed faster than you anticipated. However, if your strategy appears to be obsolete, redo it. Many elements of business plans, such as cash flow projections and marketing plans, are similar. And many of them share common objectives, such as raising funds or convincing a partner to join the firm. However, no two business plans are alike, just as no two businesses are alike.

You may require a very different type of business plan than another entrepreneur, depending on your business and the purpose of your plan. The length, appearance, detail of content, and emphasis placed on various aspects of the business vary greatly. The significance of plan selection stems from the fact that it significantly impacts your plan's overall impact. You want your plan to present you and your company in the best possible light. Regardless of how you intend to use your plan, if you wish to present it at a venture capital conference, or whether it will never leave your office or be seen outside of internal strategy sessions. (MANAGE, 2013)

Types of Plans

There are roughly four types of business plans.

Mini plan: It used to have one to ten pages, and it should provide at least cursory attention to critical issues such as business concept, financing requirements, marketing plan, and financial declarations, primarily income projection cash flow, and balance sheet. It's a great way to quickly test a business idea or gauge the interest of a potential partner or minor investor. It can also serve as a valuable prelude to a more comprehensive plan later on. However, a mini-plan is not meant to be used in place of a full-length plan. Therefore, sending a mini-plan to an investor looking for a comprehensive one is not good.

The Working Plan: A working plan is used to run your business. It should be provided in detail, but it may be presented briefly. When creating a working plan, you can probably afford to be a little more candid and informal than when creating a mini-plan.

An arrangement planned exclusively for internal use may likewise overlook a few components that would be necessary for one expected for somebody outside the firm. For example, you most likely don't have to include an appendix with critical leaders' resumes. Product photos, for example, would not help a working plan. Inner consistency of raw data is similarly significant in an operational plan, focusing on outsiders. You don't need to worry about errors in the text, totally adjusting to business style, being reliable with date designs, etc.

Presentation Plan: Take a working plan with a low accentuation on beauty care products and impressions. Turn the handle to expand how much consideration is paid to its appearance, and you'll get a show plan. This plan is suitable for presenting to bankers, investors, and other stakeholders outside of the company.

Essentials

- Practically all the information in the working plan is similar to the presentation plan. However, it could be styled unexpectedly. For example, standard business vocabulary should be used rather than the informal jargon, slang, and shorthand that is useful in the workplace and appropriate in a working plan. Keep in mind that these readers will be unfamiliar with your company. Unlike the working plan, this plan serves as an introduction rather than a reminder.
- Information on all competitive threats and risks is one of the due diligence requirements for investors. Therefore, even if you only mention a few minor concerns, you must address them by providing the information.

- The main difference that can be observed between a presentation and a working plan is in polish and appearance. A working plan can be printed on a standard office printer and stapled in one corner. A presentation schedule should be printed on high-quality paper, preferably in colour. It must be expertly bound into a durable, easy-to-read booklet. Charts, graphs, tables, and illustrations should all be included.
- A presentation plan should always be precise and internally consistent. A minor error here could be interpreted as a deception perpetrated by an uncaring outsider. (MANAGE, 2013).

Meaning of Project Report

A project report is like a guide. It is a functioning document. A project report, otherwise called a business plan, is a composed assertion of what the business person expects to do. It is a sort of guide frost or strategy that frames what the business entrepreneur desires to achieve in his business and how he expects to achieve it.

Formulation of Project report

Creating a business plan necessitates a lot of tasks and decisions. For example, decisions about the project's product or service, the availability of raw materials, and the marketing infrastructure must be made in a succession of difficult choices. The project report is the final product of the project planning process.

A project report contains all relevant information on the planned enterprise unit. Financial aid is required by the many developmental agencies or organisations that help set up the unit, particularly financial institutions and banks. The report should be created to give all information requested by financing institutions to appraise the project. A well-prepared project report will save the banker time and energy and aid the entrepreneur by reducing banker objections and questions.

In India, a lot of published data about project feasibility is ready to use. The Small Industries Development Organization (CIDO) has produced useful publications on several elements of industry in the country. With so much prepared information available, all that an entrepreneur has to do to start an industrial unit is:

1. To choose the kind and degree of industrial activity.
2. To match public funds with the necessary expenditure.
3. Report on your work.

The preparation of a project report is assisted by organisations such as the Institute for Entrepreneurship Development (IED), Small Industries Service Institutes (SISI), State Industrial Development Corporation (SIDC), or the State Small Industries Development Corporation (SSIDC). These organisations all assist. Afterwards, the banks will be referred to them. In addition to these institutions, a number of commercial banks assist in this regard.

Content of Project report

We will now briefly discuss the various factors presented in a project report.

1. General information.
2. Project description.
3. Market potential.
4. Capital costs and sources of finance.
5. Assessment of working capital requirements.
6. Other financial aspects.
7. Economic and social variables.
8. Other details.

1. General information

To begin with, some information of general nature should be provided. The following got some aspects:

a) **Bio data of promoters-** It includes the name and location of the entrepreneur and their qualifications, expertise, and other capabilities.

b) **Industry profile-** Here's a quick guide to researching the industry in which your project is set up.

c) **Constitution and organisation-** The following details and the company's constitution and organisational structure must be provided. Whether a registration certificate from the Directorate of Industries or the District Industries Centre has been obtained or will be received later in the case of a partnership.

d) **Product details-** Products that are useful and have a wide range of applications. Even the product designs or drawings could be included in the. The advantages of proposed items over their substitutes should also be mentioned.

2. Project description

The project report should briefly describe the project covering the following aspects.

a) **Site:** The weather site is a zoned industrial area that has been permitted. Is it appropriate for the type of enterprise that is being contemplated? It is necessary to clarify whether an open or covered place is available or whether one is required. If the location is in a residential neighbourhood, a copy of the municipal authority's certificate of no objection should be sent with the application.

b) Physical infrastructure:

   Raw material- Whether or not it is necessary to import raw materials. If this is the case, what are the chances of obtaining raw materials consistently at reasonable costs, and if the required licence has been obtained?

   Skilled labour- Whether or not the area has access to qualified workers. Is there a plan in place to teach the workers new skills?

   Power- A project's operation may be hindered by a lack of electricity supply or a high cost per kilowatt-hour. The project report should include power requirements, load-sanctioned stability of power supply, and the cost of electricity at different consumption levels.

   Fuel- No matter what type of energy source is needed (coal, gas or oil), state the availability of such resources.

   Water- Breweries, tanneries, ice plants, and chemical plants depend on water. In these circumstances, the source and quality of the water must be disclosed.

c) Pollution control: Most industrial plants produce trash or emissions that could pose a big problem to the government. Different forms of emissions, such as gaseous ones, may be emitted. The extent of dumps, the sewage system, and the sewage treatment facility should be clearly defined.

d) Communication system: Communication options, such as telephone, fax, Internet, email, etc., should be included.

e) **Transport facilities-**Material inputs must be delivered over a specified distance, and the present and probable modes of transportation and any anticipated bottlenecks must be specified.

f) **Other common facilities-**Availability of facilities such as electrical repair shops, machine shops, welding shops, etc.

g) **Manufacturing process-** The specifics of the manufacturing process that is involved should be fully described. In addition, specify the period required for conversion from raw materials to completed goods. It is necessary to give a flow chart of the process.

h) **List of machinery and equipment-**A comprehensive list of all machinery and equipment should be included as information on their type, size, and cost (where applicable). It is also necessary to provide information on the sources of supply for capital equipment and construction services.

i) **Capacity of the plant-** It is necessary to specify the installed licenced capacity. Additionally, the state weather unit will operate on a single, double, or triple shift schedule.

j) **Technology is selected-**Is it current and appropriate for the situation? What other units are employing the same technology as this one? What are the outcomes of this technological advancement? How is it planned that the necessary know-how will be arranged?

k) **Balancing of plant-**Declare whether or not there is sufficient capacity in the various plants at various production phases while describing the various stages of production. It is necessary to estimate the amount of rebalancing equipment required at a later stage and the increase in capacity that will result.

l) **Quality control or testing and inspection-**A system may have been developed to check quality constantly. Quality marks such as ISI, Q, and AGMARK build consumer confidence by demonstrating consistency and reliability.

m) **Research and development-**Besides the quality control, whether any study or improvement of quality is proposed to be formed in the enterprise?

3. Market potential

The following aspects relating to market potential should usually be covered in the project report.

a) **Demand and supply position-** Provide information on the predicted demand for the product and the current supply situation. What portion of this gap will be covered by the planned unit is unclear.

b) **Price expected to be realised-** To determine the margin of profit, an estimate of the expected price should be provided. A comparative statement of the selling prices of competitors should be beneficial.

c) **Marketing strategy-** What sales strategy is being proposed to be implemented for the products in question? Is it possible to determine whether any arrangements are made with reputable suppliers and distributors to increase production? Sometimes, particularly in the case of electrical items, the owners of well-known brands will agree to a contract with the manufacturer to lift the entire show. And then sell it when they have registered their trademark on it.

d) **After-sales service-** It is essential in some cases. Because of a loose screw or snapped wire, the consumer may discover that the instrument is either not working or working poorly, and if the product does not receive after-sales support, the product will earn a bad reputation. The majority of the time, it has been discovered that money invested by a manufacturer on after-sales care is repaid several times over in the long run.

e) **Seasonality factor-** Whether or not the items' sales are subject to seasonal changes. The arrangements for warehousing or stocking the items during the off-season should be specified if this is the case.

f) Transportation- Whether the unit will be reliant on public, private, or own transportation for the movement of goods is still being determined. In the case of phone transport, the costs and support required are specified.

4. Capital costs and sources of finance

An estimate of the various components of capital items required by the unit should be given in the report. These components may be.

- Land and building.
- Plant and machinery.
- Installation costs.
- Other miscellaneous assets, like furniture or fixtures, vehicle, tools, etc.
- Preliminary and preoperative expenses.
- Contingency cushion against price rise or unforeseen expenses.
- The margin for working capital.

The report should include information on potential financing sources and cost concerns. The funding sources for a project must be sufficient to cover the total cost; otherwise, the project would be unable to finish in its entirety. Loans from banks or other financial institutions are expected to be made accessible in addition to the money raised through the owners' funds, loans and deposits, and other sources. Finance assessments for cost factors worldwide should be realistic and precise, just as they should be in the United States. Numerous units face severe financial problems due to an erroneous assessment of their financing requirements.

5. Assessment of working capital

Planning for working capital requirements is equally crucial for an entrepreneur. While estimating the capital, costs and margin for working capital were taken into account; any unit will be able to function only when adequate working capital funds are available.

6. Other financial aspects

Profitability or providing a means of subsistence is a fundamental purpose of starting a business. Additionally, the project structure must be capable of repaying investments made throughout the project's lifecycle. This is only possible if items are developed and proven to be profitable. This would entail the creation of a projected financial statement, which would include projections of expected sales revenue, manufacturing costs, and profit margins. These estimates, particularly those concerning sales revenue, should be reasonable. Additionally, a projected balance sheet and cash flow statement would be necessary to demonstrate the financial position and requirements of the project at various stages of development. After all, the unit's effectiveness is contingent upon the availability of sufficient funds to meet numerous commitments.

7. Economic and social variables

What will abatement cost be, defined as the cost of preventing environmental damage? In the case of pollution, the cost of abatement is the value of the additional engineering and technology necessary to clean effluents and pollutants. Is there a possibility that this initiative will have a beneficial social and economic impact?

- **Employment generation-** The number of people proposed for employment about the job situation in that location may be indicated.
- **Import substitution** can indicate how it will be accomplished and how much advantage is expected.
- **Ancillarisation-** Is it likely that the unit will require subcontracting duties of such a nature that additional industrial units will be promoted to meet them?
- **Exports-** Products planned for manufacture are likely to be exported in whole or part.

- **Local resource utilisation-** Certain local resources that are currently being wasted could be put to good use once the project is up and running.
- **Development of the area-** How will the unit's establishment affect overall growth in the region of its operation?

8. Other details

a) **Project implementation schedule-** If a separate or CPM chart cannot be appended to the project report, the expected dates of completion of the following activities might be simply provided in a tabular manner.

- Acquisition of land.
- Registration of a unit.
- Bank loans.
- Construction of building.
- Power connection.
- Ordering plant or machinery.
- Installation of plant or machinery.
- Recruitment of workers.
- Training of workers.
- Procurement of raw material.
- Trail run.
- Commercial production.

b) **Plant layout-** If possible, include a copy of the plant layout in the project report. This will aid in establishing the sufficiency of the area for current and future growth needs.

c) **Appendices-** The following is an illustrative list of appendices of a project report, which may be attached along with the project report.

- Equipment required.
- Details of preliminary expenses.
- Estimates- the cost of production and profitability.
- Labour in staff requirements.
- Break-even point.
- Working capital requirements.
- Debt service coverage ratio.

Planning Commission's Guidelines for Formulating Project Report

India's Planning Commissions have issued guidelines for preparing/formulating practical industrial projects to process investment proposals and make decisions. The feasibility report is located between the stages of project formulation and appraisal and sanction. The enterprise identifies investment options in consultation with the Administrative Ministry, the Planning Commission, and other relevant authorities during the project formulation stage. Recognising the significance of these guidelines, we are now presenting them more concisely.

1. **General Information:** The feasibility report should include a market analysis of the project's industry. It should take into account the industry's past performance. A description of the type of industry, such as the priority of the sector, increase in production, the role of the public sector, allocation of funds for investment, technique choice, and so on, should also be provided. This should also include details about the company submitting the feasibility report.
2. **Preliminary Alternatives Analysis:** The gap between demand and supply of current data of output should be produced, information on the limit that would be accessible from projects that are underway or under execution at the time the report is ready, and a total list of all current plants in the industry, including limit and level of production accomplished, and a list of all projects for which letters of intent/licenses have been given. All technically feasible options should be considered at this early stage. The location of the project, as well as its implications, should be investigated. Foreign exchange requirements should also be taken into account. It is also necessary to provide information on the profitability of various options. The rate of return on investment should be calculated and presented in the report. Cost-to-return calculations should be presented in a variety of ways.
3. **Project Description:** The feasibility report should include a brief description of the project's chosen technology/process. In addition, information relevant to determining the optimality of the selected locations should be included. To aid in evaluating a project's environmental impact, every feasibility report must present information on specific points such as population, water, air, land, flora and fauna, effects of project pollution, other environmental discretions, etc. In addition, the report should include a list of the plant's operational requirements, water and power needs, personnel requirements, the proposed organisational structure, transportation costs, activity-based construction phasing, and influencing factors.
4. **Marketing Plan:** Incorporate the following elements into your marketing strategy:

a) Marketing data plan

b) For each service area, supply for demand and potential

c) The domestic collection is presented with estimates using various methods and data, and a selection of market areas

d) Price sensitivity approximation should be studied and provided.

e) A previous price trend analysis report should be studied.

5. **Capital Requirements and Costs**: Reasonably accurate and complete estimates should be performed. All cost items' information should be meticulously gathered and presented.

6. **Operating Requirements and Costs**: Operating costs are incurred after commercial production begins. All operational costs, including raw materials and intermediates, fuel, utilities, labour, repair and maintenance, selling, and other expenses, should be documented.

7. **Financial Analysis**: This analysis aims to present some metrics for determining the project's economic viability. A proforma Balance Sheet should be presented for the project data. Depreciation should be allowed by the Bureau of Public Enterprises guidelines. The Department should approve any foreign exchange requirements of Economic Affairs. The feasibility report should consider income-tax breaks for priority industries, incentives for underserved areas, accelerated depreciation, and other factors. The sensitivity analysis should also be included. Finally, the rate of return on change in the level and pattern of product prices must be examined in the report.

8. **Economic Analysis:** The enterprise's costs and returns data must be adjusted for social profitability analysis. One critical type of investment requires a cost and input correction to reflect the true value of foreign currency, labour, and capital. The company should try to figure out how its operations affect foreign trade. In addition, the report should include indirect costs and benefits. If they cannot be quantified, their importance should be highlighted.

9. **Miscellaneous Aspects**: The three primary areas apply to nearly every new small business. Other items may be deemed important enough to be included in the project report, depending on the size of the operation and the specifics of a particular project. For example, in some small businesses, minicomputers or other electronic data processing services, cash flow statements, accounting methods, and so on may be highly beneficial.

Common Errors in Project Formulation

The creation of a project is an essential but difficult step. But on the other hand, entrepreneurs frequently make mistakes when creating project reports and business plans. Some of the most common mistakes in project formulation are as follows:

1. **Product Selection-** Some entrepreneurs have been observed to make mistakes by selecting the incorrect product for their businesses. They choose the product without considering other product-related factors such as the size of the product market, future demand, competitive position, lifecycle, labour availability, raw materials, and technology. As a result, when selecting a product, consider all factors.
2. **Capacity Utilisation Estimates-** Entrepreneurs overestimate the utilisation of available capacity as often as possible. Projections made are based entirely on incorrect assumptions. Estimates are made for current enterprise performance, conditions for the current market, environment competitiveness, technical difficulties, or other factors. A business plan written in this manner is susceptible to financial deception. As a result, avoid such temptations when estimating capacity utilisation for your business.
3. **Market Study-** The end goal of product development is to sell it. As a result, product market research is critical. Unfortunately, market research is still a grey area. On the other hand, some entrepreneurs disregard this aspect of their business plan entirely. Based on their hazy ideas and scant and scattered information on demand and supply for their proposed product, they conclude that the market is just waiting to be trapped. This is a faulty attitudinal block. Keep away from it.
4. **Technology Selection-** Depending on the nature of the product, the need for technology varies. Entrepreneurs can be swayed by reported profit margins and plan for a technology that is impossible to implement with limited financial resources. As a result, without technological feasibility, a business is doomed to fail. As a result, ensure the technical feasibility of your project.
5. **Location Selection-** Entrepreneurs frequently make two types of mistakes when choosing a location for their business. First and foremost, they are completely swayed by the government's offer of financial incentives and concessions in exchange for locating industries in a specific location. This becomes their primary concern, completely ignoring other factors such as market proximity, raw material availability, workforce, and infrastructural facilities. Second, even though it is not an appropriate location, entrepreneurs choose a location for their businesses solely because it is their hometown or

own ancestral land there. Make certain that you do not succumb to such temptations.

6. **Ownership Form Selection-** Numerous businesses fail because their ownership structure is inappropriate. Therefore, after considering all of the factors that influence the choice of a form of ownership, select a suitable form of ownership.

The six steps to writing a successful business proposal are as follows:

i) Gather the required information

ii) Project Objectives & Scope are defined

iii) Cost and labour are estimated

iv) Begin writing your business proposal

v) Revise your business proposal

vi) Distribution of your business proposal and follow up

References

Chandra, Prasanna (1996). Projects, Planning, Analysis, Selection, Implementation and Review; Tata McGraw-Hill Publishing Company Limited, New Delhi, Fifth Reprint.

Desai, Vasant (1996). Dynamics of Entrepreneurial Development of Management; Himalaya Publishing House, Mumbai, Reprint.

Gupta, V. (1998). Steps in setting up a small enterprise.

IGNOU. (2017). *eGyanKosh: Unit-6 Preparation of Business Plan and Project*. https://egyankosh.ac.in/handle/123456789/10847

Indian Council of Agricultural Research. (2020). *Handbook of agricultural extension.* Indian Council of Agricultural Research. Directorate of Knowledge Management in Agriculture.

Jerry Jinnett Pinson (1999). Anatomy of a Business Plan, D arbom Trade.

Joseph A. Covello, (1994). The Complete Book of Business Plans: Simple Steps to Writing a Powerful Business Plan.

MANAGE. (2013). *Agri-business and Entrepreneurship Development*. https://www.manage.gov.in/moocs/structure.asp

Mike P. McKeever (2005). How to write a Business Plan.

Nabhi Publication (2004). How to Borrow from a Baking and Financial Institution; Nabhi Publications, New Delhi, Edition.

Rao, C. B. (2018). *India as Global Start-up Hub/ : Mission with Passion*. Notion Press. https://www.amazon.in/India-Global-Start-up-Hub-Mission-ebook/dp/B07DGBD73R?asin=B07DGBD73R&revisionId=&format=2&depth=1

Teamwork (N.A). Critical Success factors in project management. Retrieved April 16, 2022, from https://www.teamwork.com/project-management-guide/critical-success-factors-in-project-management/

Yarbrough, Q. (2021). What is a critical Success Factor? A Quick Guide. Retrieved April 16, 2022 from https://www.projectmanager.com/blog/critical-success-factor

12

Financing of An Enterprise

Sapna Jarial, Sharad Sachan, Haobijam James Watt and Devina Seram*

Department of Agricultural Economics and Extension
School of Agriculture, Lovely Professional University, Phagwara, Punjab

**Department of Entomology, School of Agriculture*
Lovely Professional University Phagwara, Punjab

Introduction

Finance is vital to entrepreneurship. With limited resources starting a business is a challenge. Earlier generations of entrepreneurs establishing a business were different. They first guaranteed that money would be available to start—the business. So, if one wanted to build up a unit for a business, one would undertake market research and then approach the bank. Then activities like product development, ordering equipment, determining the site, acquiring land for the facility, what government policies are applicable etc., were considered. Before starting a business, an entrepreneur considers these factors. That was the old regime.

But today, the new-age entrepreneurship or the start-up space is the idea that is the spark for entrepreneurship. A start-up is the largest group of people you can convince of a plan to build a different future. (Thiel, 2014). The entrepreneur does not wait until all money, location, and other concerns are secured before moving with the enterprise. So, the greater risk is taken because the ideas are unique, innovative, and need to be developed into goods or services. The entrepreneur cannot take for granted that the future will be better. We need to work to create it today. (Thiel, 2014). So, means the challenges for raising finances in a new start-up domain or a new entrepreneurial domain are significantly much more different and much more challenging than they are in conventional entrepreneurship. The present chapter will focus on raising financial resources for an entrepreneurial firm and a start-up.

Keywords

Enterprise financing: Enterprise financing can be defined as forming plans on ways to obtain money for a business start-up

Financial analysis: Analysing project cost, capital source funding, break-even point, loan repayment period, cost of production and profitability estimates is the financial analysis

Cost of the project: The project's cost is a precise estimation to decide on the project's financing pattern and economic sustainability.

Debentures- The instruments are long-term debt obligations secured by a charge against the assets of the entity that issued the instrument.

A term loan is a long-term loan with a set interest rate that can be repaid in equal semi-annual payments over 5 to 10 years.

Public deposits- Particularly essential short-term and working cash sources, especially for small businesses.

Break-even analysis- The production level at which a unit is neither lucrative nor losing money is referred to as the unit's break-even point.

Debt-equity ratio- The business's financial structure should demonstrate an appropriate balance of internal resources, equity, and borrowed capital.

Net present value (NPV)- The net present value is the sum of the current value of all the cash flows associated with the project.

Nano-enterprise: Start-up entities that cater to one product and one small market segment are best-termed *nano enterprises.*

Bootstrapping: Is a method of financing a start-up through the creative use of resources, trade channels and other stakeholder relationships without raising equity from equity investors or loans from banks.

Enterprise financing can be defined as forming plans on ways to obtain money for a business start-up. Commercial loans and schemes are available from various banks and financial institutions. Therefore, it is critical to comprehend and select those schemes that will meet your needs. Different banks have various financial plans or schemes, each with its own set of terms and conditions. Therefore, we should select those readily available schemes on reasonable terms for our company. The project report serves as the starting point for approaching financial institutions. If you intend to seek loans from banks or financial institutions, it is preferable if you can identify a guarantor for your loan, as the financial institution may require it. Typically, financial institutions will request collateral for a bank loan for a business.

Financial analysis of project

Financial analysis is required for the entrepreneur to put the project together and for the financial institutions and banks providing loans to the project's investors. Other organizations that have invested in the project's equity and all those who have participated in the project's appraisal are also included. Financial analysis is a prerequisite for determining the sustainability of a project. There have been numerous instances where a project has been ill due to an inaccurate financial evaluation performed early in the project's life cycle. The financial analysis of projects is intended to determine whether or not cost, capital sources of funding, break-even point, loan payback time, cost of production, and profitability estimations have been effectively completed. .(Chole et al., 2012).

A. Cost of project and means of finance

The project's cost is a precise estimation to decide on the project's financing pattern and economic sustainability. If the project's cost is underestimated and there is an overrun, we will have to raise additional resources, which may cause the project to be delayed. It may also have an impact on the viability of the project. Higher commitments are made if the project cost is overstated, resulting in unnecessary commitment charges. (Chole et al., 2012).

Cost of project

Following are the major components of the cost

1. Land and site development
2. Cost of laying roads, fencing and gates
3. Various buildings like the main factory, administrative building stores, utilities, canteen, essentials, housing, etc.
4. Plant and machinery like the cost of equipment, speared, duties and taxes, packing and forwarding, freight, foundation and commissioning.
5. Technical know-how like fees, expenses on drawings, consultancy fees etc.
6. Training and deputation of foreign technicians.
7. Cost of miscellaneous fixed assets like furniture, office, machinery and equipment, vehicles, laboratory, experiment, telephone, Internet, workshop equipment, etc.
8. Preliminary expenses related to the formation of the company cost of raising capital by public issue.

9. Preoperative expenses mean expenses during preoperative or construction before the start of commercial production, i.e. establishment expenses like salaries, rent, travelling and conveyance etc.
10. Contingencies because of unforeseen factors, foreign currency value fluctuations, and inflation. Usually, 5% to 15% contingency provision is made.
11. Margin money for working capital can be estimated with the inventory quantum for materials, consumables, stores, work in process and finished goods.

Banking for working capital should be given with a margin of 25 to 40%, depending on the size of the project and the risk value of the security, such as inventory or bills of exchange. Bank funding is subtracted from total working capital to arrive at the working capital margin. Therefore, long-term resources must cover this expense, included in the project's budget.

Means of finance

After estimating the project's overall cost, the pattern of financing the task to meet the cost of the project must be decided. The following means of finance can be considered.

Generally, sources of business capital can be divided into two parts.

1. **Owned funds**- Share capital and flowing back of profit.
2. **Borrowed funds**- Debentures, term loans, public deposits, commercial banks and intercompany deposits.

1. **Sources of own funds**- Own capital refers to the capital that has been put in a company unit by the owners themselves. A joint-stock company can collect share capital as owned capital, and profits can be re-invested back into the company or a particular business unit. There are two types of owned capital: share capital and profit, to put it simply. (Chole, 2010)
   a) **Share Capital-** A joint-stock company may issue shares to gather owned capital, according to the Company Act of 1956. A joint-stock company's ability to raise significant amounts of cash through the issuance of shares is a hidden attribute. The share capital of a firm is divided into tiny bits, and each of these little parts is referred to as a share. A shareholder is someone who owns stock in a corporation.
   b) **Flowing back of profits**. If a joint-stock company makes a lot of money, it may put some in a reserve fund instead of paying it all as dividends. The earnings held aside as a reserve are subsequently used to fund the

company's activities, a process known as "flowing back of profit." Profits of this type can be used for various goals, including corporate development and modernization. Furthermore, due to the higher flow back of earnings, a company can exist even during a recession and can deal with financial difficulties more easily. As a result, the company's financial stability improves.

2. **Sources of borrowed funds or capital:** Any business activity in today's environment demands a large amount of funds expenditure. Such high capital requirements will not be met just by the owner's capital. As a result, the businessman also uses borrowed funds. Essential sources of borrowed funds are:

   a) Debentures

   b) Term loans

   c) Public deposits.

   d) Commercial banks and

   e) Intercompany deposit.

   a) **Debentures-** The instruments are long-term debt obligations secured by a charge against the assets of the entity that issued the instrument. If a corporation needs long-term financing but is not in a position to redeem that capital, the company can issue debentures to raise funds. It is a recognition of debt, delivered under the company's seal, containing a contract for the repayment of principal, some at a defined date, and the payment of interest on the outstanding debt. (Chole et al., 2012)

   b) **Term loans-** This sort of financing is also known as term finance. It is a long-term loan with a set interest rate that can be repaid in equal semi-annual payments over 5 to 10 years. Aside from banks and state-owned financial institutions, development organizations such as IDBI, ICICI, and LIC provide term loans to enterprises to support medium- and long-term assets and permanent working capital. The lending institution's interest rate is decided by the overall level of interest rates, the company's financial status, the lender's risk perception, and the manner and length of time for repayment. Term loans are approved following a thorough review of the investment proposal. .(Chole et al., 2012)

   c) **Public deposits-** Public deposits are particularly essential short-term and working cash sources, especially for small businesses. Under the Company Rules of 1978, a corporation may take public deposits from investors. The general public makes deposits in the company with their savings. It is possible to make public deposits for a period ranging from 6 months to 36 months. The interest rate is generally between 10 and 14 per cent, owing to the greater interest rate on government bonds. Public deposits are more elastic in terms of earning greater rates of interest because the corporation can return such deposits upon maturity and therefore relieve itself of the burden of interest payments. The maximum amount of public deposits accepted is up to 25 per cent of paid-up capital and free reserves.

d) **Commercial banks in India**. Commercial banks assist firms with meeting their working capital and other short-term obligations. Deposits from the general public are typically made for a fixed period, and the money saved is utilized to assist small & medium-sized businesses with financial help. In India, commercial banks assist in various ways, including loans, overdrafts, cash, credit, bills, discontinuing, export, and credit guarantees. Commercial banks provide support in compliance with the Reserve Bank of India's requirements. At the moment, the Reserve Bank of India (RBI) is pressuring commercial banks to lend to small firms, tiny and medium-sized enterprises (SMEs). .(Chole et al., 2012)

e) **Intercompany deposit in India-** Many management groups control various branches like Tata, Birla Reliance, Bajaj Group etc. Such an organization owns ownership of several enterprises. So in such a group of companies, if there is a surplus capital fund in a company, this is lent to the company having its requirement for a short period. Sometimes a firm makes a deposit capital fund in another company of the same group in the form of a call deposit. So by intercompany deposit, a company can acquire financial aid with a cheaper interest rate and without legal formalities. Yet, the Government of India has imposed numerous limits on intercompany deposits.

3. **Deferred credits**. Often, suppliers of machinery offer deferred credit, which allows for the payment of machinery purchases over a duration of time.

   a) **Capital subsidy and development-** The government subsidizes capital investments in industries located in backward or hilly areas. Additionally, some state governments provide development assistance, loans, or the sale of text loans to aid in the growth of an area.

   b) **Unsecured loans and deposits-** Occasionally, promoters are needed to make unsecured loans to bridge the gap between the statutory promoter contribution and the capital that the promoter can raise. These are supplementary loans to institutional loans.

c) **Promoters' contribution.** The promoters must have a financial interest in the venture. To this end, the supporters should contribute a specific amount of the project's cost. The promoter's involvement is determined by the project's location and the promoter's background. For technical and female entrepreneurs, the margin is small.

B. **Cost of production:** In arriving at the product's cost of production, we have to look at the various factors outlined below.

1. Material and consumable stores
2. Utilities
3. Repairs and maintenance
4. Rent, insurance
5. Wages and salaries
6. Administrative expenses
7. Expenses on marketing
8. Royalty
9. Excise duty
10. Financial expenses
11. Depreciation

C. **Financial projections**

Cash flow statement- Cash flow predictions are created to guarantee that the unit has the finances it needs and does not face a liquidity crisis. Estimated cash flows consider both the sources of financing and the depositions or uses of those funds. During the construction phase, predicting production cash flow is critical to ensuring adequate cash can meet the project's requirements. Several sources of funds have been described under means of finance earlier in this chapter.

a) Capital expenditure
b) Preliminary expenses.
c) Current assets-Increase in the level of inventories and book debts.
d) Decrease in term loans or debentures or deferred credit.
e) Decrease in unsecured loans or deposits.
f) Repayment of bank borrowings.
g) Interest
h) Dividends
i) taxation.

The difference between the sources and uses of funds indicates the net surplus or deficit. Accordingly, one has to take a business decision regarding the management of funds. .(Chole et al., 2012)

Projected balance sheet- The projected balance sheet is created using the profit and loss statement, cash flow, and other financial statements. The position of the company's share capital, term loans, creditors, bank borrowings, current assets, and other assets is chosen at the end of each year based on the movement reflected in cash flow and profitability expectations, among other factors. The balance sheet is a snapshot of the company's financial condition at the end of each year, and the total of assets on one side of the balance sheet will equal the sum of liabilities on the other.

D. **Financial analysis**

Break-even analysis- The production level at which a unit is neither lucrative nor losing money is referred to as the unit's break-even point. Performing a break-even analysis aims to determine the cost-volume relationship and, as a result, the amount of production or sales at which the company breaks even.

Cost contribution = Sales revenue-Variable cost.

Contributions assist units in recovering their fixed costs. The point at which a contribution fully recovers its fixed costs is the break-even point. The break-even point denotes the level of production required to avoid losses. Profits are generated when sales exceed the break-even point. The break-even point should be low for units anticipated to have marketing challenges, material shortages, power shortages, or other obstacles in reaching full capacity utilization. For example, when variable costs exceed the sale price, and the situation is unlikely to change shortly, a businessman will prefer to close this factory. By stopping the factory, only the fixed costs are lost; however, by operating the plant, both the fixed costs and the excess variable costs over the sale price are lost.

Payback period- The payback period is the amount of time required to recover the initial capital expenditure in a project. The project will be more appealing if the payback period is as short as possible.

Profit to total capitalization ratio- This is worked out by dividing profit before taxes by long term debt. This measures the earning power of both owned and borrowed capital.

Debt service coverage ratio (DSCR) - Financial institutions that provide the majority of long-term finance for industrial projects evaluate financial viability primarily using DSCR and internal rate of return calculations.

$$DSCR = \sum_{i=1}^{n} \frac{\text{Profit after tax+Depreciation+Interest in term loan}}{\text{Term loan installments+Interest in term loan}}$$

Where n is the number of years over which the loan has to be repaid. A DSCR of 2 is considered satisfactory.

Net present value (NPV)- The net present value is the sum of the present value of all the cash flows associated with the project. One may accept the project if NPV is positive, and reject if NPV is negative.

Internal Rate of Return (IRR)- The internal rate of return of a project is the discount rate, which makes the net present value equal to zero in the net present value method. We assume that the discount rate (cost of capital) is known and determines the net present value of the project. In IRR calculation, we set the NPV to zero and determine the discount rate IRR which satisfies this condition. The calculation of IRR is one of the trial and error. We try different values of discount rate till we arrive at one which makes the present value of cash inflows (profit under tax depreciation, salvage value) equal to the present value of cash outflows, capital expenditure, increase in current assets calculated over the life of the project.

Debt-equity ratio- The financial structure of the business should demonstrate an appropriate balance of internal resources, equity, and borrowed capital. Certain institutions have varying loan equity standards for different types of borrowers, ranging from 3:1 for small businesses to 1:1 for huge companies.

Current ratio- This ratio illustrates the relationship between current assets and current liabilities. Its objective is to determine the viability of the project.

Ratio of sales to capital employed- This ratio is a broad indication of capital utilization efficiency and economy.

Over the last few years, India has become a global destination for start-up investments. These investments are typically seed/angel and venture capital/ private equity investments, which are related to the stage of the firm. The first seed investment phase is usually a round of strategic investments by the promoters, their friends and families, high net worth individuals and angel investors. This phase enables the idea to take shape and go through the prototype build stage to different degrees. The second and third phases of venture capital and private equity funding must follow, which typically could occur in multiple sequential series. Venture capital funding helps start-ups take their prototypes to commercialization and beyond, while private equity funding helps start-ups scale up as mainstream companies. It is a win-win, providing exit opportunities when the start-up company accomplishes scale and value.

Macro Funding Scene

The funding scene for start-ups has changed significantly over the last five years. There is a huge spurt in start-up sub-verticals based on disruptive technologies and business trends, which have attracted increased funding interest. Globally, the financing staircase for a start-up follows a typical path:

Financing the entrepreneurial journey is very challenging; it is also very evident in today's situation that there are multiple avenues of finance available for start-ups compared to the availability for the earlier generation entrepreneurs. So, they typically start from one's own personal and family savings, then move on to angel and seed funding, then move on to the venture capital several series funding. Finally, when entrepreneurs are in the growth phase, they move to private equity funding. During the expansion and diversification phase, a combination of private equity funding and an initial public offer is the source of funding.

- At the **ideation stage,** personal savings and institutional grants
- In the **prototyping phase**, financial support from angel investors and seed funds.
- In the **testing phase**, bridge funding by angels and venture capital firms
- In the **growth phase**, more structured venture capital funding in multiple series
- For the **major expansion and diversification phase**, private equity investments

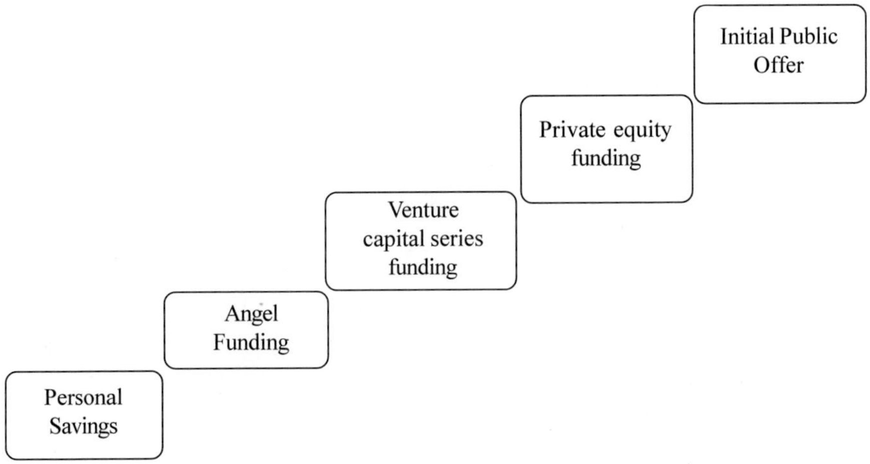

Figure 1. Funding staircase of Start-ups

The economic models of venture capital are patient in terms of returns but expectant in the magnitude of returns. The predicted or received returns by angel investors, venture capitalists, and private equity investors are not publicly available. The returns are influenced by the entry and exit prices and dividends and bonus shares earned. Angel investors, similar to micro venture capitalists, can expect low single-digit returns, whereas venture capital and private equity companies can expect mid- to high-single-digit returns. While angel investors may expect their sub-million (or million, in certain circumstances) dollar investments to pay off in two or three years, venture capital and private equity firms may be willing to wait five to ten years for their multimillion-dollar investments to pay off. Recent IPOs of high-growth start-ups and other companies that have seen partial or full exits by private equity investors have seen share prices range from 25 to 250 times the par value of each share of Rs 10 per. For virtuous equity-led development models, these thumb rules imply that start-ups should aim for sustained and profitable growth. (Bhaktavatsala, 2019)

Indian Start-up Funding & Investment Trend Seed money is typically accessible from USD 50,000 to USD 1 million. In contrast, equity funding is usually available in amounts ranging from USD 500,000 to USD 2.5 billion. The continuous dominance of consumer internet and e-commerce platforms, which cater to everyday consumer and consumption demands, is essential in India. Healthcare, fintech, big data, logistics, Cloud SaaS solutions, and artificial intelligence are all becoming hot topics at the same time. Bengaluru continues to lead in start-up activity, with Mumbai, Pune, Chennai, Gurugram, and Hyderabad making the top five.

Rather than basic research and development (R&D), India's start-up investments are driven by product and service digitization. Unlike in the West, where foundational research by start-ups is acquired by global giants, in India, value creation in India is dependent on market consumption.

Enterprises in the Making

Start-up entities which cater to one product and one small market segment are best termed as *nano enterprises*. Only one individual, the owner, usually operates a nano enterprise. We see and depend on several self-employed persons each day but do not see them as *nano enterprises*. It is amazing how the nano-entrepreneurial effort is surviving in India despite the formal economic system's lack of attention to it. Societies must be guided to take an enterprise view of self-employment and support *nano enterprises* in upskilling and upgrading.

Own/Family Financing

Typically, passionate entrepreneurs/founders invest their employment savings or family money to start such businesses. Given India's strong family and societal ties, the family ecosystem is vital to entrepreneurial growth. Working CEOs should set aside a tiny amount of their profits to build their start-up fund or support other firms.

This method is useful for university professors, company researchers, and technicians naturally inclined to pursue entrepreneurship. Working executives might use this method to fund nano-enterprises in India that cost less than Rs 100,000. (USD 1500). Even retired personnel can re-invest a portion of their pension funds to start their micro-enterprises, whether a corner store or a community service. Aiming to create *a few nano-entrepreneurial ventures* per year.

Community Financing

Adding to the idea, gated communities and apartment associations can have a bigger impact. Gated communities and apartment associations often have more pooled resources and a captive consumer demand base. These organizations can assist build nano-businesses that efficiently serve local communities. There are numerous chances for gated residential communities to create nano enterprises, ranging from security to automated laundry and library to documentation. The nano and micro-foundations of business can increase as these gated communities emerge into new suburbs and mini-cities. Individuals and communities have significantly more power than they know to develop nano entrepreneurs.

Angel Funding

Hi-net-worth individuals (HNIs) invest independently or through angel networks in early-stage firms. Angel Networks follow an organized procedure of inviting start-up applications, reviewing them through third-party agencies, and investing in them. For the HNIs and to grow the corpus for future investments, Angel Networks typically aim to cash out during the following Series Funding rounds. In addition to receiving personal contributions, start-ups engage with individuals to be introduced to the Angel Network. Angel networks in India are mostly geographically based. However, they welcome applicants from anywhere. Unlike venture capital and private equity organizations, angel investors do not place constraints on board membership or other governance standards. **Examples of Top angel investors of 2021**: Kunal Shah, Ramakant Sharma and Binny Bansal Co-founder, Flipkart. (Saini, 2022)

Incubator Support

Incubators are infrastructural platforms that provide start-up companies with plug-and-play facilities, co-working spaces, legal and patenting support, and mentoring. Start-ups can use incubators to overcome some of their resource constraints and become more organized. In addition to scaling up existing incubators, the Indian government has established Atal Incubation Centres (under the Atal Innovation Mission) in the public and private sectors. Furthermore, several state governments have established incubation centres at the state level. In addition, incubators are well-positioned to assist companies in pursuing their programmes, thanks to grants.

Incubator Support for Not-for-Profit Start-ups

Some Incubators and Accelerators provide specific investment support for start-ups set up with not-for-profit motives. Such platforms are beneficial to encouraging and sustaining social entrepreneurship that aims at improving the Quality of Life in the country. N/*Core* is one such incubator set up with participation from Cisco, Ford Foundation, and IRB Infrastructure. *N/Core* recently unveiled Series/N to provide funding for 30 start-ups over 5 years, ranging up to Rs 2 crore for each start-up. In addition, N/Core has senior executives from various IT and other companies to mentor and nurture start-ups. Incubators typically provide their funds in any of the four forms of grants, debt, quasi-equity and equity. (Bhaktavatsala, 2019).

Bootstrapping as a Source of Finance

Bootstrapping is a strategy of funding a business that involves making creative use of resources, trade channels, and other stakeholder relationships rather than obtaining money from investors or taking out loans from banks. Founders benefit greatly from bootstrapping since their equity is not diluted and loans are not contracted; they keep the entire worth of the company. Leasing real estate and equipment can be a cost-effective strategy to establish a start-up's initial foundation. Bootstrapping can work in product development when potential buyers have a stake or interest in the product and are ready to pre-fund it. To be successful at bootstrapping, founders must be skilled at managing their working capital. Bootstrapping should not be viewed as a long-term or total financial solution, as it can lead to a resource-constrained impasse. Instead, bootstrapping should be utilized to develop internal talents and provide value to a firm while avoiding stock dilution and interest costs. According to reports, the founders of today's leading tech companies all went through a bootstrapping phase in the early stages of their entrepreneurial careers. Demonstrating the importance of developing a product concept and prototyping it on a low budget.

Alternate Investment Funds

In India, Alternative Investment Funds (AIFs) are defined in Regulation 2(1) (b) of the Securities and Exchange Board of India (Alternative Investment Funds) Regulations, 2012. AIF refers to any privately pooled investment fund (from Indian or foreign sources) in the form of a trust, a company, a body corporate, or a Limited Liability Partnership (LLP).

Hence, in India, AIFs are private funds that otherwise do not come under any regulatory agency's jurisdiction in India. As per Securities and Exchange Board of India (Alternative Investment Funds) Regulations, 2012, Alternative Investment Funds shall seek registration in one of the three categories:

- **Category I:** Mainly invests in start-ups, SME's or any other sector that which Govt. considers economically and socially viable.
- **Category II:** These include Alternative Investment Funds such as private equity funds or debt funds for which no specific incentives or concessions are given by the government or any other Regulator
- **Category III**: Alternative Investment Funds such as hedge funds or funds that trade to make short-term returns or other open-ended funds for which the government or any other Regulator gives no specific incentives or concessions.

Venture Capital Model

Venture capital is money given to businesses and entrepreneurs. It can be given at any stage of development, but it is most common in the early and seed rounds. Investors must be accredited to invest in venture capital funds. After World War II, venture finance became a sophisticated business with various stakeholders that helped promote innovation.

VC businesses flooded into the Indian industrial landscape in the 1990s, accompanied by economic policy liberalization. The VC firms entered because the Indian government decided to allow international finance corporations to invest in Indian companies.

Venture capital firms have helped a number of first-generation companies improve their equity basis and list on the bourses by taking 10 to 25% holdings in their capital structures. Venture capital funds help organizations grow from small start-ups to mature businesses by providing equity finance for new technology or markets. Because companies aren't normally public at that stage, venture capital firms buy shares at a discount to the promoters. Start-ups rely on seed and Series A, B, and C investments to survive.

Indian Start-up and Financing Ecosystem

India is the world's 3rd largest start-up ecosystem, with yearly growth of 12-15 per cent. In 2018, India had 50,000 start-ups, of which 8900-9300 were technology-based. In 2019 alone, 1300 new IT start-ups were born, averaging 2-3 every day.

Corporations as Investors

Many start-ups focus on digital applications, including e-commerce and digital technologies, while established corporations with a strong brick and mortar business have only peripheral digital applications. Established corporations could gain a lot by investing in strategically aligned and technologically reinforcing start-ups for their businesses. Reliance Industries, for example, has taken up a start-up initiative covering modern technologies; for example, physical products such as wind turbines, solar and hydro-electric plants, logistics, artificial intelligence, robotics and data analytics. Take solution is an example of how a corporate investment of Rs 2 crore by Shriram Group enabled the company to become a mainstream software solutions company. Mahindra Group's Rise project focuses on grants for start-ups in the energy and transportation sector, while Godrej Group's venture capital fund focuses on agricultural and consumer products. If every successful corporation begins investing in and starts mentoring start-ups in related technologies and products, India would see a significant level of product innovation and delivery. Reliance Industries has invested in 11 start-ups to reinforce its digital ecosystem (Agarwal, 2019).

Quite apart from such value chain participation, another way is to leverage a corporation's resources to reach out to the wider population, create awareness and harness passion in association with Non-Governmental Organizations (NGOs) and Not for Profit Organizations (NPOs). (Rao, 2018).

Crowdfunding of Start-ups

Crowdfunding is the technique of generating finances online from many people giving modest amounts. Crowdfunding harnesses the collective power of the people to fund beneficial causes. The idea has been used for start-up creation. While start-up crowdfunding is structured and legal in the US, it is not yet in India. Crowdfunding platforms may also help start-ups market and sell their products. They help build user communities that support the start-up and benefit from product customization in exchange for guaranteed sales and community buzz.

Financial Instruments

Equity, convertible debt, and venture debt are three principal forms of raising finance for start-ups. The instruments are chosen based on the stage of the company, the business model, and the valuation levels. Equity is typically obtained from angel investors or private equity funds, with the issuance by the company to them.

Venture debt is a senior secured loan that sits on top of the funding pile in liquidation preference (repaid before all other debt or equity holders). Venture debt is typically issued by more aggressive banks or venture debt investors. An asset pledge usually secures such debt. All these instruments, typically, have a timeframe of 6 to 18 months for conversion or redemption. The three instruments differ in terms of dilution to founder equity structure and influence or get influenced by valuations that are pre-determined or determined at the conversion time. A revenue model is necessary to support the valuations in all types of financing but is essential for the third route of debt. Variations exist for each investor protection condition, including first rights where equity issuance is involved. An excellent summary of the financial instruments is available in the Forbes article "Comparing Equity, Debt and Convertibles for Startup Financings". (Deeb, 2014).

Microfinance Corporation Support for Start-ups

Professor Muhammad Yunus, the founder of "Grameen Bank," reasoned that if financial resources can be made available to the poor people on terms and conditions that are appropriate and reasonable, "these millions of small people with their millions of small pursuits can add up to create the biggest development wonder." Grameen Bank (GB) has reversed conventional banking practice by removing the need for collateral and creating a banking system based on mutual trust, accountability, participation, and creativity. (Bank, n.d.). The success of the Grameen Bank and the global recognition it secured is reflective of the potential of directed micro credit. Today the Grameen Bank has become more diversified in its product offerings, leading to a greater generation of wealth for its customers.

In India, the microfinance corporations (MFC) sector quickly took root over the last two decades. Some of them even received small bank licenses under the new regulations of the Reserve Bank of India. While MFCs played a stellar role in supporting social entrepreneurship and women's self-help groups, upon conversion into small banks, shifted focus to high-cost business loans.

MUDRA

What is Mudra Loan?

According to the Department of Financial Services, Ministry of Science and Finance, Government of India's letter number 27, dated May 14, 2015, MUDRA loans under the Pradhan Mantri Mudra Yojana (PMMY) can be defined as loans given by all public sector banks, regional rural banks, state cooperative banks, and urban cooperative banks to non-farm income-generating enterprises in manufacturing, trading, and service whose credit needs are less than Rs.10,00,000. These loans may be covered by Mudra's refinance and credit enhancement products.

In addition to these banks, NBFCs and MIFAs operating across the country can extend credit to this segment to obtain financial assistance from Mudra Limited, provided they meet the approved eligibility criteria. The eligibility criteria for institutions seeking to refinance or financial assistance from Mudra have been finalized and are available on the Madras website.

To begin, Mudra has enrolled 27 public sector banks, 17 private sector banks, 27 regional rural banks, and 25 microfinance institutions as partner institutions for channelling assistance to the ultimate borrower based on eligibility criteria.

1. Process Flow Diagram

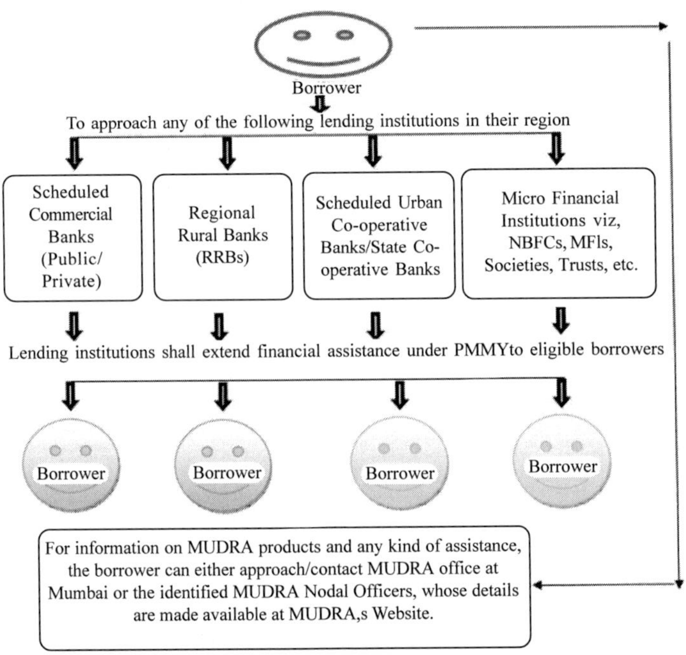

Figure 2. How to apply for MUDRA loan

Who to approach for assistance under PMMY?

Borrowers interested in receiving assistance under the PMMY should contact the local branch of any of the institutions mentioned above in their area. The amount of assistance will be determined by the eligibility criteria of the lending institution.

4. Whom to contact for assistance?

Mudra has designated 97 nodal officers at various sit by regional offices or branch offices to serve as Mudra's first point of contact. For information on Mudra products and assistance, the borrower can approach or contact the Mudra office in Mumbai or the identified Mudra nodal officers whose contact information is available on the Mudra website. Under the Pradhan Mantri MUDRA Yojana (PMMY), MUDRA has created several products and services as below:

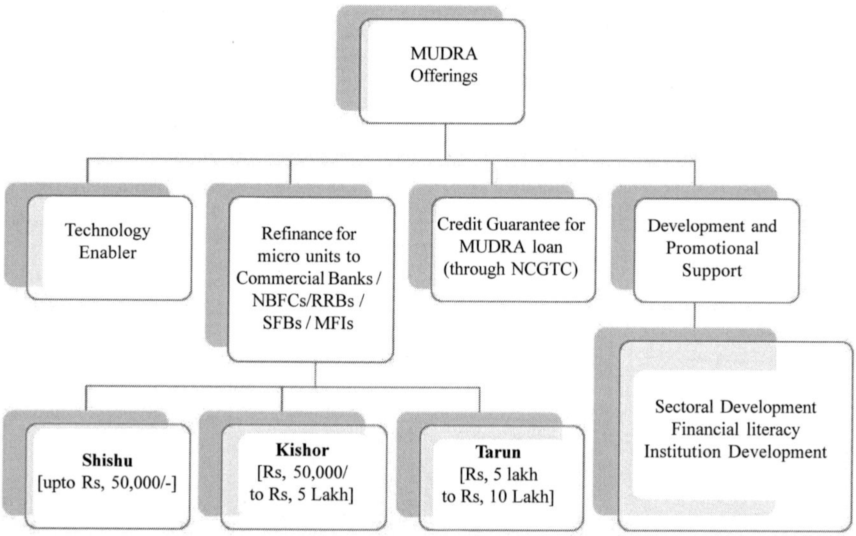

Figure 3. Product and services of MUDRA*(MUDRA, n.d.)*

Limits Collaterals

Margins High Interest

Indian Banking Platforms for Start-ups

With the government's increased focus on 'Startup India', numerous public and private sector banks have launched initiatives to meet start-up entrepreneurs' funding and non-funding needs. The RBI has set up a special mailbox for the start-up industry. It has also set up a FOREX helpline to give cross-border regulatory services and FEMA advice (Foreign Exchange Management Act). Another announcement abolished the Angel Tax to encourage investment. Following RBI's lead, the **AXIS Bank** "Thought Factory", the **Federal Bank** "Launchpad", the **HDFC Bank** "Smart Up", the **ICICI Bank** "start-up Garage", the **Kotak Mahindra Bank** "Kotak Business Boosters", and the State Bank of India has developed an 'IT Innovation Start-up Engagement Programme' are such examples. (Trivedi, 2017)(*IT - ISEP - Business*, n.d.)

Conclusion

Finance is vital to entrepreneurship. With limited resources starting a business is a challenge. In the new regime of entrepreneurship, banking initiatives focus on advisory services, information and support, and in certain circumstances, capital for start-ups. This would help break down the information barrier and provide new chances for aspiring businesses. However, the financial sector still has a lot to do to help start-ups. For example, a loan often requires collateral, but collateral is tough to come by for young entrepreneurs coming out of college. Only venture capitalists or angel investors are eligible for collateral-free loans from some banks, leaving students with creative ideas and entrepreneurs from isolated rural areas out of the loop. The above-mentioned services will undoubtedly revitalize the already lively start-up environment further.

References

Agarwal, M. (2019). *11 Indian Tech Startup Acquisitions And Investments By Reliance*. https://inc42.com/features/indian-tech-startup-acquisitions-and-investments-by-reliance/

Bank, G. (n.d.). *Grameen Bank*. Retrieved March 22, 2022, from https://grameenbank.org/introduction/

Bhaktavatsala, R. (2019). *Entrepreneurship*. NPTEL. https://drive.google.com/file/d/1CWJTsv2SQvvbf4lgzpiGKAOueKAZdH4b/view

BSEINDIA. (n.d.). *BSEINDIA*. Retrieved March 22, 2022, from https://www.bseindia.com/Static/about/alternative_investment_funds.aspx

Chole, R.R., Kapse, P.S., and Deshmukh. (2012). Entrepreneurship development and Business Communication Skills. Scientific Publishers,

Deeb, G. (2014). *Comparing Equity, Debt And Convertibles For Startup Financings*. https://www.forbes.com/sites/georgedeeb/2014/03/19/comparing-equity-vs-debt-vs-convertibles-for-startup-financings/?sh=40cf839d69ff

GoI. (n.d.). *Incubation Support*. Retrieved March 21, 2022, from https://www.startupindia.gov.in/content/sih/en/compendium_of_good_practices/incubationsupport.html

Hayes, A. (2022). *Venture Capital Definition*. https://www.investopedia.com/terms/v/venturecapital.asp

Indian Start-up Ecosystem. (n.d.). Retrieved March 22, 2022, from https://www.startupindia.gov.in/content/sih/en/international/go-to-market-guide/indian-startup-ecosystem.html

IT - ISEP - Business. (n.d.). Retrieved March 22, 2022, from https://sbi.co.in/web/business/information/it-isep

MUDRA. (n.d.). *Mudra - Micro Units Development & Refinance Agency Ltd.* Retrieved March 22, 2022, from https://www.mudra.org.in/

Rao, C. B. (2018). *India as Global Start-up Hub/ : Mission with Passion*. Notion Press. https://www.amazon.in/India-Global-Start-up-Hub-Mission-ebook/dp/B07DGBD73R?asin=B07DGBD73R&revisionId=&format=2&depth=1

Saini, T. (2022). *Top 70 Angel Investors of 2021 in India - StartupLanes.com*. https://www.startuplanes.com/top-70-angel-investors-of-2021-in-india/

Thiel, P. (2014). *Zero to One. Note on Start-ups or How to Build the future*. Crown Business.

Trivedi, A. (2017). *Indian banks responding to the growing start-up ecosystem!* https://yourstory.com/mystory/7570536365-indian-banks-responding-to-growing-start-up-ecosystem-/amp

13

Opportunities for Agri-entrepreneurship and Rural Enterprise

Sapna Jarial, Sharad Sachan, Haobijam James Watt Devina Seram* and Roop Kumar

Department of Agricultural Economics and Extension School of Agriculture Lovely Professional University. Phagwara, Punjab

**Department of Entomology, School of Agriculture Lovely Professional University Phagwara, Punjab*

Introduction

India has been an agricultural economy since its inception. Several mechanisms are used in agribusiness, such as forward and backward linkages with secondary and tertiary sectors, such as manufacturing and service sectors. Opportunities in agriculture and related sectors can be identified at various stages of the farming process. Generally, agribusiness opportunities exist at the input stage, the farming stage, the value chain, the output processing and marketing stage, and the related services stage. As a result of globalisation and a more interconnected global market, the scope and potential of agribusiness opportunities is expanding. For entrepreneurs, there are numerous potential opportunities. Many different inputs are required in the agricultural process, such as seeds, fertilisers, pesticides, and innovative and localised farm technology. As a result, the aforementioned areas create agribusiness opportunities in developing and producing these inputs.

There are numerous opportunities for entrepreneurship in bio-pesticides, bio-fertilisers, vermicomposting, soil testing and amendment, and so on. The growing emphasis on organic farming is creating even more options. In terms of seed development, there is much room for research and development. Even in unfavourable climatic conditions, these seed varieties are expected to serve. To maximise revenue and improve the living conditions of our farming community, crop productivity should be increased, which is possible with good management practices and high-quality inputs. Unfortunately, India can only produce half of the average global output per hectare.

Furthermore, there is a lot of potential in agro-tech products. Chemically intensive fertilisers and pesticides are gradually being phased out in favour of natural manure and pesticides. This gradual shift reveals enormous potential and opportunities for developing and marketing bio-pesticides, eco-friendly agrochemicals, and natural manures. At this farming stage, the primary goal is to maximise output while taking advantage of seasonal advantages. There is an opportunity to be innovative in balancing fertilisers and pesticides and agrochemicals, adopting multiple cropping and crop rotation to protect, preserve, and improve soil quality, using agri-tech machines to reduce cultivation costs and labour drudgery, and so on. Opportunities are felt in the postharvest stage, value chain, output processing, and marketing. Changes in agricultural produce supply chain management are allowing new businesses to emerge. Agri-processing units are rapidly expanding. There are opportunities in the distribution and logistics sectors. To be more specific, opportunities for Agri-preneurship development include farming vegetables, fruits, food grains, pulses, oil seeds, and so on, developing greenhouse concepts, herbal plantation, dairy and poultry development, animal husbandry, grading and packaging of agri-products, establishing food processing units, establishing cold storages, sericulture, horticulture, and so on.

Areas of Agri-preneurship

The Fourth Industrial Revolution is revolutionising many industries, including agriculture. Unaware of their actions, young male and female farmers abandon agriculture. Agriculture using the Internet of Things (IoT) can be more sustainable. IoT helps both progressive and small farmers. IoT applications include drones, robotics, precision irrigation, livestock tracking, and crop disease surveillance in agriculture. Agritech uses IoT to track livestock and monitor crop disease. (Jarial, 2022).

Agri Horti entrepreneurship in India

India is a major producer of vegetables such as potatoes, onions, eggplant, and cauliflower. The flavour of its spices, red chilli, and coriander has spread throughout the country. Aside from the aforementioned enterprises, several others have a high potential for growth as agribusinesses, such as fisheries, custom hiring, agri-clinics, etc. In India, the total production of fruits is 99069 thousand M.T. and vegetables 191769 thousand M.T. (NHB, 2022). Entrepreneurs in India can benefit from ongoing government incentive programmes using cooperative root contract farming and the poultry sector. Agricultural development in the agro-industry is essential to increase agriculture's profitability and create more employment opportunities at all stages of production and sales.

Postharvest activities like processing and freezing agricultural products for global distribution make up a large part of the agricultural business. For agro-industries, agricultural output is recognised as a source of economic activity. Food isn't just what grows in the fields; it's a wide range of products made from the crop. Other emerging markets like India rely on agriculture. Our journey from manufacturing to industrial capacity development led us to a comprehensive classification of agriculture. A village industry relies solely on manual labour and minimal automation. Small-scale industries require little capital and equipment, like oil mill management. Large-scale industries like rice mills require a lot of money and automation to run. Since India's independence, agriculture has been its main economic driver.

India is primarily an agricultural country, and its economy is heavily reliant on agricultural products. Massive developments in various industries are being made to change the country's economy. In India, the agricultural input industry has enormous potential. The agricultural input industry consists primarily of industries related to the main agricultural inputs, namely seed, fertiliser, pesticides or agrochemicals, farm machinery, and food processing. To understand the country's agricultural input industry, it is necessary to understand the seed industry, fertiliser industry, pesticide industry, farm machinery industry, and food processing industry. (GOI, 2022a).

An overview of the Indian Seed Industry

Seeds are a fundamental and critical input for long-term growth in farm production, frequently encouraging the use of new methods, machinery, and yield-boosting agro-inputs. India has the world's fifth-largest seed market, valued at approximately US$1,500 million and growing at a rate of 12–13 per cent per year. Private companies place a high value on R&D, investing 5–10% of their revenue in such activities. Private firms integrate these functions, unlike the public sector, where research is separate from seed production and marketing. The private sector has prioritised the development of hybrids/high-yield varieties because they are more valuable and offer higher margins. The private sector accounts for roughly 70% of total commercial seed turnover. Most seed companies began with agrochemicals and diversified into seeds, which have become essential for their portfolios. According to the Department of Agriculture, Cooperation and Farmers Welfare, some 540 private seed firms, both Indian-owned and multinational, operate in the country. Around 80 companies have their R&D programmes. The others produce and market public sector seed and do not produce breeder seed. Most private seed companies produce foundation and certified/truthfully labelled seeds, according to the survey. (Jadhav, 2021).

In 2020, the Indian seed industry was worth $4.9 billion. The commercialisation of agriculture, increasing public-private partnerships, rising consumer income, and developing hybrid seed varieties are some of the drivers driving the Indian seed industry. However, due to the sudden COVID-19 pandemic, several agricultural supply facilities were temporarily shut down. In addition, the lack of migrant labour has also hampered harvesting in India. The Indian seed industry is divided into four types: grain seed, oil seed, vegetable seed, and fruit seed. Currently, grain seeds dominate the market.

The Indian market is divided into Uttar Pradesh, Madhya Pradesh, West Bengal, Rajasthan, Punjab, Maharashtra, Andhra Pradesh, Bihar, and Karnataka. Advanta, DuPont, Kaveri Seeds, Syngenta, and J K Seeds are prominent companies in the Indian seed sector. (IMARC, 2022). The state sector's portion of seed production fell from 42.72 per cent in 2017-18 to 35.54 per cent in 2020-21, while the private sector's share grew from 57.28 per cent to 64.46 per cent during the same period. (Jadhav, 2021). The primary data by the Indian Council of Agriculture Research (ICAR) shows that 53.25 per cent share of the public sector and 46.75 per cent of the private sector is in the total formal system of the seed supply. Most of the varieties multiplied and marketed by the private sector companies are from the public sector. (Jadhav, 2021). Currently, seed export by India is less than Rs 1,000 crore per annum, and the annual global seed trade is $14 billion (Rs 10,460 crore). Therefore, India has the potential to capture a 10 per cent share, which is $1.4 billion or Rs 747 crore, by 2028, as per the FSII data. (Jadhav, 2021).

An overview of the Indian Fertilizer Industry

The Indian fertiliser industry is one of the most important industries in the Indian economy because it produces a critical raw material for agriculture. The fertiliser industry in India has enormous potential in the future. It is critical for the fertiliser industry in India to progress in terms of technologically advanced manufacturing processes and innovative new-age products. In 1906, India's first fertiliser manufacturing unit was established in Ranipat, Chennai. The Indian fertiliser industry has been a critical support system for the Indian agricultural sector. Farmers' increased use of chemical fertilisers was the secret of the nation's so-called green revolution of the late 1960s. The fertiliser industry in India has played a critical role in enabling the necessary increase in the use of plant nutrients to achieve the goals of food grain self-sufficiency and accelerated and continuous agricultural growth.

Indian Pesticide or Agrochemical Industry

Agrochemicals, also known as pesticides, are substances or mixtures of substances used to prevent, eliminate, or control pests or unwanted plants or animals that cause harm to crops or impede the normal growth process. According to a 2002 Government of India estimate, the value of crop losses caused by pesticide non-use was around Rs. 90,000 crore. Assuming losses grew at a 2% annual rate, total losses in 2009 would have totalled Rs. 1,01,355 crore, or 2.2 per cent of India's GDP. In 1952, India's pesticide industry began with the import of BHC. By 1958, India had produced five basic pesticides. However, during the 1990s, there was a greater emphasis on Integrated Pest Management(IPM) and biological control. Pesticide use has not increased further as a result. Consumption of chemical pesticides in India 62193 unit (Unit: Quantity in M.T. tech. grade). (GOI, 2022b)

Currently, 44 technical grade pesticides with 110 formulations are produced. Pesticides are manufactured in India by private and public sector companies or corporations. Pesticides are manufactured in 25 large units and 450 smaller ones. Currently, production stands at 80,000 tonnes, compared to a capacity of 1.07 lakh tonnes. Pesticide consumption per hectare is currently around 328 grams, lower than in advanced countries. USA: 1600 grams/hectare; Japan: 2000 grams/hectare. Until the 1990s, there was a rapid increase in pesticide consumption. (Chole, 2012).

Pesticides are marketed by manufacturers who appoint 69 distributors for each region, either in the cooperative or private sector, and are distributed to farmers through dealers. Dealers can come from the private sector, agricultural service centres, agri-clinics, agribusiness centres, cooperatives, and the Farm Machinery Industry in India. In Indian agriculture, there has been a gradual shift from Draft Animal Power (DAP) to mechanical power because DAP and manual labour were insufficient to meet the workload of intensive agriculture. Mechanical power is becoming increasingly important for making the best use of other resources and completing various operations in intensive farming on time. As a result, mechanisation has become a critical input in agricultural development. Farmers use power-driven equipment such as tractor-drawn mould board ploughs, cultivators, disc harrows, seed drills, and seed drills in most states. Commercially available combines include self-propelled and tractor-driven reaper harvesters and potato and groundnut diggers. Agriculture must diversify. Due to the increasing size of tractors used by farmers, custom renting of farm equipment will become more common, as multi-farm use will be the only method to keep farm equipment running expenses low-agrochemicals' role: Realising a USD 5 trillion economy by 2025 (PWC, 2020).

An overview of the Indian agriculture products industry

India is the world's leading milk producer, contributing 209.6 million tonnes in 2020-2021 and contributing to 23 per cent of global milk production. Livestock management and cattle rearing have always been a part of our daily lives (Invest India, 2022). Farmers can benefit from the breeding of improved breeds and their proper management. The total livestock reared in India is 53.65 crore, and the milk & meat production is around 198.4 & 8.6 million tonnes, respectively. (GOI, 2019). Uttar Pradesh (16.3 per cent, 30.52 MMT), Rajasthan (12.6%, 23.69 MMT), Madhya Pradesh (8.5 per cent, 15.91 MMT), Andhra Pradesh (8 per cent, 15.04 MMT), and Gujarat are the top five milk production states (7.7 per cent, 14.49 MMT). (Invest India, 2022).

The complementary nature of Indian agricultural products creates a wealth of export options for the country's agricultural exports. Unlike Western countries, India is on the verge of revolutionising the food supply chain. Since the country's agricultural output is expected to double in the next ten years. International Dairy Federation's World Daily Situation 2007 claims that China and India would see the greatest increase in dairy consumption in Asia. An estimated 15% of the world's total milk production occurs in India each year, and that percentage will only grow in India in the future. Dairy and animal products account for 7% of the country's total income and 26% of the country's total agricultural activity in India. There is a wide variety of items that can be made from dairy products made by women: milk curds like lassi and paneer; frozen desserts like kulfi; high-fat dairy products such as butter; and sweets like ice cream. Entrepreneurs can build their production facilities or form a cooperative depending on the nature of the created product.

Process food products from India are exported in large quantities. Many semi-processed commodities are exported from the country, but it also sends bulk shipments of tea and coffee that are neither marked nor packaged. The food industry in India used to be tough for many enterprises to penetrate, but this has changed dramatically in the last few years, making it much easier for businesses to establish themselves there. Factors such as a rapidly expanding middle class of more than 50,000,000 dwellings, rising salaries, and expanding technology are important. The average Indian individual spends about 53 per cent of their salary on food. Currently, the country's domestic market for processed goods is valued at roughly 90 billion dollars, increasing at pace with the economy. As a result, processed food producers in India must take a firm position while also customising their products to the needs of the Indian customer, according to experts in the industry.

A few international companies have been in India for a more extended period and have earned a considerable market share in India. These companies include ITC and Nestle. It is possible to learn from these examples and gain a foothold in the upper echelons of the home market, which will allow you to secure some of the export markets. A combination of large-scale investment and the application of cutting-edge technology has been developed as a result of these revelations. Dairy products have become a significant part of the Indian agricultural industry because of aggressive marketing, partnerships with foreign firms, and the creation of a distinctive brand. The country has made remarkable achievements in milk and dairy product processing, suggesting that it has a lot of promise. However, be aware that just 15% of the country's total milk production is processed, a crucial fact to keep in mind. Diabetes and heart disease affects a large section of the Indian population today. In large quantities, sugar-free foods and fat-free dairy products are hard to come by. Increased soy milk production, for example, is needed in the country.

There is a lot of room for growth in the country's shrimp and fish exports. On the other hand, there are no cold storage or modern processing facilities throughout the year. Another area in which India might make money through exports is herbal medicine. A rising number of people realise that herbal products don't cause any harm to the body. Many herbal products have been tried and tested in the country's long history of experimentation, and the country's knowledge and experience in this area are unparalleled. However, there is a lack of strict quality control systems, appropriate packaging, and distinctive brand identity in this field. Nevertheless, positive signs are emerging in India, and modern merchants, are tackling this pressing issue through new packaging and labelling regulations and increased expenditures in the supply chain, among other things. For more than 10,000 years, Indian agriculture has evolved into a modern enterprise with unique qualities.

Beekeeping: Because of the country's diverse flora and fauna, there is a vast potential for honey production and beekeeping. This is such a growing industry that even illiterate and resource-poor men and women can start their own with no need for land. In the last five years, honey production has increased by 32%. Now the total production of honey in India is 1,25,000 Metric Tons. (National Bee Board, 2021).

Food processing industry

While food is an essential economic product, only a few countries thrive in agricultural production. Most agricultural goods require a lot of lands, which only the largest countries have. Four of the world's major food producers—

China, India, the U.S., and Brazil-are also among the ten most significant countries. (Ross, 2021)

The establishment and operation of food processing businesses should be done in an environmentally responsible manner. Raw materials, infrastructure, and skilled labour must support the manufacturing process. Cleaning and hygienic conditions are essential in the food processing business. Assert stringent quality control throughout the entire process, from the collection of raw materials to the finished product. Product shelf life can be extended without any contamination or deterioration throughout this period. Creating food that is safe and healthy, as well as tasty, is an integral part of the process. The things made should be in high demand and give employment and income. The end of the year should be both financially sustainable and socially desirable (Chole, 2012).

An overview of the food processing industry in India

While food is one of the most fundamental economic products, only a handful of countries excel in agricultural production. Most agricultural commodities require a lot of land area, and land area is something only the largest countries have in abundance. Four of the world's dominant food-producing countries-China, India, the U.S., and Brazil-rank in the top ten countries for total geographic land area. Agriculture, horticulture, animal husbandry, and fisheries are part of the food processing industry, a huge industry encompassing a wide range of operations. Additionally, it contains other sectors that use agricultural inputs to produce consumable items. India is second in producing potatoes, onions, cauliflowers, brinjal, cabbages, etc. The country has the most bananas (26.08%), papayas (44.05%) and mangoes (45.89 per cent). (APEDA, 2022)

The massive manufacturing base requires the backing of a strong food processing industry to be successful. Fruits and vegetables processed in India include tomatoes and mangoes prepared for use as juice, cane fruits processed into jam and pickle (as well as frozen fruit), dehydrated freeze-dried veggies (as well as canned mushrooms), and a variety of other products. With a vast number of units, especially at the cottage or home scale and small scale, India's fruit and vegetable processing business is highly decentralised. According to the definition of food processing, segments such as carbonated beverages, mineral water, and alcoholic beverages are included, but they are not included in the investigation. Because of the perishable nature of food, it is a particularly suitable business for small-scale companies. Small companies dominate the bottom part of the food market, supplying unbranded products tailored to specific regional tastes and preferences. Most multinational corporations have restricted themselves to premium Western products such as jam sauces and chocolates, except a few companies like Hindustan Lever Limited; very few have entered the mass market, where growth prospects are the greatest, but risks are also the greatest.

The population of cattle in India is the largest in the world. India's buffalo meat exports remain at $3.17 billion in 2020-21. India sells buffalo meat to 70 countries, including Hong Kong, Vietnam, Malaysia, Egypt, Indonesia, Iraq, Saudi Arabia, the Philippines, and UAE (E.T. Bureau, 2021). When modern slaughter and cold storage facilities are established, buffalo meat has the potential to become a significant source of foreign revenue for the country. Another perspective category within the business is milk and milk products, including infant milk, malted food, condensed milk, and cheese. Infant milk is a particularly promising component within the sector.

The country produces all major grains, including paddy wheat, maise, barley, guar, and ragi. With a 20 per cent market share, India is the world's second-largest rice producer behind China. Basmati rice from India, on the other hand, has always been in high demand on the worldwide market. When it comes to the success or failure of the proposed Indian food market, the Indian middle class will determine the outcome. More ready-to-eat food options are available to this sector, primarily comprised of dual-income, nuclear families with more disposable cash. This area has provided the fuel for the growth of the Indian food processing industry. The most significant impediment to expanding the food processing business, both in terms of investment and exports, is a lack of suitable infrastructure, particularly in a solid and stable cold chain. Even at the current output level, a vital sector such as the food processing industry, which relies primarily on perishable products, will be unable to exist and grow. According to the USDA, approximately 30 to 35 per cent of farm food, mainly fruits and vegetables, is wasted every year due to insufficient storage space, transportation cold chain facilities, and other infrastructural assistance.

Another major small industry that can be easily started is producing various fruits and vegetables preserved items such as potato chips, potato fingers, potato papad, mango and litchi squashes, jam, jelly marmalade, mixed vegetables, and tomato pickles, tomato sauce, ketchup, and so on. India's exports of Processed Food were Rs. 36,946.20 Crores/ 4,987.76 USD Millions in 2020-21. (APEDA, 2021).

An overview of the fish processing industry in India

India ranks third in fish production and the second largest aquaculture country behind China. The Blue Revolution in India proved the sector's relevance. The industry is expected to play a crucial influence in the Indian economy shortly. Inland fisheries have recently emerged as a major contributor to fish output, rising from 36% in the mid-1980s to 70%. Inland fisheries have benefited from a change from capture to culture-based fisheries. (GOI, 2022c)

The fish and fisheries products processing industry mainly focuses on exports, with just a tiny amount of goods coming into domestic markets. With the rise of India's fish and fishery products export industry, there has been a parallel development in the country's fish processing industry. Historically, fish was dried and cured by traditional practices, and it was primarily sold locally during the 1960s and 1970s. On the other hand, fishery processing saw a quick shift as fish began to be sold more widely, first within the country and then to foreign markets. The techniques of freezing and canning were initially used in the early 1960s. From 1960 to 1990, India's fish and fishery products exports increased by 10% per year, or from 1654 metric tonnes (M.T.) to 133653 metric tonnes (M.T.). Traditional exports of Indian fish and fisheries products have taken the country to more than 300 major markets. The European Union, Japan, and the United States account for over 85 per cent of this total, with Japan alone responsible for nearly 45 per cent of this total. Indian exports of fish and fisheries products are dominated by frozen shrimp, which accounts for the total exports.

Status of Indian farm machinery industry

The Indian agricultural machinery market is expected to develop at a cumulative agricultural growth rate (CAGR) of 4.9 per cent (2022-2027). (Mordor, 2022)

Drought animal power has gradually given way to mechanical power in Indian agriculture due to a lack of animal and manual labour capacity to handle the increased workload of intensive farming. Intensive farming requires mechanical power to maximise the use of other resources and complete multiple processes in a timely manner. As a result, mechanisation has become a critical component in agricultural development. Due to a lack of labour, farmers are increasingly turning to farm mechanisation, such as tractor-drawn cultivators, disc harrows, plant protection devices, tractor-operated combines, harvesters, and potato and groundnut diggers.

Individual farmers who cannot afford farm machinery can form cooperatives or groups to pool their resources to buy agricultural equipment. Rural craftspeople, small-scale businesses, the state-owned Agro Industries Corp., and organised tractor power tiller and engine makers all make Indian machinery in India. Organised farm machinery producers create agricultural tractors, Power Tillers and farming tools and implements. More than a million rural communities use bullock-drawn implements and equipment, including steel flow, cultivator partners, sewing devices, cane crushers, and bullock carts. New tools are necessary for agricultural diversification, and farmers' willingness to use them increases. Multi-farm use will be the only way to keep the operating expenses of farm equipment at an acceptable level in the future. Therefore bespoke hiring of farm equipment will be considerably expanded. We should expect to see more and more utilisation of high-performance equipment in the near future if it has been proven helpful in the field recently.

Changes in food processing technology

All food processing techniques must be combined to obtain the desired changes in the raw materials. The majority of these can be grouped as unit activities, each of which has a distinct, detectable, and predictable effect on us and our environment. A process comprises a collection of unit actions that are grouped. The ultimate product's nature is determined by how the procedures are combined and performed in succession. Change has occurred due to industrialisation, urbanisation, and the resulting changes in the people's way of life.

In contrast to previous generations, consumers no longer demand food to have a shelf life of several months at room temperature for the vast majority of their purchases. As family and lifestyle changes occur and an increase in the ownership of freezers and microwaves, there is an increase in the demand for foods that are easy to prepare, ideal for cruises and cold storage, and have a moderate shelf life at room temperature. Many customers are interested in foods that contain fewer synthetic ingredients or have experienced fewer alterations during the production process. These foods are more closely related to their original essential components and have a more positive reputation for being healthy and natural. Natural alternatives to synthetic additives, such as colourants and flavours, have been introduced by producers in response to consumer demand. In addition, manufacturers have created new low-fat, sugar-free, and low-salt product lines in practically all sub-sectors.

As a result of increased investment in capital-intensive automated processes designed to reduce labour and energy costs, a shift in philosophy from quality assurance attained through testing final products to a more sophisticated approach to quality assurance that includes all management aspects has occurred. Several industries have profited because of the widespread raw material availability and ingredients worldwide. However, this has been broadened to encompass other sectors to reduce costs and ensure supply continuity. In the past few decades, several factors have contributed to technological advancements, including significant increases in energy and labour prices due to public pressure and legislation to limit the adverse environmental impact of processing, particularly air or water pollution and energy consumption. Because food processing technology is getting highly advanced in its level of control, processing expenses for the consumer are being reduced. Ensure that it can transition fast between shorter production runs to improve quality and provide better records for management decision-making to reduce costs.

Case studies

A successful case study is a narrative that shows how a specific action, intervention, or process resulted in a positive change in the situation. Texts, video, audio, and even infographics can be used to tell the story. First, however, one that explains how a process resulted in the desired transformation in someone, a community, a business, or a family. (Emmanuel, 2020). A successful case study amuses interest in learning more about procedures, implementing activities, and looking for new opportunities. Such is the power and determination it possesses. Marketers, promoters, funders, and Implementing Partners are all aware of the significance of these narratives. As a result, they develop a successful case study and strategically impact it. Project managers, in particular, help businesses build successful case studies to present the organisation to funders and investors, but there's more to a success story than that.

15 successful agricultural case studies in this article. That will inform the reader about the current state of agriculture and its success story, which must be examined for greater explanation and comprehension.

Agriculture is the practice or science of farming, which includes the cultivation of the soil for crop growth and the keeping of animals for the production of wool, food and other products.

Indian Agriculture's gross domestic product (GDP) plays a crucial role in the country's overall economic and social well-being. Agriculture is a major source of income, employment, and national food security, employing over 59 per cent of the country's workforce. Farmers are included in this sector, as are farm labourers and those employed in agriculture-related industries and services, such as the textile and sugar processing industries. However, agriculture cannot be understood solely as farming in this perspective. Instead, it should be considered a whole agriculture value-chain (AVC) system comprising cultivation, aggregation, processing, and retailing. (Sen, 2021). Agriculture is the country's largest business, and a business can only thrive if it can continually grow. Due to scientific research, inventions, technological developments, and enhanced extension services, India has made remarkable progress in food production, transitioning from a food deficit to a surplus country.

The Ministry of Agriculture and Welfare established several programmes to promote agriculture and related activities. As a result, farmers are guided and inspired to adopt scientific and contemporary agriculture enriched with innovative technologies under the programmes. Modern scientific agriculture, with a changing approach to agricultural technologies and farming techniques, is the need today, as it will assist farmers in increasing their efficiency and judicious use of natural resources to fulfil the world's food, fuel, and fibre needs.

Farmers are informed about research and recommendations from experts and scientists from various fields from State Agricultural Universities. In addition, officers from the Departments of Agriculture, Horticulture, and ATMA contact farmers directly to obtain information about their problems and provide solutions. On the ground, extension employees answer questions and provide solutions constantly. On the ground, extension professionals answer questions and provide solutions to farmers regularly. Farmers now have access to a proper farming environment due to this (MA&FW, 2021).

Below are 15 successful farmer case studies that have inspired millions of other farmers and motivated and boosted their self-confidence, leading to agripreneurship.

1. Protected cultivation and farm mechanization for better income and sustainable livelihood

Smt. Bhavana Nikam is a well-educated woman. She is a forward-thinking farmer. Even though she has a Bachelor's degree, she is not looking for a salaried position. Instead, she has chosen agriculture as a career and has established herself as a known progressive farmer in the area by successfully implementing various agricultural strategies. In 2016, she built a 2000-square-meter polyhouse in her hamlet of Dabhadi. She began cultivating capsicums, grapes, and vegetables. She has a farm pond, a polyhouse, a shade net house, a tractor, and a rotavator, among other agricultural equipment.

Krishi Vigyan Kendra and the State Agriculture Department provided her with training on the Integrated Farming System and related activities on multiple occasions as part of several programmes. With her family's guidance and support, she could develop a model integrated farm via her hard work and dedication. Polyhose, shade net house, mulching, grading, and packaging are some of the newer technology she has implemented on her farm. Her farm became a biodiversity model hub after collecting all the innovative and unusual varieties of vegetables and other crops from the exposure visits. Sharing such seeds and plants with farmers who want to cultivate them attracts visitors and scholars to their farms. The rainwater collection system and water storage ponds are other farm concept that can be replicated. The ponds generate a good income from fish farming, and the water storage helps with irrigation during the dry season. (MA&FW, 2021).

Achievements

- Vegetable production using drip irrigation and polythene mulching
- Grape cultivation
- Farm mechanisation
- Fish farming
- Her land is a showcase for various innovative and modern technology, such as irrigation, spraying, and diverse farming operations.
- Capsicum, tomato, and bean production in a poly house.
- Poultry and fish farming in a farm pond.

Importance for Farmers

Many farmers and youth come to her farm regularly to see how successful she has been, and many have followed in her footsteps. Within the Dabhadi Circle, she became a role model for women farmers. She was honoured during ATMA's Mahila Kisan Diwas ceremony.

Recognition

- 2019- Shivaji Maharaj Krushi Sanman Award
- 2019- Best Woman Farmer Award (Krushiratn Award, Shetinishth Award, Rotary Club Adarsh Mahila Shetakari Award)
- 2021-Innovative Woman Farmer Anman Patra By Hon. Dadaji Bhause, Agriculture Minister)

2. Flourishing Entrepreneur in Unique Activity

Smt. Sarbjit Kaur is a landless woman from a joint family who had been educated until elementary school and lived in the hamlet of Bhagoran in the Saheed Bhagat Singh Nagar (SBS Nagar) and earned is around Rs. 6000/- per month. In the academic year 2014-15, she approached KVK to undertake a vocational training course on value addition. KVK piqued her interest in acquiring new talents and techniques, and she was able to supplement her family's income. In the following years, she will also participate in other training programmes on processing, garment enrichment, food preservation, environmentally friendly cleaning agents, and printing procedures, among other topics. She joined Sukhmani Self-Help Group, a Gramin Bank-registered organisation in the district of SBS Nagar, to participate in inter-lending to meet her family's needs regularly. She started her modest business in her home with the support of a self-help group, investing Rs.

5000/-Smt. Sarbjit Kaur wanted to be a demand-driven entrepreneur. She also wanted to start her business with a product that may generate larger profits. After consulting with KVK specialists and receiving advice, she began her business in 2016-17 by producing an eco-friendly liquid cleaning product (Phenyl) for her family and neighbours. The village's desire for her items grew gradually. Later, she decided to mass-produce various eco-friendly cleaning agents such as hand soap and dish soap, as well as phenyl, and sell them in local communities. Due to the high cost of ready-made cleaning chemicals on the market, they are out of reach of the average villager. She also believed that the products should be sold at a reasonable price so that every household in the community has access to cleansers such as handwash, dishwash and phenyl, among other things.

Regular skill-based short-duration on-campus and off-campus training on the creation of various cleaning agents, such as handwash, dishwash, and phenyl, were organised using a standardised approach and delivered for three years (2014-15, 2015-16 and 2016- 17). Following the standardisation of technology, skills in packaging, labelling, and marketing were also taught. The group also learned about purchasing raw materials, processing, packing, and labelling items, among other things. Under technical specialists' supervision, boxed goods were labelled at the KVK Campus. To encourage the progressive farm women's training and free exhibition booths, the District Agriculture Department has developed agreements with NABARD, SUTS-NGO, and ATMA. Direct and indirect marketing strategies such as door-to-door product sales, sales in neighbouring villages, sales inside villages, exhibits, and online sales were used (WhatsApp, apnimandi, kvk portal etc.). Small bottles of handwash (200ml), dishwash (250ml), and phenyl (1lt) were also packed and sold at affordable prices to direct customers. On a demand basis, bulk packaging was delivered straight to the offices of the dist. SBS Nagar (MA&FW, 2021).

Achievements

- After 2017, she began holding eco-friendly cleaning chemical exhibitions, which brought in a lot of money. With the help of self-help group members and constant family support, she also won various honours.
- She has been selling her wares at Kisan melas hosted in several districts across Punjab for the past three years.
- During 2018-19, she sold handwash kits (n=200) as a member of the Sukhmnai self-help group as part of the project "Reproductive Health" in collaboration with the College of Community Science, Punjab Agricultural University, Ludhiana, to promote healthy hygiene and sanitation practices for rural women on a no-profit, no-loss basis.

Importance for Farmers

- She married at a young age but strongly desired to master skill-based strategies to supplement her income and assist her family. She is beautifully groomed and has motivated other women in their town to start small businesses and succeed. Snawa, Dalutpur, Langroya, Jadla, and Sloah in Punjab's district SBS Nagar, among others, have looked up to her as an inspiration.

Recognition

- On International Women's Day in 2017, 2018, and 2019, she received the 'Mahila Shakti' award from PAMETI, KVK SBS Nagar, and the district's Agriculture Department. She joined "The SBS FPO" organization in May 2019 and began promoting her items through them.

3. Success Story of a progressive Farm Woman and a true leader

Smt. Rohini Subbaiah finished her PUC and decided to work for herself. SHG members work in rice cultivation, coffee production, and pepper production. Farm women also farm their Self-Help Groups to supplement their income. All of her family members backed her up in all of her endeavours. She is now a successful entrepreneur in cattle, honey bees, paddy agriculture, vegetable cultivation, masala powder manufacture, pickles, wine preparation, and fisheries. The Agriculture Department paid a visit to her field and praised her work.

She is an engaged businesswoman and a forward-thinking woman who received mushroom and nursery training from KVK Gonikoppa. She participated in ATMA offline and online training and bamboo cultivation and honey beekeeping training at the College of Forestry in Ponnampet. She taught her groups how to use these training methods. She brought mushroom spawns from KVK Gonikoppa and began small-scale mushroom gardening. She has become an entrepreneur due to her several failures in mushroom farming and has provided training to a variety of other groups.

She cultivated bamboo in her field in addition to mushroom farming, as well as vegetable production for her home needs. In addition, a farm school was held in her field by ATMA staff to encourage other local farmers.

Her husband brought her here for Mahaila Sangha Groups training on value-added products and post-harvest technologies. She sought advice and information from KVK scientists and academics at the Forestry College and the Agriculture Department. She took part in training organised by the ATMA Scheme. KVK and the Horticulture Department provided seeds, and their scientists assisted in adopting technology for the best productivity. She also purchased small mills for generating masala and ragi powders for the group. She raised fish such as common carp, catla, rohu, and grass carp in agricultural ponds and used the bunds to plant trees. She demonstrated the cultivation of novel paddy varieties with great yields. She also participated in a farmer-scientist engagement session to help them learn more (MA&FW, 2021).

Achievements

- She accomplished everything via hard work and the instruction and support of her family members, and she gradually learned how to use tactics. She is the President of the 14-member "Nagra Sri Shakthi" SHG. She encouraged all her organisation members to participate in the ATMA scheme's training, exposure trips, and demonstrations. This group engages in vegetable and mushroom cultivation, as well as the preparation of value-added goods and income generation. She also earns roughly Rs. 8.00 lakhs per year from mushroom farming, masala powder preparation, rice agriculture, and coffee production.

Recognitions

- Smt. Rohini Subbiah has inspired and mobilised over 50 women Self-Help Groups in the Virajpet block to pursue entrepreneurship. She also used integrated farming practices, which means that if one activity fails, the other operations may succeed in earning money and improving socio-economic standing. In 2019, she received the KVK Gonikoppa, Kodagu district's Best Farmer award for her IFS model. In 2015, the College of Forestry gave her the Best Farmer award for her achievement with the IFS concept. In 2015, she was named "Best Progressive Farm Women and Entrepreneur" by UAHS Shimoga.
- The Agriculture Department recognised her efforts and nominated her as a BFAC member under the ATMA and a member of the State Farmer Advisory Committee (SFAC).

Importance for Farmers

- For better returns, she founded a Self-Help-Organization in her hamlet and began marketing mushrooms and value-added goods through the group.

4. Inspiration Success Story of Smt. Iravya Shivanand Mathapati

Smt. Iravva Shivanand Mathapati is a formally educated woman from a poor farming background. She married when she was younger. She and her husband toiled away in a stoney, arid terrain with no irrigation system. She sought assistance from the Department of Agriculture. She recognised the importance of water-saving methods, which she implemented in her barren 10-acre property. She grew fruit trees and cultivated crops. However, due to the dominance of intermediaries, she first suffers a loss in marketing for her produce. Because of this traumatic event, she decided to market her produce independently. She overcame this threat by creating her marketing channels and adding value to her products. As a result, she became one of the most successful Woman Entrepreneurs in a short period, with a financial turnover of more than 45 lakhs.

She owns 10 acres of agricultural property in Ramdurg Taluk's Mudakavi hamlet. With an annual rainfall of 562mm, this region is classified as in the Northern Dry Zone. On her farm, she planted 300 mango trees, 300 sapota trees, 35 Jamun trees, 200 citrus trees, drumstick trees, aonla trees, guava trees, Curry leaf trees, Mahogani trees, Pomegranate trees, and Sandalwood trees. To collect rainwater, trenches were dug between rows of planting. Then, the entire property is irrigated using drip irrigation to efficiently use available water and collect water in a farm pond. In addition, her farm has a biodigester tank, vermicompost pits, biogas plant, power tiller, pickle vehicles, pickle manufacturing equipment, and pickle storage godown.

She has been practising organic farming for 20 years and has never purchased anything from other sources. Every agri-input required for farm operations is generated on her farm in situ, including manure, seeds, Jeevamrut, and compost. On her farm, she has several units such as a biodigester tank, a vermicompost pit, a Gokrupamrut-jal, and a jeevamrut preparation, among others.

Intermediaries take the lion's portion of the profit, which she avoided using direct marketing channels like @mandis, rural hats, and e-marketing.

Exposure to various farm technology through ATMA and exposure tours and knowledge gained through ATMA training inspired and bolstered her confidence to do better. Her success as a Farm Woman Entrepreneur is largely due to departmental support. She is a member of the Belgaum district's ATMA District Level Farmers Advisory Committee (DFAC).

Water collection trench bunding procedures keep runoff water and soil erosion at bay. This strategy assisted her in increasing the output of horticultural crops and improving the fertility of stony and barren soil. Her sensible decision to plant high-input generating fruit crops in millet-growing areas using drip irrigation was wise (MA&FW, 2021).

Achievements

- She grows organic fruits and vegetables and makes value-added products such as pickles, chutneys, and spreads, earning over Rs. 7.00 lakh each year.

Recognitions

- In 2011, she received the Shreshta Krushi Mahila award from the University of Agricultural Sciences in Dharwad.
- In 2018, she was awarded the National Mahila Kisan Award by Door Darshan Chandana and ICAR in New Delhi.

Impotance for Farmers

- Her farm serves as an experimental station for agricultural and related branch students who receive instruction in agriculture, horticulture processing, and value addition from Mrs Iravva Mathapati. Many State Agriculture University students pay a visit to her farm during their state exposure visits. She is teaching organic agricultural practices to farmers in and around Mudakavi and the entire district of Belgaum.

5. Beekeeping- A Sustainable Income Success Story

Smt Hmangaihkimi, 31, owns 5 acres of land and farms alongside his husband, a teacher and a passionate farmer, to support their family. For their family, it has proven to be a very stable source of income. Though they do not rely only on farming and beekeeping for a living, they have stated that their standard of living has improved since they began beekeeping because it provides a reliable source of revenue.

Agricultural Technology Management Agency (ATMA), Siaha District, Mizoram, in collaboration with State Agriculture Management and Extension Training Institute (SAMETI), Aizawl, Mizoram, and National Institute of Agricultural Extension Management (MANAGE), Hyderabad, held a skill-based training programme on 'Beekeeping' in March 2019 that helped her gain knowledge and skills in identifying the Queen in bee boxes, hiving of honey bee colonies, division and uniting (MA&FW, 2021).

Acheivements

- Based on the knowledge she obtained during the training, she made the following changes to her traditional beekeeping practises:

- Replaced some of her traditional bee boxes with contemporary bee boxes when she discovered that modern bee boxes produce more honey.
- She inserted a stick/other material in her typical bee box to allow the bees to build their hives more readily, simply, and economically.
- She inspects her farm more frequently to look for intruders/pesticides, which is the first and most important step in any infestation.
- She can adequately care for queens, but previously, she, like many other kids, was unable to locate the Queen. She can now not only split colonies to avoid swarming, but she also understands the importance of time and concepts like colony strength. She made a monthly net income of Rs 28,000/- by implementing creative methods.

Importance for Farmers

- As a result of her progress, three community members began large-scale beekeeping. Still, due to delayed rainfall, there was a report of wildfire, which also affected their farm, forcing them to continue on a smaller scale. She has also inspired and motivated other farmers to use scientific rather than traditional beekeeping procedures and management.

6. Enhancing Farm Income Through Integrated Farming System Approach- A Case study of Kullu Valley

Smt. Veena Bharti, a successful women Agri-entrepreneur and a sedulous and creative farmer who is constantly eager to adopt new ideas and technology, is 52 years old and matriculated. Initially, she used traditional methods to grow only wheat, maize, and local pulses. Still, with the help of KVK and other agencies (agriculture, horticulture, and animal husbandry), she could incorporate all of the major components of Integrated Farming Systems for diversified agriculture and increase her farm income. She is currently the Gram Panchayat's Pradhan and a role model for other agribusiness women in the district who use the Integrated Farming System. She has 2.80 hectares of property, with 1.3 hectares dedicated to fruit crops and the remaining 1.5 hectares to vegetables. With the help of the state agricultural department, around half of the land is rainfed. At the same time, the rest is irrigated by perennial streams and nallah using a portable sprinkler system. With the help of the state agricultural department, a vermicompost unit of 4-5 vermi-pits has been built. Around 40 quintals of manure are produced yearly and utilised to cultivate various crops. She has purchased farm implements/machinery such as a power sprayer, foot sprayer, power weeder, grass cutter, and a power chain to reduce drudgery and boost efficiency in agricultural operations. She also runs a small dairy farm with two milking cows. She also has a small mushroom farm to supplement her income from this business.

She is a passionate farmer interested in agricultural awareness camps hosted by KVK and other organisations. She is a regular visitor and trainee at KVK Kullu, where she has received advanced instruction in vegetable growing, horticulture, vermicomposting, water management, post-harvest and value addition, and other topics. Her fervour, commitment, and frequent personal connection with KVK experts have propelled her to the forefront of progressive and innovative farming (MA&FW, 2021).

Acheivements

- Smt. Bharti organises the marketing of her produce in such a way that she makes the most money with the least amount of effort. She offers contract fruit crops such as plum and pear, apple, persimmon, and peach, among other fruits and vegetables, at wholesale fruit and vegetable market yards (Sabji mandis). She gathers information about the rates in other mandis before taking the produce to the market to receive the best price. She sells the mushrooms to local vegetable sellers as well as directly to clients. Customers call her if they require large quantities of mushrooms for parties, weddings, or other events. As a result, she reaps the advantages of her hard work efficiently, earning a commendable profit of around seven lakh annually from all agricultural operations.

Importance for Farmers

- Smt. Veena Bharti is an encouragement to other women who work in agriculture. She is always willing to lend a hand and provide assistance. She also urges farm women in the nearby villages to embrace new and innovative farming methods with the support of KVK scientists and other specialists.

Recognitions

- CSKHPKV's Krishi Doot Samman (2003)
- CSK HPKV, Palampur, 2013 State Level "Innovative Farmer" Award
- Department of Agriculture Best Farmer Award 2016
- Member of Scientific Advisory Committee, KVK Kullu (2015-2018)
- CSKHPKV, Palampur, member of the Extension Council (2003-05)

7. Diversified Farming- Nursery unit and Vegetable Farming

Smt. Sunita Kumari had a modest existence before turning to farming as a source of income. Her spouse made a modest living by renting a cycle repair shop for Rs. 3000 each month. However, her husband suffered a significant health problem in 2007, forcing him to stop working as a cycle mechanic. As a result, Sunita Kumari was forced to work as unskilled labour in her village to support her family. Still, her wages were insufficient to cover her family's and children's necessities. As a result, she chose farming as a vocation to survive.

Smt. Sunita, a modest female farmer, has only 2.0 hectares of land. The majority of the land in the village was watered once the lift irrigation project was installed, and she began cereal cultivation. Despite the difficulties, she continued to farm, and in 2008-09 she leased an additional 3.0 hectare of property in her hamlet. She began cultivating vegetables in addition to grains, and due to the larger yields from vegetables, she acquired confidence. As a result, she concentrated on vegetable production. She also has two Jersey cows, which she uses to meet her farm's Farm Yard Manures and supplement her income through milk sales.

Smt. Sunita met KVK Mandi in 2009-10 when she faced difficulties and wanted to talk about her choices in agriculture. KVK specialists inspired her little land holding to undertake vegetable cultivation as a source of revenue. Experts from KVK urged her to develop and raise vegetable crops in an organized manner to maximise profits. She received vocational training at KVK, Mandi, and UHF Nauni, Solan, in scientific nursery rearing of vegetable crops, their production, and protection technologies. She was also associated with the Department of Agriculture's ATMA programme. She was recruited as a women SHG leader in 2010 for agricultural diversification through producing vegetables as cash crops.

From 2009-to 10, KVK Mandi did numerous FLDs, OFTs, and method demonstrations on various vegetable crops, which boosted her confidence and inspired other women farmers in the area. She also received vocational training in high-yielding and high-quality vegetable seeds, fertilisers, disease and pest management strategies, and other necessary knowledge for a sustainable life. She began cultivating enhanced hybrids in 2010 after learning about the performance of FLDs and OFTs, and her yields have been steadily increasing since then. In Rabi season, she grew cauliflower, broccoli, radish, spinach, peas, turnip, and potato; in Kharif season, she grew cucumber, bottle gourd, bitter gourd, and summer squash, as well as French bean, capsicum, and tomatoes. KVK also encouraged her to cultivate seedlings for sale to neighbouring farmers and the surrounding area to supplement her income. She subsequently began producing onion, cole crops, and solanaceous vegetables in scientific nurseries, as well as poly tube nurseries of cucumber, bottle gourd, bitter gourd, and summer squash, among other things, early in the season. Ms Sunita regularly keeps in touch with KVK, and scientists visit her vegetable farm/nursery unit for technical support (MA&FW, 2021).

Acheivements

- Smt. Sunita is a hardworking woman farmer who can quickly comprehend and integrate new technology. She is actively involved in the farm's day-to-day operations and marketing. She continues to employ new and sustainable farm practices that have resulted in increased returns, and she has devised a model of sustainable vegetable farming that small farmers can replicate. She makes a net profit of Rs. 50,000/- from selling vegetable seedlings from a 500 m2 vegetable nursery operation. She makes Rs. 2.30 lakh yearly from the sale of fresh seasonal vegetables grown on her modest farm. Sunita used to sell vegetables in her village before. Vegetable sellers from the surrounding areas now come to her fields to buy her produce. She also manages and supervises two Vegetable Self-Help Groups in her community. KVK, the Department of Agriculture, and ATMA give technical and financial assistance to improve yield. Family members also contributed to the success of the complete operational task, from sowing to selling.

Importance for Farmers

- Small landowners may adopt these vegetable farming innovations. She has inspired two Self Help Groups (each with 40 women) and other women farmers from nearby villages (Jaral, Ghanjal, Chhathar, and Sayanah) to start vegetable gardening and nursery production as a business to supplement their family's income. Farmers are inspired to adopt her success strategy after visiting her farm. Her vegetable farming and nursery unit concept have not only supplied employment to all family members throughout the year but have also ensured the family's food and nutritional stability. She is wholly delighted with her business because she now has more social acceptance and can produce a consistent income. She is currently a successful entrepreneur who serves as an inspiration to other women farmers in the area and neighbouring villages. She attributes her accomplishment to the KVK's ongoing technical assistance.

Recognition

- Her women's self-help group got the Department of Agriculture's Best Farmer Group Award and a Rs 20000/- incentive under the ATMA for accomplishing an outstanding job in vegetable production.

8. Empowering Women Through Natural Farming

Smt. Leena Sharma is from a modest household. However, she is well-educated and supports and cares for her family's wants and requirements. Her family consists of four members. Her husband works as a science teacher at a nearby village school. Leena Sharma had little interest in farming before joining Natural Farming, and as a postgraduate, she planned to work in education.

She has a total of five bighas of rain-fed land. She is the proud owner of a desi Pahari cow. She cultivates her fields by paying fees and does not have any of his machines. Instead, she's organised a group of 20 female farmers. In this hamlet, all of the women farmers labour together and have covered an area of 80 bighas with Natural Farming. Over a hundred farmers have likewise adopted natural farming in her immediate vicinity.

She received a six-day Natural Farming course from Padam Shree in 2018 on behalf of the Agriculture Technology Management Agency (ATMA) District Mandi Himachal Pradesh. Shubhash Palekar lives in Shimla's Kufri District. She was blown away by his lectures and planned to implement ecological farming in her fields. Her husband backed him up in his decision to develop a natural agricultural system. She chose natural farming in her lands after receiving Natural Farming training. After that, she prepared jivamrit, ghanjivamrit, beejamarit khatti lassi, agniastra, and other natural agricultural components in her sansadhan bhandar and employed them regularly in her fields, with excellent results in the first year. After seeing the results, the ladies in the community learned her method and utilised it in their fields, eventually adopting her farming practice (MA&FW, 2021).

Achievement

- In the rabi season, she grows peas, garlic, coriander, fenugreek, and French beans, while in the Kharif season, she grows maize, mash, soybean, til, and kodra, and bhindi. Their production cost has decreased significantly due to this farming, and good quality products have also been achieved as a result of the sound output. In her fields, she also grows these crops' seeds, which she then distributes to other farmers in the village for cultivation.

Recognitions

- On the occasion of Independence Day, she was honoured by SDM and MLA Karsog for her outstanding work in natural farming, as recommended by the Agriculture Department. In June of this year, the Honorable Vice-President of NITI Aayog shared her personal experience with fellow farmers.

Importance for Farmers

- She inspired other farmers in the village to begin using this approach of Natural Farming in their fields, and people from the surrounding villages flocked to him to learn about it. She also teaches natural farming to youngsters in schools and NSS camps and provides training in this area to farmers in her Block's several panchayats. Farmers from different districts flock to her farms to see what she offers. Leena Sharma was the only woman farmer from India to participate in an international webinar on the influence of agricultural activities on the environment and economic cooperation, including the usage of energy, water, and food.

9. Mixed Farming with Coconuts for Livelihood Support

Smt. Linishawas, a progressive farmer who has made a name for herself in agriculture, was first uninterested in agriculture. She was initially interested in fashion design, but after receiving support, confidence, and encouragement from a Facebook Agriculture group in which she was an active member, she decided to pursue farming. She began producing vegetable bag cultivation with around 50 bags and now has over 300 bags with vegetables such as cabbage, cauliflower, carrot, beetroot, annual moringa, capsicum, brinjal, amaranth, chilli, tomato, okra, kasturi turmeric, and others. In addition to tapioca, elephant foot yam, banana, and dragon fruit as intercrops under coconut, she raises rabbits, fowl, and other animals on her farm.

In December 2020, she participated in a week-long training programme on 'Nursery Management' as part of the Skill Training of Rural Youth (STRY) programme. Krishi Vigyan Kendra, Indian Institute of Spices Research (ICAR), Kozhikode, organised the programme for rural youth with the help of ATMA, Kozhikode and MANAGE Hyderabad. She used the knowledge and skills she gained throughout the programme to boost her farm revenue and establish herself as a role model farmer and entrepreneur for others to follow (MA&FW, 2021).

Achievements

- As a secondary enterprise, she practises coconut-based mixed cropping with vegetables, fruits, cattle, poultry, rabbit raising, and ornamental fish culture. She also cultivates and propagates a variety of indoor and ornamental plants. In addition, she keeps about 100 layer chicks, rabbits, and ornamental fishes at her house as a side business.

Importance for Farmers

- She sells vegetable seeds to local farmers and organically grown veggies from her garden. She also provides quality desi girls to those in need. Her farm attracts many school children and enthusiastic farmers, and she is keen to educate and motivate them in various farming approaches. She owns a cake production unit with an FSSAI licence and supplies value-added cakes made with eggs from her farm, assuring healthy and affordable cakes for the poor.

Recognition

- Through a Facebook group, I received an award from Principal Krishi Officer for the finest kitchen garden (grow bag cultivation) (2019).
- The State Agriculture Minister presented me with an award for best coconut-based intercropping through a Facebook group (2019).
- Recognized by a local school for several agricultural endeavours (2020).

10. Innovative Seed Grower & Producer of Certified and Foundation seed

Ms Monika Pandurang Sharma, a 46-year-old farmer from Maharashtra's Jalna district, has been with KVK, Jalna-I, for the past seven years. She came from a farming family and was educated up to the ninth grade. She participated in various KVK activities, including training, seminars, and exhibitions. Mr Pandurang Sharma, her spouse, is also a full-time farmer. She is the owner of 5.20 hectares of arable land. However, in a joint family of nine members, the total land is 20 ha.

She has also established an SHG called "Shivkrupa Mahila Bachat Gat", through which she creates natural Holi colours, flax seed products, and other processed items creatively to generate more income for her SHG's other women. Ms Monika Sharma is a firm believer in sustainable agriculture, conservation of natural resources, and organic farming. She keeps a total of 41 animals, including six bullocks, 35 Desi cows, and one Pandharpuri buffalo. For sustainable soil health management, she has embraced new methods such as composting, green manuring using sun hemp, pulse intercropping, and so on. She has also used IPM approaches in pigeon pea and chickpea to reduce cultivation costs, such as using bird perches, NSKE, pheromone traps, trap crops, etc. In addition, she uses and maintains innovative tools, machinery and equipment, such as a rotavator, tractor, rippers, BBF sowing machine, and others, to improve agricultural operations while lowering costs of farm expenditures.

In KVK, she received instruction in seed production, natural colour preparation, processing, and value addition of pulses, fruits, and vegetables. Farmers in the district have praised her efforts and successes. Moreover, through her interactions, motivational presentations, and involvement in exhibitions, she has inspired many women. She has also completed ASCI skill training at KVK, Jalna-I (MA&FW, 2021).

Achievements

- Through her SHG, she has created and promoted eco-holi colours, soya products like Soya Dal and Soya Flour, flax seed mouth freshener (Mukhwas), Niger chatni, and other products. She earns around 30% more money than other farmers by producing more than 100 q certified and foundation seed, 3-5 q natural colours, and 2-3 q soya goods each year. Her inventive nature has also resulted in a 50 per cent reduction in production costs.

Importance for Farmers

Under KVK's supervision, she gathered and marketed more than 10 tonnes of watermelons by door-to-door marketing during the lockdown period, avoiding losses due to the lockout and fetching better prices.

Recognitions

- She is a pioneering seed farmer and producer of certified foundation seeds for oilseeds and pulses such as soybean, pigeon pea, chickpea, green gramme, black gramme, and others. At KVK, she produces and supplies seeds to the seed hub for pulses. With the support of KVK, she uses all of the most recent crop varieties.

11. Income generation through Pulse Processing and Other Allied Activities.

In the Maharashtra state, the Latur district is famed for its pulses and Tur dal. Most farmers in the region sell their crops as raw grains at a low price with no added value. Though pulses are grown on a big scale in the Latur district, most dal mills are located in the district's MIDC area.

During the 2014-15 school year, Smt. Jayashree Kolate Patil participated in a vocational cum skill development training given by KVK. At KVK, pulse-growing farm women, SHGs, and rural adolescents received a seven-day business model training (MA&FW, 2021).

Achievements

- Under the direction of Krishi Vigyan Kendra, she built her tiny dal mill unit in April 2015, along with additional interventions such as a vermin-compost production unit, chicken unit, and nutritional garden, raising her social, economic status and net profits to 7 to 8 lakhs per year. She made a net profit of almost Rs. 3.00 lakh from the sale of farm crops. Her net profit from the mini dal mill was Rs.3.24 lakh, and she devised her marketing methods by creating the "Single Horse" brand. Other businesses include backyard poultry for 0.60 lakh and produced vermicompost for her own land and vermiculture for 0.05 lakh each year. The veggies from the edible garden are consumed mainly by the family, with the remaining Rs 0.20 lakh being sold.

Importance for Farmers

- Mrs Jayashree Kolate Patil's dal processing business became a successful example for the Latur district's farming community. Several groups and individual farmers came to these units to start their businesses. She also serves as a master trainer for KVK in pulse processing and vocational training. Farmers' market value of red gramme and Bengal gramme has increased as a result of this activity, while commercial purchasing of dal at retail rates has declined in this area. Because the sale of produced dal is increasing daily, she opened a selling counter at the Agricultural Produce Market Committee in Latur to expand the sale of produced dal. Mrs Jayashree employs herself and four other family members who labour in the field and establish businesses such as a dal mill and a poultry unit throughout the year.

Recognition

- KVK, Latur, has acknowledged her on several platforms and has hired her as a master teacher in their training programme.

12. The Nutritional Garden- A Long-Term Model for Food and Nutritional Security

Smt. Anjali Waman, a 44-year-old graduate farmer from Pune's Junnar taluka, hails from Kalwadi village. She has a 5-acre plot of land where she grows papaya and bananas. Most farmers in the tehsils of Junnar and Ambegaon are small and marginal farmers who use a monocropping technique. As a result, they rely on a weekly bazaar outside of villages for their family's vegetable needs. Their diet is less diverse because fruits and vegetables are not readily available regularly. Following the assistance of KVK, Mrs Anjali Waman created a 200 sq.m backyard nutrition garden for easy availability of veggies to the locals.

KVK Narayangaon, Pune II, took the lead in organising a farmer's seminar on nutrition gardens and demonstrating how to prepare them. As a result, 150 Aganwadi sevikas were trained to administer nutrition gardens in their respective areas. KVK created a Nutrition Garden seed kit containing 25 species of vegetables and four types of fruit seedlings after training in 2019-20 as part of a project financed by UNICEF, MS Swaminathan Research Foundation, Chennai, and ATARI Pune's "NARI Project." In total, 670 households in six villages were trained, with 250 families receiving inputs from the NARI project and 190 families receiving inputs from other initiatives. At the KVK Farm, a model of a nutrition garden was created, and women farmers were given tours of the garden. As a result, she was the one who received organic farming training and began growing organic veggies. The arrangement is based on the area available in the village's backyard for a Nutritional Garden. At KVK Farm (200 sq.m.), KVK created its own eight-petal circle model, with 25 types of vegetables cultivated in 100 sq.m. and NADEP, Vermicompost, poultry, and goat raising in 100 sq.m. (MA&FW, 2021).

Achievements

She began selling veggies after meeting the needs of her own family by making weekly baskets and delivering them to nearby city locations. It provided her with additional income. She has enlarged the area for the nutrition garden in response to increased demand.

Importance for Farmers

The success of Kalwadi village has inspired other villages to adopt the nutrition garden concept. She organised 100 women in her village into SHGs and encouraged them to develop their own Nutrition Gardens. As a result, organic Nutrition Gardens was founded by over 100 farm women.

Recognition

- Her efforts have been honoured by KVK Pune on many platforms throughout the district, and she has been presented as a role model to other farmers, particularly women farmers.

13. A Journey of Prosperity Through Value Addition

The head of Kangra's 'Gayatri Self Help Group,' Smt. Shikha Chaudhary is a one-of-a-kind example of an agri-entrepreneur farm woman. She used to prepare processed food products only for domestic consumption and share numerous farm chores. Almost every housewife prepares traditional processed products like pickles, seera, barian, etc., for the household during lean periods due to a lack of off-farm job possibilities in the district. Smt. Shikha Chaudhary has established herself as a successful agri-entrepreneur by focusing on the tremendous market potential of value-added products. Her family owns a ten-kanal plot of land where they grow wheat, paddy, and vegetables. Smt. Chaudhary additionally increased the family's earnings by growing button and oyster mushrooms.

During the year 2016, she took part in a vocational training programme run by the KVK. She learned about various areas of scientific processing and the marketing of value-added food items throughout this course. The plan was designed and conceptualised using a participatory approach (intervention of technologies/ techniques in processing through method demonstrations, training, exhibitions, and exposure visits), skill-oriented income-generating training courses on fruit, vegetable, cereal/grain processing and value addition were organised for the group, and regular guidance and support for technological backstopping for establishment were provided. The group also learned about purchasing raw materials, finding equipment, packing and labelling products, etc. For training sponsorship, links were formed with the Agriculture Technology Management Agency (ATMA) and the Japan International Cooperation Agency for Technical Cooperation (JICA). Panchayat Raj Institutions, likewise, prepared for training places. Soon after, the pioneer lady gained experience and led the group to start a business (MA&FW, 2021).

Achievements

- The group made dried mango powder, fortified nuggets and vermicelli, Triphala powder (a combination of harad, bahera, and aonla powder), Seera (a local product made from wheat grains), Sepubadi (nuggets made from black gramme lentil), Dalia, and pickles made from local and underutilised fruits, vegetables, and mushrooms. They incorporated papaya pulp into the nugget batter to value these items. Similarly, dried spinach powder/pulp and beetroot powder/pulp were added to the vermicelli, which improved the colour as well as the nutritional value of the products. The group's output was limited to only five quintals in 2017-18, but it increased to 12 quintals in 2019-2020, and it now earns a net profit of Rs1 38,700/-. They've acquired much traction in her job that she's now cultivating and marketing oyster mushrooms and providing value to agricultural produce. The concept of door-to-door selling techniques was taught to the aspiring entrepreneur for them to generate commission-based revenue. In addition, authorization from the District Collector of Dharamsala has requested to market the products through an outlet at the DC office.

Importance for Farmers

- Inspired by this entrepreneur's accomplishments, additional SHGs from neighbouring towns have expressed interest in adopting these activities.
- Shikha recruited other unemployed kids as helpers, service providers, and intermediaries in addition to running her own business.

Recognition

- Won prizes for value-added products shown at several Kisan Melas during Kissan Samman Samaroh for outstanding performance in the processing sector.

14. Entrepreneurship Development Through Sorghum value-added products

Sorghum is Maharashtra's principal crop, farmed on about 4.3 lakh ha in the Solapur district. However, it fetches a low market price due to excess arrival and minimal value addition. It has a nutritional value of 12.96 per cent, is an excellent energy source without gluten, has a high availability of minerals and vitamins, is the best food for diabetics, and lowers cholesterol and blood sugar levels. Sorghum is a nutrient-dense cereal that contributes to a balanced diet. However, sorghum is used in only one traditional product (Roti). Schoolchildren also avoid Sorghum Roti. As a result, KVK chose to raise awareness about new technologies by promoting value-added sorghum products created by ICAR-IIMR, Hyderabad, and MPKV, Rahuri. It is a tradition in the Solapur district for farmers to invite their friends and family to their farm to eat hurdle when the sorghum grain is in its green state. Green corns are roasted in a tiny pit dug after grain filling, filled with cow dung, and then threshed by expert labour after roasting. Shenga chatani is served with separated roasted grains. Solapur KVK-I've taken the lead in popularising the Hurda variety produced by MPKV, Rahuri, among farmers. Hurda requires 30 to 40 days less time than regular sorghum.

Sorghum is a crop that is almost universally grown, so there is room for processing because it is so widely available. Therefore, one of the main areas of attention was sorghum processing. Jowar Kadak Roti is one of the processed items. It can be used to make Roti, Cake, Biscuits, and Hurda (Roasted Green Grains). KVK has attempted to improve farm women's skills in preparing the above-mentioned processed products (MA&FW, 2021).

Achievements

- KVK has held nine vocational trainings on sorghum processing, which benefitted 230 farm women/SHG women, 12 Mahila Ghoshti, 1728 farm women, and 14 lectures, 1240 farm women. In addition, 22 women entrepreneurs participated in 16 separate sorghum product displays held on various platforms, benefiting a total of 45155 visitors. With 68 women entrepreneurs, exposure tours were planned at ICAR-IIMR in Hyderabad and other sorghum processing operations. The preparation of value-added sorghum products has expanded in the area due to KVK's continual technical backstopping and advisory. KVK Solapur has registered the Shabari Fresh trademark for sorghum rawa, sorghum cake, and sorghum biscuits. KVK Solapur's sorghum goods were also FSSAI-registered, and sorghum processing women entrepreneurs were helped. Serving Hurda in Agro Tourism Centers has become the district's main point of attraction in the past ten years, thanks to KVK Solapur's promotion. Farmers' fields were also used to demonstrate the variety Phule Madhura, which was explicitly designed for Hurda. To encourage business in the district, 219 farmers were given 450 kg of Phule Madhura seed. The Hurda producers have been linked to 7 Agro Tourism Centers and ten merchants through the KVK.

Importance for Farmers

Ex-KVK trainees started 42 processing units due to the impact of vocational trainings. They make sorghum cake, biscuits, rawa, sahi laddu, and chakali for a monthly net income of Rs 7000 to Rs 10000 per unit. The technology has reached 102 villages, benefiting almost 42000 families in the district. After 110-130 days, farmers usually receive the lowest payment of Rs. 25-30 per kilogramme from sorghum. Hurda, on the other hand, is ready to harvest 85-90 days after planting and can be sold the same day. That is, it is a business that focuses on producing money in a short period. As a result, farmers choose to grow Hurda types alongside grain varieties. Currently, 20 young farmers are selling their Hurda for Rs 210 per kg to various agro-tourism centres, malls, and merchants. Hurda pays farmers seven times more in 90 days than normal sorghum, which sells for Rs. 30 per kg in 120 days. This type covers an average of 0.10 hectares. On average, rural youth made a net profit of Rs 20500 per hectare or Rs 205000 per hectare. Due to rising health consciousness and the popularity of processed foods, sorghum has a low price and a significant market.

15. A case study of Belmati Women Cooperation of Tehri Garhwal

Uttarakhand Gramya Vikas Samiti (UGVS) registered Belmati Women Cooperative in village Kathud Gaja, block Chamba, Tehri Garhwal, Uttarakhand, to improve the socio-economic situation of rural women. On June 15, 2015, the Cooperative was founded to provide small loans to farm women to obtain agriculture inputs and livestock to continue their livelihood. In 2015, 45 women's organisations with 478 members were founded in the Tehri district to sell their agricultural produce at rates set by the women's organisations in the UGVS rural hart. Initially, the government-aided women by providing a monetary benefit of Rs. 3600 per woman for the purchase of seeds, manures, and fertilisers. Mushroom cultivation, food processing, poultry, and dairy processing received an additional fund of Rs. 3600/- for livelihood and income-generating activities. Aside from that, the Cooperative set aside Rs. 10 lakh as a Cash Credit Limit (CCL) in the bank, allowing economically disadvantaged women to borrow money at a reduced interest rate (1 per cent). The government aimed to reduce migration rates while preserving the district's nutritious traditional crops (Barah Anaz-Koda, Jhangora, Ogal, Lobia, Chaulai, Bhatt, Rajmah, Urad, Naurangi, Tor, Til, and Gahat). However, agriculture offers marginal and low returns due to the mountainous terrain. The women of the cooperative group have a total of 150 hectares of land, animals (Buffalo 386, Cow 55, Goat 1550), farm machinery (Power Tiller 18), processing machinery (Dry-Wet Pulverizer-1, Vacuum Packaging Machine-1, Packaging and Labeling Machine-1, Sealing Machine-1, Grinder-3), and other resources.

Previously, the women in this category lacked technical knowledge in food production, processing, and value addition. Their products were organically cultivated, yet they sold them at a low wholesale price in the rural hart, which was created as a cooperative. These organisations met with KVK, Tehri Garhwal, in 2017. The KVK scientists taught the participants how to process the products and add value to them. In 2018, the cooperative brand name "Hilans" was formed with the support of the Uttarakhand government. They received training from KVK on how to grade, sort, and package their organically cultivated pulses and cereals. Milling and vacuum packing machines were installed at their cooperative centres in 2018, thanks to financial support from the International Fund for Agriculture Development (IFAD).

The methods for developing healthy foods from native small millets were passed on to cooperative organisations; following the successful sale of these products, the government-funded Hilans to open a block-level outlet to promote their wares. These women's clubs are committed to working and earning a modest living. Regularly, technical support was provided with the material collection, grading, sorting, and preparation of value-added products, iron-rich laddoos, and amaranthus laddoos. KVK supported them in setting up of minimal processing plant in their cooperative centres. KVK assisted them in establishing a small-scale processing factory in their cooperative centres. KVK assisted them in establishing marketing connections to sell their products. Under the Kishori Shakti Yojna Scheme, the Ministry of Women Empowerment and Child Development consented to purchase their iron-rich Laddoos produced from soybean, finger millets, and barn millets to cure anaemia among adolescent girls in the district. This Belmati Cooperative was tied to both government and private players via KVK. The government also provided rural outlets for these cooperatives to sell their produce at the nine-block level (MA&FW, 2021).

Achievements

- Their business abilities improved their self-esteem, self-respect, and family respect, as well as their independence. Individually, they got an income of around Rs. 10,000/- each month, allowing them to raise the standard of living of their families and provide their children with a better education.

Importance for Farmers

- The Belmati Women's Cooperative has served as an example to other women in the surrounding areas.
- Other women in the district were inspired to join the cooperative to sell and learn processing skills.
- Due to the effectiveness of these groups, the total number of women groups has expanded to 65 from 19 adjacent communities in 2020. These 65 women's organisations presently number 607 women who operate in the Belmati cooperative.

Recognitions

- Mrs Sangeeta Aswal (Head of Belmati) was recognized at the district level by the Hon'ble MLA for her Cooperative's efforts.
- During National Nutrition Day, Hon'ble CDO thanked Mrs Sangeeta Aswal (Head of Belmati) for actively participating in the anaemia campaign.

Conclusion

Successful agricultural stories and agri-partnerships have provided insights into how farmers adopted a specific technique or solution and how it impacted their farming/agripreneur enterprises. Hopefully, these success stories will provide other farmers with valuable visions of the farming process that they may use to improve their farming/agripreneur business.

References

APEDA. (2021). *Annual Report, APEDA*. https://apeda.gov.in/apedawebsite/about_apeda/About_apeda.htm

APEDA. (2022). *Fresh Fruits and Vegetables*. https://apeda.gov.in/apedawebsite/six_head_product/FFV.htm

Chole, R.R., Kapse, P.S., and Deshmukh. (2012). Entrepreneurship development and Business Communication Skills. Scientific Publishers.

E.T. Bureau. (2021). India allays buffalo meat export concerns, says meat is safe. *The Economic Times*. https://economictimes.indiatimes.com/news/economy/foreign-trade/india-allays-buffalo-meat-export-concerns-says-meat-is-safe/articleshow/82797205.cms

Emmanuel, J. (2020). *Meaning of a Success story-The definitive guide*. Retrieved June 9, 2022, from https://livingwordmission.org.ng/success-story/

GOI. (2019). *20th Livestock Census | Department of Animal Husbandry & Dairying*. https://dahd.nic.in/division/provisional-key-results-20th-livestock-census

GOI. (2022a). *Annual Report Department of Chemicals & Petro-Chemicals, MoC&F, GoI*. https://chemicals.nic.in/document-report/annual-report

GOI. (2022b). *Directorate of Plant Protection, Quarantine & Storage*. http://ppqs.gov.in/

GOI. (2022c). *Inland Fisheries, Department of Fisheries*. https://www.dof.gov.in/inland-fisheries

IMARC. (2022). *Seed Industry in India | Share, Size, Growth, Trends and Forecast 2021-2026*. https://www.imarcgroup.com/seed-industry-in-india

Invest India. (2022). *Dairy Industry In India - Growth, FDI, Companies, Exports*. https://www.investindia.gov.in/sector/food-processing/dairy

Jadhav, R. (2021). *Private sector's share in India's seed industry expands to 65 per cent - The Hindu BusinessLine*. https://www.thehindubusinessline.com/data-stories/data-focus/private-sectors-share-in-indias-seed-industry-expands-to-65-per-cent/article35101260.ece

Jarial, S. (2022). Internet of Things application in Indian agriculture, challenges and effect on the extension advisory services – a review. Journal of Agribusiness in

Developing and Emerging Economies, Vol. ahead-of-print No. ahead-of-print. https://doi.org/10.1108/JADEE-05-2021-0121

MANAGE. (2013). *Agri-business and Entrepreneurship Development.* https://www.manage.gov.in/moocs/structure.asp

Ministry of Agriculture & Farmers Welfare, (2021). Success stories of Progressive Women Farmers and Agripreneurs. Retrieved June 10, 2022, from https://agricoop.nic.in/sites/default/files/Success%20Story%20For%20approval.pdf

Mordor, I. (2022). *India Agricultural Machinery Market 2022 - 27.* https://www.mordorintelligence.com/industry-reports/india-agricultural-machinery-market

National Bee Board. (2021). *National Bee Board.* https://nbb.gov.in/aboutus.htm

NHB. (2022). *National Horticulture Board.* http://nhb.gov.in/

PWC, F. (2020). *The role of agrochemical: Achieving the vision of a USD 5 trillion economy by 2025.* https://ficci.in/spdocument/23379/Knowledge-Report-Agrochemicals-Conference-20.pdf

Ross, S. (2021). *4 Countries That Produce the Most Food Worldwide.* https://www.investopedia.com/articles/investing/100615/4-countries-produce-most-food.asp#citation-16

Sen, S. M. (2021). *Why we must listen to farmers. Idr.* Retrieved June 10, 2022, from https://idronline.org/why-we-must-listen-to-farmers-agriculture-value-chains/

Bibliography

Abdullah F. (2009). Developing a framework of success of Bumiputera entrepreneurs, Journal of Enterprising Communities, Vol. 3 No. 1, 2009 pp. 8-24

ACABC. (n.d.). Retrieved March 6, 2022, from http://www.agriclinics.net/scheme-home.htm

Adhia, N. (2015). The History of Economic Development in India since Independence. 20 (3): 18–22.

Adoram, G. (2011). Gender differences and their impact on Entrepreneurial Ventures Advances in Management, Vol 4 (2), pp. 13-18

Agarwal, M. (2019). *11 Indian Tech Startup Acquisitions And Investments By Reliance*. https://inc42.com/features/indian-tech-startup-acquisitions-and-investments-by-reliance

Agriclinics available at: http://www.agriclinics.net/ACABCGuidelines 2018.pdf

Anonymous (2021). Entrepreneur Skills: Definition and Examples. Retrieved April 10, 2022 from https://in.indeed.com/career-advice/career-development/entrepreneur-skills

Anonymous. (2021). Annual Report. Government of India, Ministry of Micro, Small and Medium Enterprises, New Delhi.

APEDA. (2021). *Annual Report, APEDA*. https://apeda.gov.in/apedawebsite/about_apeda/About_apeda.htm

APEDA. (2022). *Fresh Fruits and Vegetables*. https://apeda.gov.in/apedawebsite/six_head_product/FFV.htm

Arafat, M.Y., Saleem, I., Dwivedi, A.K. and Khan, A. (2018). Determinants of agricultural entrepreneurship: a GEM data based study. International Entrepreneurship and Management Journal, Vol.1,pp.1-26.

Atkinson, J. W., & Feather, N. T. (1966). *A theory of achievement motivation*. New York: Wiley.

Ayadurai, D. (1987). The Employer, the Employee and the Law in Malaysia, Butterworths: London.

Azqueta Díaz de Alda, A. (2017). *El concepto de emprendedor: origen, evolución e introducción*. https://idus.us.es/handle/11441/74177#.Yg-gkoK-tLw.mendeley

Babu, M. S. (2020). *Why 'Make in India' has failed - The Hindu*. https://www. thehindu. com/opinion/op-ed/why-make-in-india-has-failed/article30601269.ece

Bank, G. (n.d.). *Grameen Bank*. Retrieved March 22, 2022, from https://grameenbank.org/ introduction/

Baumol, J. W. (1990). Entrepreneurship: Productive, Unproductive and Destructive, Journal of Political Economy. Vol. 98, no. 5, 1990.

Beliaeva, T., Ferasso, M., Kraus, S. and Damke, E. J. (2020). Dynamics of digital entrepreneurship and the innovation ecosystem. International Journal of Entrepreneurial Behavior & Research, Vol. 26 No. 2, pp. 266-284.

Berry, R. S. (2020). *10 essential skills you need as an Entrepreneur.* Retrieved April 10, 2022 from https://hivelife.com/essential-entrepreneurial-skills/

Bhaktavatsala, R. (2019). *Entrepreneurship*. NPTEL. https://drive.google.com/file/d/ 1CWJTsv2SQvvbf4lgzpiGKAOueKAZdH4b/view

BSEINDIA. (n.d.). *BSEINDIA*. Retrieved March 22, 2022, from https://www.bseindia.com/ Static/about/alternative_investment_funds.aspx

Cabral, C., & Dhar, R. L. (2019). Skill development research in India: a systematic literature review and future research agenda. *Benchmarking*, *26*(7), 2242–2266. https://doi.org/ 10.1108/BIJ-07-2018-0211/FULL/XML

Cantillon, R.(1755). Essay on the nature of general commerce. Henry Higgs, Trans, Macmllan, London.

Carland, J. W., Hoy, F., Boulton, W. R., Ann, J., & Carland, C. (1984). Differentiating Entrepreneurs from Small Business Owners: A Conceptualisation. *Source: The Academy of Management Review*, *9*(2), 354–359.

Cavallo, A., Ghezzi, A., Dell'Era, C. and Pellizzoni, E. (2019), "Fostering digital entrepreneurship from startup to scaleup: The role of venture capital funds and angel groups. Technological Forecasting and Social Change, Vol. 145, pp. 24-35.

Ced available at: https://ced.gujarat.gov.in/vision-and-mission

Chand, S. (n.d.). *Function of State Financial Corporation's (SFCs) in India*. Retrieved March 19, 2022, from https://www.yourarticlelibrary.com/banking/function-of-state-financial-corporations-sfcs-in-india/24817

Chandra, Prasanna (1996). Projects, Planning, Analysis, Selection, Implementation and Review; Tata McGraw-Hill Publishing Company Limited, New Delhi, Fifth Reprint.

Chaudhary, R. D. (2015). *Japan's $12 billion "Make in India" fund to push investments - The Economic Times*. https://economictimes.indiatimes.com/news/economy/ finance/japans-12-billion-make-in-india-fund-to-push-investments/articleshow/ 50154789.cms

Chole, R.R., Kapse, P.S., and Deshmukh. (2012). Entrepreneurship development and Business Communication Skills. Scientific Publishers.

Chowdhary, G. (2014). *Live coverage: Launch of Modi's Make in India campaign - Hindustan Times*.https://web.archive.org/web/20140925055526/http://www.hindustantimes.com/business-news/live-coverage-launch-of-modi-s-make-in-india-campaign/article1-1268119.aspx

Clement, C and Dhar, R. L. (2019). Skill development research in India: a systematic literature review and future research agenda. Benchmarking: An International Journal. 26(7): 2242-2266. doi:10.1108/BIJ-07-2018-0211. ISSN 1463-5771

Cote, C. (2020). *Must-have entrepreneurial skills for aspiring business owners*. Retrieved April 10, 2022 from https://online.hbs.edu/blog/post/entrepreneurial-skills

Cromie, S. (2000). Assessing entrepreneurial inclinations: some approaches empirical evidence", European Journal of Work and Organizational Psychology. Vol.9 No.1,pp.7-30.

Cullen,H., Calitz,A., and Chandler,L. (2014). Business incubation in the Eastern Cape: A case study. International Journal for Innovation Education and Research, Vol 2(05): p-76-89.

Cunningham, J., Damij, N. and Modic, D. (2022). An Exploratory Study of High-Performance Computing Technology Adoption over the Stages of Entrepreneurship. International Journal of Entrepreneurial Venturing.

David Z. and Edward B. (2011). Personal characteristics and strategic orientation: entrepreneurs in Canadian manufacturing companies, International Journal of Entrepreneurial Behaviour & Research, Vol. 17 No. 1, pp. 82-103 |

Deeb, G. (2014). *Comparing Equity, Debt And Convertibles For Startup Financings*.

Deen. A Shepherd, Wiklund, J., & Haynie, J. M. (2009). Moving forward: Balancing the financial and emotional costs of business failure. *Journal of Business Venturing*, 24(2): 134-148.

Desai, V. (2001). Dynamics of Entrepreneurial Development and Management, Himalaya Publishing House, New Delhi.

Desai, Vasant (1996). Dynamics of Entrepreneurial Development of Management; Himalaya Publishing House, Mumbai, Reprint.

Dilli, S., Elert, N., & Herrmann, A. M. (2018). Varieties of entrepreneurship: exploring the institutional foundations of different entrepreneurship types through 'Varieties-of-Capitalism' arguments. *Small Business Economics*, *51*(2), 293–320. https://doi.org/10.1007/S11187-018-0002-Z/TABLES/12

Dolores Martínez García, M., María Moreno Meneses, J., & Valencia Sandoval, K. (2022). View of Theoretical Review of Entrepreneur and Social Entrepreneurship Concepts. *Journal of Administrative Science*, *3*(6), 19–26. https://repository.uaeh.edu.mx/revistas/index.php/jas/article/view/7687/8332

Dong, J. Q. (2019). Moving a mountain with a teaspoon: Toward a theory of digital entrepreneurship in the regulatory environment. Technological Forecasting and Social Change, Vol. 146, pp. 923-930.

Dwivedi, Y. K., Hughes, L., Ismagilova, E., Aarts, G., Coombs, C., Crick, T., Duan, Y., Dwivedi, R., Edwards, J., Eirug, A., Galanos, V., Ilavarasan, P. V., Janssen, M., Jones, P., Kar, A. K., Kizgin, H., Kronemann, B., Lal, B., Lucini, B., Medaglia, R., Le Meunier-FitzHugh, K., Le Meunier-FitzHugh, L. C., Misra, S., Mogaji, E., Sharma, S. K., Singh, J. B., Raghavan, V., Raman, R., Rana, N. P., Samothrakis, S., Spencer, J., Tamilmani, K., Tubadji, A., Walton, P. and Williams, M. D. (2021). Artificial Intelligence (A.I.): Multidisciplinary perspectives on emerging challenges, opportunities, and agenda for research, practice and policy. International Journal of Information Management, Vol. 57, pp. 101994. https://www.forbes.com/sites/georgedeeb/2014/03/19/comparing-equity-vs-debt-vs-convertibles-for-startup-financings/?sh=40cf839d69ff

E.T. Bureau. (2021). India allays buffalo meat export concerns, says meat is safe. *The Economic Times*. https://economictimes.indiatimes.com/news/economy/foreign-trade/india-allays-buffalo-meat-export-concerns-says-meat-is-safe/articleshow/82797205.cms

EDHEC (2021). *Entrepreneurial skills: Top 7 skills required for successful entrepreneurship.* Retrieved April 10, 2022 from https://online.edhec.edu/en/blog/skills-needed-to-be-entrepreneur/

EDII available at: https://www.ediindia.org/

Ehigie, B.O. and Umoren, U. E. (2003). Psychological factors influencing perceived entrepreneurial success among Nigerian women in small-scale businesses. Journal of International Women's Studies, Vol. 5(1), pp. 78-95.

Elenurm, T.(2001). Development needs of Estonian entrepreneurs and managers for international business. 4th McGill Conference on International Entrepreneurship, Vol. 1,

Emmanuel, J. (2020). *Meaning of a Success story-The definitive guide*. Retrieved June 9, 2022, from https://livingwordmission.org.ng/success-story/

Entrialgo, M., Fernandez, E. and Vazquez, C. (2000). Characteristics of managers as determinants of entrepreneurial orientation: some Spanish evidence. *Enterprise and Innovation Management Studies*, Vol.1No.2,pp.187-205.

Ernst & Young (2008). The Global Executive Report 2008. URL: http://www.ey.com/Publication/vwLUAssets/Global_Executive_2008/$FILE/GE_2008_Global_Executive.pdf [Accessed on 18 March 2016].

ET Bureau. (2017). *To boost Skill India Mission, Govt sets aside Rs 17,000 crore in Budget - The Economic Times*. https://economictimes.indiatimes.com/news/economy/policy/to-boost-skill-india-mission-govt-sets-aside-rs-17000-crore-in-budget/articleshow/56944089.cms

Etzkowitz, H. (2002). Innovation as a Triple Helix of University: Industry Government Networks. Svience and Public Policy. Vol 29(2): p.115-128.

Evens, George Herberton (1949). Entrepreneur and Economic Theory. American Economic Review, p.338.

Express News Service. (2015). *Start-Up India plan on Jan 16: Modi on Mann ki Baat | India News, The Indian Express*. https://indianexpress.com/article/india/india-news-india/action-plan-on-startup-india-to-be-unveiled-on-jan-16-pm-modi/

Friedman, B.A.(2011). The relationship between Governance Effectiveness and Entrepreneurship.

Functions of Commercial Banks: meaning, functions, types, example. (n.d.). Retrieved March 6, 2022, from https://byjus.com/commerce/functions-of-commercial-banks/

Ghani, E Kerr, W. R. and O'Connell, S.(2019). Spatial Determinants of Entrepreneurship in India," in Entrepreneurship in a Regional Context.International Journal of Humanities and Social Science, 1(17): p. 221-225.

GOI. (2019). *20th Livestock Census | Department of Animal Husbandry & Dairying*. https://dahd.nic.in/division/provisional-key-results-20th-livestock-census

GOI. (2022a). *Annual Report Department of Chemicals & Petro-Chemicals, MoC&F, GoI*. https://chemicals.nic.in/document-report/annual-report

GOI. (2022b). *Directorate of Plant Protection, Quarantine & Storage*. http://ppqs.gov.in/

GOI. (2022c). *Inland Fisheries, Department of Fisheries*. https://www.dof.gov.in/inland-fisheries

GoI. (n.d.). *Incubation Support*. Retrieved March 21, 2022, from https://www.startupindia.gov.in/content/sih/en/compendium_of_good_practices/incubationsupport.html

Greene, F., (2012). Should the focus of publicity provided small business assistance be on start-ups or growth businesss? Ministry of Economic Development, New Zealand.

Gupta, V. (1998). Steps in setting up a small enterprise.

Hayes, A. (2022). *Venture Capital Definition*. https://www.investopedia.com/terms/v/venturecapital.asp

https://www.investopedia.com/articles/personal-finance/080615/5-skills-every-entrepreneur-needs.asp

https://www.zeebiz.com/small-business/news-live-national-startup-day-2022-how-entrepreneurs-are-applauding-pm-narendra-modis-decision-quotes-who-said-what-176273

IBEF. (2022). *Make In India Programme, All About The Manufacture in India Initiative*. https://www.ibef.org/economy/make-in-india

IGNOU. (2017). eGyanKosh: Unit-6 Preparation of Business Plan and Project. https://egyankosh.ac.in/handle/123456789/10847

IMARC. (2022). *Seed Industry in India | Share, Size, Growth, Trends and Forecast 2021-2026*. https://www.imarcgroup.com/seed-industry-in-india

India. https://www.livemint.com/Industry/NIK7XM3p7ochGKFtDruhUL/After-Digital-India-Oracle-seeks-to-participate-in-Make-in.html

Indian Council of Agricultural Research. (2020). *Handbook of agricultural extension.* Indian Council of Agricultural Research. Directorate of Knowledge Management in Agriculture.

Indian Start-up Ecosystem. (n.d.). Retrieved March 22, 2022, from https://www.startupindia.gov.in/content/sih/en/international/go-to-market-guide/indian-startup-ecosystem.html

Invest India. (2022). *Dairy Industry In India - Growth, FDI, Companies, Exports.* https://www.investindia.gov.in/sector/food-processing/dairy

IT - ISEP - Business. (n.d.). Retrieved March 22, 2022, from https://sbi.co.in/web/business/information/it-isep

Jadhav, R. (2021). *Private sector's share in India's seed industry expands to 65 per cent - The Hindu BusinessLine.* https://www.thehindubusinessline.com/data-stories/data-focus/private-sectors-share-in-indias-seed-industry-expands-to-65-per-cent/article35101260.ece

Jain, M. (2019): 5 Essential Skills Required to succeed as an Entrepreneur. Retrieved from https://www.entrepreneur.com/article/339531

Jarial, S. (2022). Internet of Things application in Indian agriculture, challenges and effect on the extension advisory services – a review. Journal of Agribusiness in Developing and Emerging Economies, Vol. ahead-of-print No. ahead-of-print. https://doi.org/10.1108/JADEE-05-2021-0121

Jawad, M., Naz, M. and Maroof, Z. (2021). Era of the digital revolution: Digital entrepreneurship and digital transformation in emerging economies. Business Strategy & Development, Vol. 4 No. 3, pp. 220-228.

Jerry Jinnett Pinson (1999). Anatomy of a Business Plan, D arbom Trade.

Joseph A. Covello, (1994). The Complete Book of Business Plans: Simple Steps to Writing a Powerful Business Plan.

Kala, S., Singal, S. and Gover, I. (2002). Economics of stitching enterprises run by tribal

Kanungo, Rabindra N. (Ed.) (1998). Entrepreneurship & Innovation: Models for Development, New Delhi, Sage Publications.

Kathewadi, H. (2015, July 15). Government to train 40 crore people under Skill India initiative. The Economic Times, Retrieved on March 3, 2022.

Kaur, H. (n.d.). Understanding The Concept Of Entrepreneur Competency. *Journal of Business Management & Social Sciences Research.* Retrieved February 18, 2022, from www.borjournals.com

Kenton, W. (2017). Strength, Weakness, Opportunity, and Threat (SWOT) Analysis Definition. https://www.investopedia.com/terms/s/swot.asp.

Khadi and Village Industries Commission. (n.d.). Retrieved March 6, 2022, from https://www.kvic.gov.in/kvicres/aboutkvic.php

Kirzner, I. (1973). Competition and entrepreneurship, Chicago, Chicago University Press.

Kraus, S., Palmer, C., Kailer, N., Kallinger, F. L. and Spitzer, J. (2018). Digital entrepreneurship: A research agenda on new business models for the twenty-first century. International Journal of Entrepreneurial Behavior & Research.

Krishna, P. (2017). Pradhan Mantri KaushalVikas Yojana: Boon Or Bane. Business world. Retrieved on March 3, 2022.

Laghu-Udyog available at: http://www.laghu-udyog.gov.in/righttoinformationact05.doc

Lalitha Rani, D. (1996). Women entrepreneurs, APH Publishing Corporation, New Delhi. p. 9.

Livestock Entrepreneurship: National Institute for Small Industry Extension Training (NISIET). (n.d.). Retrieved March 6, 2022, from http://ecoursesonline.iasri.res.in/mod/page/view.php?id=73731

Madsen, Dag Øivind (2016). "SWOT analysis: a management fashion perspective". International Journal of Business Research. 16 (1): 39–56.

MANAGE. (2013). Agri-business and Entrepreneurship Development. https://www.manage.gov.in/moocs/structure.asp

McClelland, D. C. (1961). *The achieving society*. Princeton: Van Nostrand.

McClelland, D. C. (1985). *Human motivation*. Glenview: Scott Foresman.

McClelland, D. C., Atkinson, J. W., Clark, R. A., & Lowell, E. L. (1953). *The achievement motive*. New York: Appleton.

McClelland, D. C., Koestner, R., & Weinberger, J. (1989). How do self-attributed and implicit motives differ? *Psychological Review, 96*, 690–702.

Melih Bulu (2005). The Characteristics Of Turkish Entrepreneurs, Global Business And Technology Association.

Micro Small Scale Industries Board India | Micro SSI Board Meeting India |Micro Small & Medium Enterprises India. (n.d.). Retrieved March 6, 2022, from http://laghu-udyog.gov.in/msme-do/sidoboard.htm

Micro, Small and Medium Enterprises available at: http://laghu-udyog.gov.in/msme-do/sidoboard.htm#:~:text=The%20Small%20Scale%20Industries%20Board, in%20the%20Government%20of%20India.

Mike P. McKeever (2005). How to write a Business Plan.

MindTools (N.A.). Entrepreneurial skills The Skills you need to Start a Great Business. Retrieved from April 10, 2022 from https://www.mindtools.com/pages/article/new CDV_76.htm

MindTools. (n.d.). SWOT Analysis Model and Examples - Business Strategy Skills. Retrieved May 23, 2022, from https://www.mindtools.com/pages/article/newTMC_05.htm

Ministry of Agriculture & Farmers Welfare, (2021). Success stories of Progressive Women Farmers and Agripreneurs. Retrieved June 10, 2022, from https://agricoop.nic.in/sites/default/files/Success%20Story%20For%20approval.pdf

Ministry Of Heavy Industries & Public Enterprises. (2014). *Focus on Make In India | Business Standard News*. https://www.business-standard.com/article/government-press-release/focus-on-make-in-india-114092501206_1.html

Models of Entrepreneurship in Basics of entrepreneurship development in agriculture. https://www.agmoocs.in/beda/#/lecture/824

Modgil, S., Dwivedi, Y. K., Rana, N. P., Gupta, S. and Kamble, S. (2022). Has Covid-19 accelerated opportunities for digital entrepreneurship? An Indian perspective. Technological Forecasting and Social Change, Vol. 175, pp. 121415.

Mondal, Sagar. (2019). Fundamentals of Agricultural Extension Education. Kalyani Publications. India

Mordor, I. (2022). *India Agricultural Machinery Market 2022 - 27*. https://www.mordorintelligence.com/industry-reports/india-agricultural-machinery-market

Mudra. (n.d.). *Mudra - Micro Units Development & Refinance Agency Ltd.* Retrieved March 22, 2022, from https://www.mudra.org.in/

Mueller, S.L. and Thomas, A.S. (2000). Culture and entrepreneurial potential: a nine country study of locus of control and innovativeness. Journal of Business Venturing, Vol. 16 No. 1, pp.51-75.

Mukherjee, P. (2016). *Modi's "Make In India" racks up $222 billion in investment pledges | Reuters*. https://www.reuters.com/article/modi-make-in-india-investment-pledge-idINKCN0VR1S0?edition-redirect=in

Murray, H. A. (1938). *Explorations in personality*. New York: Oxford University Press.

NAARM available at: https://naarm.org.in/announcements/careers/

Nabhi Publication (2004). How to Borrow from a Baking and Financial Institution; Nabhi Publications, New Delhi, Edition.

Nag, R.; Hambrick, D. C.; Chen, M.-J (2007). What is strategic management, really? Inductive derivation of a consensus definition of the field". Strategic Management Journal. 28 (9): 935–955. CiteSeerX 10.1.1.491.7592. doi:10.1002/smj.615.qn|date=June 2018

Nambisan, S. (2017). Digital entrepreneurship: Toward a digital technology perspective of entrepreneurship. Entrepreneurship theory and practice, Vol. 41 No. 6, pp. 1029-1055.

Nandapurkar, G.G. (1982). Small farmers – A study on their entrepreneurial behaviour Metropolitan Book Co. (Pvt. Ltd.) New Delhi pp. 1-2.

Nandram S. & Karel Samsom (2007). Entrepreneurial Behaviour, NRG Working Paper no. 07-04

National Bee Board. (2021). *National Bee Board*. https://nbb.gov.in/aboutus.htm

National Institute for Small Industry Extension Training (NISIET) available at: http://ecoursesonline.iasri.res.in/mod/page/view.php?id=73731

National Skill Development Corporation. (2015). Scheme Document of PradhanMantriKaushalVikas Yojana. http://www.pmkvyofficial.org/App_Documents/News/PMKVY_Scheme-Document_v1.1.pdf

Ngoasong, M. Z. (2018). Digital entrepreneurship in a resource-scarce context. Journal of Small Business and Enterprise Development, Vol. 25 No. 3, pp. 483-500.

NHB. (2022). *National Horticulture Board.* http://nhb.gov.in/

NIMSME available at: https://www.nimsme.org/

Noor H. et al (2009). Is entrepreneurial competency and business success relationship contingent upon business environment? A study of Malaysian SMEs, International Journal of Entrepreneurial Behaviour & Research, Vol. 16 No. 3, 2010, pp. 182-203

NSIC available at: https://www.nsic.co.in/Corporate/AboutUs

Olan, F., Liu, S., Suklan, J., Jayawickrama, U. and Arakpogun, E. O. (2021). The role of Artificial Intelligence networks in sustainable supply chain finance for food and drink industry. International Journal of Production Research, pp. 1-16.

Oni, E.O. and Daniya, A. (2012). Development of Small and Medium Scale Enterprises: The role of Government and other Financial Institutions. Arabian Journal of Business and Management Review, 1(7): p. 16-29.

Oyemomi, O., Liu, S., Neaga, I. and Alkhuraiji, A. (2016). How knowledge sharing and business process contribute to organisational performance: Using the fsQCA approach. Journal of Business Research, Vol. 69 No. 11, pp. 5222-5227.

Pals,S. (2006). Factors Determining Success /Failure in Business Incubators: A Literature Review of 17 countries . Worcester Polytechnique Institute.

Panagariya, A. (2001). India' s Economic Reforms What Has Been Accomplished/ ? What Remains to Be Done/ ? no. 2.

Papzan et al (2008). Determining factors influencing rural entrepreneurs' success, African Journal of Agricultural Research Vol. 3 (9), pp. 597-600. Robbins, S.P. and Judge, T.A. (2009), Organizational Behaviour. Pearson education, New York.

Pearson C. A. L. and Helms, K.(2013). Indigenous Social Entrepreneurship: The Gumatj Clan Enterprise in East Arnhem Land, J. Entrep.

PMKVY. (n.d.). Retrieved March 19, 2022, from https://www.pmkvyofficial.org/home-page

PTI. (2016a). *17.93 lakh candidates trained under PMKVY as on July 18 | Business Standard News*. https://www.business-standard.com/article/pti-stories/17-93-lakh-candidates-trained-under-pmkvy-as-on-july-18-116072100579_1.html

PTI. (2016b). *India replaces China as top FDI destination in 2015: Report - The Economic Times*. https://economictimes.indiatimes.com/news/economy/finance/india-replaces-china-as-top-fdi-destination-in-2015-report/articleshow/51932057.cms

PTI. (2016c). *Japan to set up skill development institutes in Gujarat, Karnataka and Rajasthan - The Economic Times*. https://economictimes.indiatimes.com/news/politics-and-nation/japan-to-set-up-skill-development-institutes-in-gujarat-karnataka-and-rajasthan/articleshow/55377055.cms

PTI. (2016). *Make in India Week gets Rs 15.2 lakh crore investment commitments - The Economic Times*. https://economictimes.indiatimes.com/news/economy/policy/make-in-india-week-gets-rs-15-2-lakh-crore-investment-commitments/articleshow/51040369.cms

PWC, F. (2020). *The role of agrochemical: Achieving the vision of a USD 5 trillion economy by 2025*. https://ficci.in/spdocument/23379/Knowledge-Report-Agrochemicals-Conference-20.pdf

Raine, A. L., & Pandya, M. (2019). Three keys to entrepreneurial success: are curiosity, creativity, and commitment. Entrepreneurship Education 2019 2:3, 2(3), 189–198. https://doi.org/10.1007/S41959-019-00019-Y

Rao, C. B. (2018). *India as Global Start-up Hub/ : Mission with Passion*. Notion Press. https://www.amazon.in/India-Global-Start-up-Hub-Mission-ebook/dp/B07DGBD73R?asin=B07DGBD73R&revisionId=&format=2&depth=1

Ross, S. (2021). 4 Countries That Produce the Most Food Worldwide. https://www.investopedia.com/articles/investing/100615/4-countries-produce-most-food.asp#citation-16

Sahut, J.-M., Iandoli, L. and Teulon, F. (2021). The age of digital entrepreneurship. Small Business Economics, Vol. 56 No. 3, pp. 1159-1169.

Saini, T. (2022). *Top 70 Angel Investors of 2021 in India - StartupLanes.com*. https://www.startuplanes.com/top-70-angel-investors-of-2021-in-india/

Salem, M.I. (2014). The Role of Business Incubators in the economic developmenr of Saudi Arabia. International Business & Economics Research Journal (IBER). Vol. 13(4): p.853-860.

Sammy King-fai Hui et al (2006). International Journal of Entrepreneurial Behaviour & Research, Factors involved in the success of Hong Kong construction and property entrepreneurs , Vol. 12 No. 4, 2006 , pp. 228-245

Schiuma, G, Schettini, E., Santarsiero, F. and Carlucci, D. (2021). The transformative leadership compass: six competencies for digital transformation entrepreneurship. International Journal of Entrepreneurial Behavior & Research, Vol. ahead-of-print No. ahead-of-print. https://doi.org/10.1108/IJEBR-01-2021-0087.

Secundo, G., Rippa, P. and Meoli, M. (2020). Digital transformation in entrepreneurship education centres: preliminary evidence from the Italian Contamination Lab network. International Journal of Entrepreneurial Behaviour & Research. Vol. 26 No.7, pp.1589-1605.

Sen, S. M. (2021). Why we must listen to farmers. Idr. Retrieved June 10, 2022, from https://idronline.org/why-we-must-listen-to-farmers-agriculture-value-chains/

Serban, R. (2018). 5 Most Successful Types of Entrepreneurs And Personality Testing. available at: https://www.hubgets.com/blog/5-most-successful-types-of-entrepreneurs-personality-testing/ (accessed 16 June 2022).

Sevier, Robert A. (2001). Not SWOT, but OTSW. Thinking outside the box: some (fairly) radical thoughts on how colleges and universities should think, act, and communicate in a very busy marketplace. Hiawatha, Iowa: Strategy Pub. p. 46. ISBN 0971059705. OCLC 48165005

Shen, Y. (2022). *SWOT Analysis and Strategy Selection of Nestle Based On 2018-2020 Annual Report.*

SIDBI available at: https://www.sidbi.in/en/about-sidbi#overview

Siegel, D. S., & Wright, M. (2015). Academic Entrepreneurship: Time for a Rethink? *British Journal of Management*, *26*, 582–595. https://doi.org/10.1111/1467-8551.12116

Siggel, E. and Pradeep A.(2009). The impact of economic reforms on Indian manufacturers: evidence from a small sample survey. Eckhard Single Institute of Economic Growth.

Simeon Djankov et al (2007). What Makes a Successful Entrepreneur? Evidence from Brazil.

Srivastava, M. (2016). *After Digital India, Oracle seeks to participate in Make in India, Start-up*

Steininger, D. M. (2019). Linking information systems and entrepreneurship: A review and agenda for IT associated and digital entrepreneurship research. Information Systems Journal, Vol. 29 No. 2, pp. 363-407.

Stewart, W.H., Carland, J.C., Carland, J.W., Watson, W.E. and Sweo, R. (2003). Entrepreneurial dispositions and goal orientations: a comparative exploration of United States and Russian entrepreneurs. Journal of Small Business Management, Vol.41No.1,pp.27-46.

SWOT analysis of an entrepreneur in Basics of Entrepreneurship Development in Agriculture. (2022). https://www.agmoocs.in/beda/#/home

Tarapuez Chamorro, E., & Botero Villa, J. J. (2007). Algunos aportes de los neoclásicos a la teoría del emprendedor. *Cuadernos de Administración*, *20*(34), 39-63. http://www.scielo.org.co/scielo.php?script=sci_arttext&pid=S0120-35922007000200003&lng=en&nrm=iso&tlng=

Tarver, E. (2021). *5 skill every entrepreneur should have*. Retrieved April 9, 2022 from

Teamwork (N.A). Critical Success factors in project management. Retrieved April 16, 2022, from https://www.teamwork.com/project-management-guide/critical-success-factors-in-project-management/

Teoh, H.Y. and Foo, S.L. (1997). Moderating effects of tolerance for ambiguity and risk taking propensity on the role conûict-perceived performance relationship: evidence from Singaporean entrepreneurs. Journal of Business Venturing, Vol.12,pp.67-81.

Theories of Entrepreneurship in Basics of entrepreneurship development in agriculture. (2022). https://www.agmoocs.in/beda/#/lecture/819

Thiel, P. (2014). *Zero to One. Note on Start-ups or How to Build the future*. Crown Business.

Thomas, A.S. and Mueller, S.L. (2000). "A case for comparative entrepreneurship: assessing the relevance of culture", Journal of International Business Studies, Vol.31No.2,pp.287-301.

Timmons, J.A. (1994). New Venture Creation, Entrepreneurship for the 21st Century, 4th Edition, Irwin. University of Strathclyde, Glasgow, pp. 384-407.

TNN. (2015). *PM Modi in Mann Ki Baat: "Start Up India, Stand Up India" action plan on January 16 | India News - Times of India*. https://timesofindia.indiatimes.com/india/PM-Modi-in-Mann-Ki-Baat-Start-Up-India-Stand-Up-India-action-plan-on-January-16/articleshow/50340724.cms

Trivedi, A. (2017). *Indian banks responding to the growing start-up ecosystem!* https://yourstory.com/mystory/7570536365-indian-banks-responding-to-growing-start-up-ecosystem-/amp

Troise, C., Corvello, V., Ghobadian, A., O'Regan, N. (2022). "SME's agility in the digital transformation era: antecedents and impact in VUCA environments", Technological Forecasting & Social Change, 174, 121227, https://doi.org/10.1016/j.techfore.2021.121227. Dal 01/01/2020 ad oggi.

Upadhyay, N., Upadhyay, S. and Dwivedi, Y.K. (2021). "Theorising artificial intelligence acceptance and digital entrepreneurship model", International Journal of Entrepreneurial Behavior & Research, Vol. ahead-of-print No. ahead-of print. https://doi.org/10.1108/IJEBR-01-2021-0052

Viral acharya et al (2004). what determines entrepreneurial Success, www.ifmr.ac.in/pdf/drishtee.pdf

Visual Paradigms. (n.d.). What is SWOT Analysis? Retrieved May 23, 2022, from https://www.visual-paradigm.com/guide/strategic-analysis/what-is-swot-analysis/

Wadhva, C. (1991). India trying to liberalise/ : economic reforms since 1991, 259–84.

Weihrich, Heinz (April 1982). "The TOWS matrix—a tool for situational analysis". Long Range Planning. 15 (2): 54–66. doi:10.1016/0024-6301(82)90120-0.

Wickham, A. P. (2006). Strategic Entrepreneurship. Fourth Edition, Prentice-Hall, Esses, England.

women entrepreneurs-case study of Bihar. Maharashtra J. Extension Edu., 21 (1): 71-74.

Wood, R. and Bandura, A. (1989). "Social cognitive theory of organizational management", Academy of Management Review, Vol.14 No.3,pp.361-384.

Yarbrough, Q. (2021). What is a critical Success Factor? A Quick Guide. Retrieved April 16, 2022 from https://www.projectmanager.com/blog/critical-success-factor

Zacharakis, A. (1997). "Entrepreneurial entry into foreign markets", Entrepreneurship: Theory and Practice, Spring, New York, NY, pp.23-40.

Zeebiz. (2022). *LIVE: National Startup Day 2022: How entrepreneurs are applauding PM Narendra Modi's decision - Quotes Who said what Zee Business.*